HENRY WESTON FROST

"BY FAITH...

Henry W. Frost and
the China Inland Mission

BY DR. & MRS.
HOWARD TAYLOR

CHINA INLAND MISSION
PHILADELPHIA, LONDON, TORONTO,
MELBOURNE, AND SHANGHAI: 1938

PRINTED IN THE UNITED STATES BY THE BINGHAM CO., PHILADELPHIA

"ALPHA
AND
OMEGA"

"LOOKING UNTO JESUS
THE AUTHOR AND FINISHER
OF OUR FAITH."

FOREWORD

A PRINCETON student, Henry W. Frost by name, had turned into the room of a friend in one of the campus buildings. Blair Lee, the son of an Admiral who had served in the Civil War, was showing him an old revolver, the one which his father had carried in the navy. Not knowing that it was loaded, he was handling it without concern, when suddenly it went off, its muzzle barely three feet from the head of his companion. The bullet whizzed past, almost grazing the young man's ear, and buried itself in the wall behind. Nothing was said as the revolver was returned to its place, both men too moved for words. But to one of them came the conviction that his life had been saved for a purpose, by the watchful care of God.

·　·　·　·　·

This book is the story of a quest of faith to which that young man was led, a quest richly crowned with blessing to himself and others. It is told in his own words as far as possible, for the writers have had the privilege of access to Dr. Frost's autobiography, letters, and other records, too full for present publication. The story is incomplete, for we have the beloved Director Emeritus of the China Inland

Mission in North America still with us; incomplete, also, because faith's rewarding goes on far beyond the limits of time.

The record is written that we may gratefully "remember them that had the rule over (us), which spake unto (us) the word of God; and considering the issue of their manner of life, imitate their faith"—because the need of the world is the same; the certainty of "things not seen as yet" is the same; and above all, "Jesus Christ (is) the same yesterday, and to day, and for ever."

HOWARD & GERALDINE TAYLOR

The China Inland Mission,
Philadelphia, Penna., U.S.A.

INTRODUCTION

"By Faith"! No more appropriate title could have been chosen for this volume. It was surely given the authors by the Lord! The words at once bring to mind that great Eleventh of Hebrews with its inspired and inspiring record of Old Testament men and women of faith, and of what God wrought through them. But the chapter ends with a reminder that the record of faith's achievements was not complete but awaited later additions, and the twelfth chapter opens with an exhortation to the saints of the New Testament dispensation to enter the lists, and "run . . . the race . . . looking unto Jesus the author and finisher of faith."

The present volume, like all earlier chronicles of C.I.M. work and workers, carries forward the story of faith's quest and achievement a stage nearer the goal. Henry W. Frost in North America, just as Hudson Taylor in England and China, was a true follower of those in ancient days who "through faith subdued kingdoms, wrought righteousness, obtained promises . . . out of weakness were made strong . . ." and who "having obtained a good report through faith" still await faith's full fruition and reward at the appearing in glory of their blessed Saviour and Lord. The fact that we still have our beloved former Home Director in our midst is to us a great joy and strength.

It is quite significant that, without any human planning to that end, this book should appear just at the time of the Mission's Jubilee in North America. It thus contributes most fittingly to our commemoration of God's exceeding goodness and blessing throughout the past fifty years. And further, it serves as a stimulus to our faith and courage as we face at this time a fresh and tremendous challenge in China.

On the one hand, a greater open door is presented for the Gospel than ever before in the history of the Mission, with opportunities simply unlimited among all classes. On the other hand, the present Sino-Japanese conflict risks the closing of that open door, and a regrettable setback to missionary work. How shall we meet such an issue? In the one and only consistent and sure way—"By Faith"! Continuing to "hold God's faithfulness," the Mission faces this gravely critical situation in China not only undismayed, but with hopefulness, courage, and determination to go forward. Plans are in the making for the sending out this autumn, if the Lord will, of forty new recruits from the home lands.

To use an expression of our revered founder, Hudson Taylor, *"God is always advancing."* We must keep pace with Him. He that is with us is greater than all that are against us. His presence, provision, and power are assured "even unto the end of the age"; and so, "By Faith" shall still be our watchword and our path to victory.

ROBERT HALL GLOVER

Philadelphia
July, 1938.

"BY FAITH"

CONTENTS

ILLUSTRATIONS

PART I

FAITH'S QUEST

*"Now faith is the giving
substance to things hoped for."*
HEBREWS 11:1

*"The life of faith is the
life that uses the Lord."*
HANDLEY MOULE
Bishop of Durham

CHAPTER

I

THE OPENING STORY

IT was in the days when America was waking up to the vastness of her natural resources that Mahlon S. Frost became interested in the discovery and production of oil in western Pennsylvania. He came, far back, of a Danish family which had taken root in Cambridge, England, where they founded and endowed a hospital which, at the time of the Reformation, became the well-known St. John's College. Strange to say, Edmund Frost, who brought the name to this country, gravitated to Cambridge, near Boston, where he purchased property and became one of the founders of Harvard University. Mahlon Frost's young wife (née Frances Harriet Foster) came of stock very similar to his own. Descended from a long line of Flemish and English Knights, her forebears, like the Frosts, had emigrated to America shortly after the sailing of the *Mayflower* and settled in Massachusetts. Strong, alert, and full of initiative, Mahlon Frost moved with the times, and strenuous times they were, with "the nation growing like a weed" and apparently no

1

limit to the possibilities of development. He more than once made and lost what was then great wealth, and in spite of reverses was reckoned among the ablest financiers in the East, carrying always "the white flower of a blameless life," for he was first and above all a devoted Christian.

The younger of his sons, Henry Weston Frost, was born in 1858, when the parents were living in Detroit, near the Great Lakes. There had been a daughter, a specially lovely child, but shortly before Henry's birth she passed away after a brief illness, and the mother's grief was so poignant that he came into the world with a tendency to sadness of spirit. Life, however, was full of movement and interest. The brother, six years his senior, was a stirring companion, and their father's business activities led to frequent changes of scene as well as of fortune.

Through it all, the dark-haired little mother kept the atmosphere of home about them. She was unusually attractive in appearance and had a lovely voice. The father too was a singer. It was as members of the same church choir that they had first met, and their love of music was handed on to the second son. Among his earliest recollections is the sweetness of his mother's voice, as he sat on her knee as she told him Bible stories, or sang his favorite hymns.

There was not much discipline in those early years, though there were helpful spiritual influences that bore fruit in after life. The Bible teaching in a Brooklyn Sunday School awakened reverence for the Word of God and to some extent met the longing of the child-heart, so often unsuspected because unexpressed. But it was in home associations that the boy found most to confirm his faith.

The lives of my parents compelled me to believe that the Word of God is wholly true and also that there is a living Christ. My father's gentleness, his long-suffering patience, his ennobling companionship, and my mother's unfaltering, never-failing sweetness and love won my heart, not only for themselves but also for God. . . . If I may judge from my own experience, parental life with a child counts more than preaching, and parental sympathy more than exhortation.

School life, begun in Stamford, Connecticut, was continued in Chicago, amid the free and stimulating influences of the Middle West. Agriculture was prosperous, save in the South. Great trunk railways were being engineered across the continent and fabulous fortunes acquired in mine and factory and business.* Mahlon Frost's genius for finance found full play amid such opportunities. Though he had lost heavily in Brooklyn, through the dishonesty of a man he trusted, a year or two in Chicago enabled him to return East and establish a home again with every comfort.

To this period belonged, perhaps, the happiest days in the life of his children, for in addition to good schools, the suburbs of the city in which they settled afforded country-like surroundings. Spreading lawns about the house and a sparkling stream in the meadow beyond were a perennial delight.

More than this, about a mile away, there was an inlet of Long Island Sound, with a swimming pool, a sand bar offshore, and great neighboring docks and sheds. Oh, the long summer days of unalloyed bliss—playing in the meadow, building dams in the brook, swimming and rowing at the inlet, and watching the white-winged ships come and go! Winter too had its joys. There were snowfalls in those days that were real ones, when we were snowed in and had to dig ourselves out, and could build houses with mysterious tunnels leading to them, wherein we played Eskimos, until our fire melted the house and brought it and our visions to a sudden end.

---

* See *The Epic of America*, by James Truslow Adams, p. 277.

The next move was to a stately home in New York, at the corner of Madison Avenue and Thirty-fourth Street, where the boys found themselves launched on the full tide of city life. They attended a famous school, the Charlier Institute, where French was spoken all day long, and found in the park-like enclosure of Madison Square plenty of enjoyment for leisure hours. Another favorite haunt was Booth's Theater, a high-class playhouse not far away. The father of one of their schoolfellows was half-owner of the place, and supplied them with a pass which ensured many thrilling hours.

We were there when there were no plays, and when there were. We were sometimes before the scenes and at other times behind them. The "green room," the "red room," the "blue room," the "scene-painting room," and the "armory" were all familiar ground to us; and outside, we sat in seats or boxes as we preferred. It was the halcyon time of theater life in New York City, for an honest attempt was being made, particularly in this Theater, to purify the drama and educate its patrons' taste. Hence, great and magnificent plays were produced, Shakespeare's masterpieces predominating. In this way we saw the theater at its best and met the most reputable players of the day, including Edwin Booth and Charlotte Cushman.

With their New York house, Mr. Frost had purchased a full-sized billiard table, thinking to make home the more attractive to his sons. This it certainly did, but it gave them also an intense love of the game, for they became almost expert players. It was not until Booth's Theater was closed, as a financial failure, and the Madison Avenue house had been given up that the danger connected with these pursuits became apparent.

The time came when we moved again and had no billiard table in our home. Then, in spite of some compunctions of conscience, there was but one thing to do. I must go where the billiard tables were. And for many a day thereafter, I frequented places redolent with tobacco smoke, where stood bars patronized by men more often drunk than sober, and where profanity emphasized most of the conversation. At about twenty years of age I gave up billiard-playing, and have never since touched a cue. . . .

As it was with billiard-playing, so with theater-going. The time came when I could no longer go to Booth's Theater, and later I found myself in playhouses where conditions were anything but good. My last experience of this sort was in my college days, when I went to the Chestnut Street Theater in Philadelphia. There I became so disgusted with the play, and especially with the ballet, that I rose up between the acts and went out, never to pass through a theater door again. . . . As a result of my experience, I am constrained to express it as my conviction that the theater cannot be made a financial success except as it is made to appeal and minister to the baser passions.

Meanwhile, however, the boys enjoyed their city life, guarded by home influences that were helpful. Their father was in touch with the most spiritual movements of the day and loved to entertain ministers, missionaries, and others engaged in Christian service. Among the most welcome visitors to their New York home was a Scottish uncle by marriage, a graduate of Edinburgh in arts and theology, whom his nephews regarded with profound admiration. The Rev. James Inglis was eminent both as a preacher and writer, but it was his accurate scholarship that was the wonder of the boys who, search as they might, could never find a word he could not define as well as spell correctly. The big Webster dictionary was often called to their help, but the word that would prove their uncle's Waterloo remained undiscovered.

Mr. Inglis was the center, at that time, of the remarkable group of teachers and preachers of various denominations whose informal meetings in his office and book room were the precursors of the Bible Conference movement of our day. It is no exaggeration to say that the Niagara Conference—first of such gatherings—had its inception in the stimulating fellowship of D. L. Moody, Major Whittle, A. J. Gordon, George C. Needham, James H. Brooks, and others, who loved to forgather in that New York office with one who contributed so much of mental culture and spiritual illumination.

But Mr. Inglis was above all a man of prayer, and this it was that made him a formative influence in the life of his younger nephew in the Frost home. He himself would have been the last to suppose that, sixty years later, Mr. Henry W. Frost would write of him as "the uncle whose memory I have peculiarly revered and whose faith and works, though afar off, I have sought to follow." But it was upon this nephew, in large measure, that the mantle of James Inglis was to fall—the boy who, running into his room casually one day, was arrested to find him on his knees and to hear him earnestly praying for himself and his brother by name. Such impressions go deep in a young heart, and certainly they were needed at this time.

For when Harry was about thirteen it became necessary to dispose of the Madison Avenue property, and the family moved into the Gilsey House, one of the Apartment Hotels which were then becoming popular. There the boy entered upon what he afterwards felt to be the most critical period of his early life. Not being strong at the time, his attendance at school was irregular, and he missed his brother who was already promoted to college.

For the first time (he wrote) we were shut up in a few small living rooms, took our meals in a public dining room, moved to and

fro in crowds, and lived constantly in the midst of worldly surroundings. . . . A boy's adaptability, however, is one of his strongest characteristics, and I speedily adjusted myself to the new conditions. The hall and elevator boys became my friends, the waiters,
in spite of their august appearance, were soon regarded as familiars,
and the excitement of public life became most attractive. . . . There
were the comers and goers at the hotel to be seen; there were games
in the broad winding halls to be played. . . . Moreover, there were
the billiard room in the basement, the card-playing room next to it,
and, connecting the two, the hotel bar—all of which were open to
me as to others.

It can easily be seen why those days were critical for the
boy who was left a good deal to himself. Inwardly, he was
far from happy. He had reached the age when young people become reserved with their elders, and was facing his
problems very much alone. But there was One who perfectly understood, and who had provided a saving element
just where it seemed most unlikely. For among the families
resident in the hotel were some young girls whom Harry carefully avoided. Nothing could have been more unexpected
than that, entrapped by his brother into meeting one of
these, he should find in her the very friend he needed. Quiet
and retiring, this little maiden lived very much apart from
the influences about her. Her short white frocks and long
braids of hair put her among children, but her inner experience was that of a happy and even mature Christian.
She knew and loved the Lord Jesus and, as the boy soon discovered, was able to help him in his difficulties. How little
passers-by realized what it was that engaged the thoughts
and filled the conversation of these two, amid the distractions
of that gay hotel! To the boy, drifting and unsatisfied, this
gentle girl was like an angel from heaven.

Life to me, in those days, was big with perplexity, and I needed a friend who could see what I did not. We often found some quiet nook in the hotel and spent hours in talking seriously and even solemnly. And by this sacred influence, the spiritual life that had sadly declined was restored and saved. . . . God, through my friend, Edith Butler, came into my life anew, and by His incoming cast out things that were contrary to His will. Thus the evils of my surroundings lost their hold upon me and, in the midst of them, I was kept.

It was a change for the better when, in the interest of his sons, Mr. Frost moved to Princeton, where the elder brother continued his university education. There Henry attended a preparatory school and threw himself into the absorbing pursuits of organized athletics, especially baseball. He was fifteen by this time and found it none too soon to tackle higher mathematics, Latin, and Greek. Six years of school and college followed, brightened by delightful intercourse with a family of cousins, two boys and two girls, whose father, the Rev. W. A. McCorkle, had married a sister of Mrs. Frost's. The two families were devoted to each other, and Dr. McCorkle's ministry in the Second Presbyterian Church in Princeton led, under God, to a moving episode in the life of the college.*

For while the Frost boys were absorbed in school and college, their father became increasingly exercised about the spiritual condition of the student body of which they formed a part. He longed to bring to those hundreds of young men on the threshold of life some of the influences that were mightily stirring hearts through the preaching of D. L. Moody, Harry Moorehouse, and others. Mr. Frost had heard Moody for himself, and the evangelist had spoken highly

---

* Princeton did not become a university until 1896.

of Moorehouse, who was from England. So it was with confidence he urged Dr. McCorkle to invite both the one and the other to Princeton, and arrange for meetings in his Church.

Moorehouse came in 1874, and was entertained in the Frost home. The days that followed afforded a remarkable instance of how God loves to use "the weak things of the world" in accomplishing things that are mighty. Moorehouse had been an inveterate gambler and even a pickpocket. He was uneducated and homely in appearance. And yet, saved and transformed through divine grace, he was a mighty power in convicting and saving others. The love of God was his theme, and he would preach night after night from John 3:16, pouring out fresh treasure all the time as from an inexhaustible store.

Dr. McCorkle's Church was filled to overflowing, not only with townspeople but with students and professors. If any of the latter had been doubtful as to a man who could not speak good grammar being a channel of divine blessing, their doubts were soon swept away. "The Spirit of God moved again and again over the large audiences. . . . Hearts were bowed low, and young and old alike surrendered utterly to the claims of Christ." As a guest in the Frost home, the evangelist did some of his best work.

Here my parents gathered on several occasions a picked company of seminary students, that they might hear Mr. Moorhouse expound the Word and have the opportunity of asking him questions. I, of course, had no right in that company, but, boylike, I hovered around, attracted by the sight of the circle of eager students and the kindly teacher in their midst. I have to confess that I heard little of what was said, and understood less. But deep impressions were made upon me. I recall, among other things, the flood of questions which poured in upon the little man, and the flood of answers which came back as, Bible in hand, the quick replies were given.   And I recall how the teacher would pause at length, as one of the students would exclaim:

"Oh, Mr. Moorehouse, where do you get it all?"

"From here, just from here," he would reply, with a smile, patting his Bible as he spoke.

It was a wonderful time for some of those students, as afterdays in the ministry proved.   It was a wonderful time also for the un-noticed lad, who noticed all.

Two years after the visit of Moorehouse, Mr. Frost and Dr. McCorkle were successful in inducing the faculties of college and seminary to unite in bringing Mr. D. L. Moody to Princeton.   Harry Frost was then about to enter college. He looked on with keenest interest at the marvelous quick-ening of spiritual life that took place under the evangelist's preaching.   Princeton was moved as never before.   So many godless men were powerfully converted that the student life of that important center was "wholly transformed."   But, strange to say, young Frost was not himself brought at that time into the joy of full salvation.   Perhaps he was preoccu-pied with the experiences just before him of "Freshman year," or too much taken up with college sports.

Princeton was certainly playing wonderful baseball in the spring of 1876, their famous pitcher, McMann, having dis-covered the art of curving the ball in its flight.   Harry Frost was an ardent "fan" at these exciting games.   He found his place in college activities, both indoors and out.   He pulled bow in a four-oared crew, was pitcher on the Freshman nine, and was among the first to go in for lawn tennis.   In his studies he keenly enjoyed languages under Professor Karge, logic with Dr. Atwater, psychology and philosophy under

President McCosh, and, most of all, English literature with
Professor Hart. His student days were supremely happy,
because of satisfying friendships. He was a charter member
and the first secretary of the well-known Ivy Club,* which
gave him a congenial circle. But the chief Friendship was
neglected. He took no decided stand as a Christian. During
his college course he attended only one student prayer meeting, and was more interested in athletics, music, and good
times socially than in his studies. But through it all, as he
dimly realized, the prayers of his father and mother were
"ever wrapped about him like a mantle."

---

* The Ivy Club was formed in 1877, its first meeting place being the small
stone house at the head of Alexander Street, on the Episcopal Church grounds.

CHAPTER

II

DISCIPLINE BEGINS

AFTER three years at Princeton, Harry Frost, who was in poor health, left college to join his father and brother in out-of-door activities—the building of gas and water works. He was successful in his study of the principles of civil and mechanical engineering, so much so that when a contract was taken to supply the town of Attica, N. Y., with gas and water, he was put in charge of the construction of the works.

In the quiet life of the Wyoming Valley, the advent of a modern water supply and of gas for lighting was no small innovation. Interest and excitement grew as the reservoir was prepared three miles out of Attica, as the mains were laid during the long summer months, and as hydrants and gas posts began to appear in the streets. Hundreds of men were employed in these works, and their labors were rewarded when a full supply of clear fresh water flowed into the town and when, a little later, the first street lamps shone out on wintry nights.

But the chief interest, naturally enough, was in the young superintendent who directed these undertakings. Though he bore the stamp of a college student, he was ready to work with his men in a way that surprised conservative Attica people. And he was open to observation—more so than he could have wished—rooming in a boarding house and taking his meals at restaurants. All this enabled him to appreciate the comforts of a home when, some twelve months later, he was received as a paying-guest by Dr. and Mrs. A. G. Ellinwood of Prospect Street.

The family was an interesting one. The doctor, in addition to his local practice, was surgeon to the western division of the Erie Railroad. A man of fine Christian character, he was known and loved throughout the community. Mrs. Ellinwood, besides being thoroughly like-minded, was a woman of culture and refinement. A young son and daughter completed the household, save for a gifted elder sister who was teaching and studying in a collegiate school near New York. In such a circle, Mr. Frost found himself in touch with the best social life of the neighborhood; but he was far too busy to give much time to its enjoyment:

Water works and especially gas works (as he wrote) do not run themselves, and I soon discovered that if the one in charge should fail in any respect, the general public would give him little consideration. As I was intent upon learning the business in all its details, I assumed responsibilities which included attention to the reservoir and also the making of all the gas needed, first alone, and then with one helper. . . .

Life now meant late to bed and early to rise, and strenuous work all day long. Indeed, it sometimes implied working all night in repairing some break at the gas house or in making additional runs of gas. Even under the most favorable circumstances it involved the daily, dull routine of letter-writing, banking, drawing checks, col-

lecting bills, reading the gas meters, working at the gas house, repairing leaks in the street mains, overseeing the refining mill, and
so on.*

Thus, at last, I had plenty of thorough and continuous discipline.
But I have since discovered that the grind of those days was turning
out more than water, gas, and flour. It was, in the nature of the case,
producing a certain measure of character, and was preparing me,
including the figuring and bookkeeping, for a service later on, which
I did not in the least anticipate.

The steady application thus required had another result
of which Mr. Frost was at the time unconscious. It was
winning for him the regard of a certain member of the
Ellinwood family in whom he was increasingly interested.
For the music-loving older sister, at home for the holidays,
was induced to visit his workshop with a bevy of girl friends,
to see the process of gas-making. They found the young
superintendent occupied with his engine, clad in overalls and
streaked with grease and coal-dust—very conscious, as he
looked up, of the contrast between his appearance and theirs
in summer frocks and sashes. But amid the merry group
was one girl who received an impression of him then that
paved the way for more than friendship.

Danger as well as hard work was involved in that gas-
making process at Attica. On one occasion, Mr. Frost was
giving his machinery a thorough overhauling when, suddenly, there was an explosion which dislodged a plate of iron
above his head, weighing about two hundred pounds, almost
stunning him at the same time. What made him look up
at that moment he could never tell, but it saved his life.
For there was this falling mass of iron—and he had barely

---

* For the generous, enterprising father had purchased a flour mill in the
town, producing four hundred barrels of flour a day, and made that also
a gift to his younger son.

time to bend aside before it crashed into the pavement at his feet. Shaken as he was, the young man had to take immediate steps to prevent a more serious explosion, but when he fully realized how near death had been, he was overcome with a consciousness of the presence and protection of God.

This was renewed when, driving his Kentucky thoroughbred a little later, he came to a railroad crossing and heard the thunder of an express train in the cutting which hid it from sight. To stand still would have meant to have the train pass so close in front of him that the horse would have reared and backed, smashing the light buggy against the embankment. The whip was in his hand, and for the first time he used it to give "Nellie" a heavy cut across the flank.

The poor little creature jumped as if she had been shot, gave a leap forward, reached the farther track, and drew the buggy after her —just in time for the train to miss the hind wheels as it rushed past on the down grade to Attica. "Nellie" evidently thought the end of the world had come, and I am not sure but that I did. I succeeded in turning her to the left and guiding her on to the road which ran alongside of the track; but once there, she laid her ears back, broke into a gallop, and sped along the reach of level as if demons were after her and her one business in life was to get away from them. The only thing I could do was to let her go and keep her in the road. Fortunately, no vehicles were in sight and we were free to fly along as far as "Nellie" pleased. This proved to be a long distance. But, at last, she began to listen to my voice. She came down to a trot; one ear came up and then the other, and finally, after looking over her shoulder once or twice, she slowed down to a walk. We came to a crossroad soon after this. I turned there, took another way home, and arrived at our stables with a new affection for "Nellie" and a big, new love for God.

A different kind of danger, but one in which the deliverance was no less marked, came in connection with the flour mill in which young Mr. Frost was building up a prosperous business. On a tour of inspection, he was surprised to find some workmen stenciling the name of the mill and flour upon a shipment of barrels, with this superscription: "Made from the best Minnesota wheat."

Now, though most of our wheat was bought in the West, it did not come from Minnesota. I at once called the head miller and asked where he got the stencil. He replied that Mr. Smith, our agent in New York, had sent it to him. Telling the miller not to use the stencil again, which brought the shipment to a standstill, I wrote immediately to Mr. Smith saying that, as we were not getting our wheat from Minnesota, we could not use the stencil he had sent.

Next day I received a telegram from our agent, saying that I might expect him the following morning. In no amiable frame of mind he appeared and told me plainly that the New York market demanded the statement given on the barrel-heads, since Minnesota wheat flour was easily sold at a premium; that no one in the trade was deceived in the matter; that he, not I, must be the judge of what the trade required; and that if he could not carry on his end of the business as seemed to him best, he would have nothing more to do with it.

I admitted that the wholesale trade was not deceived, but inquired whether the retailer who purchased the flour was not. He replied that probably he was, but that he could not follow out the question as far as that; the only part he had to do with was the trade. He then advised me as a friend not to be too sensitive about such matters, saying that such a statement as was on our stencil was quite common in the milling business, and that to apply too honest a rule in advertising would mean failure of the only trade which would keep the mill going.

I knew that Mr. Smith was largely right in his conclusions. Besides, I was aware that we might not be able to get anyone else to serve us so efficiently, and that any other agent would in all probability give the same advice and make the same demands. Under these conditions, it was some moments before I had courage to speak. But finally I said:

"Mr. Smith, I am a Christian, and our business, whatever the result, must be run on Christian principles. That stencil is a lie and will not be used again in our mill."

Mr. Smith left for New York by the evening train and never sent us another order. The mill, except for our local trade, had to be shut down, for we could find no New York agent who could do for us what our former agent had done.

Through many weary and unprofitable days, the business had to be built up from a local standpoint with an entirely new constituency, and I had to learn that doing the will of God would not always mean financial prosperity, that indeed it might mean just the reverse. But I found, even under such conditions, that there were compensations for all possible losses. In the visit of our agent, I had met a great temptation and had reached what I have come to believe was a real crisis in life. If I had failed then, I know not what my spiritual end would have been. But, strengthened by God, I chose the path of obedience. And from that moment I discovered that God's way of righteousness, whatever its trials, can never be anything else but one of blessed prosperity.

CHAPTER

III

NEW LIFE INDEED

IT will be seen from the foregoing that the young mill owner was a Christian in more than name before he had been long in Attica. Outwardly religious from the first, he had joined the Presbyterian Church and had even become a teacher in the Sunday School, but his own spiritual life was so far from satisfactory that he had little power to help others. How this up-and-down experience gave place to full assurance of salvation and joy in the Lord is the inward story of those busy years.

Attica, at the time Mr. Frost settled there, had no fewer than twenty-one saloons for its population of two thousand. Deeply interested in the men employed on the gas and water works, it was with no small concern he saw most of the money he was paying out go straight into the hands of saloon-keepers. Efforts to improve the situation, while they cost him a good deal, proved anything but encouraging.

We used to pay our men on Saturdays (he wrote of this experience). Then they went in long lines to the public-houses and commenced orgies which would last through the night and the following Sunday. So we tried paying on Monday. This helped but by no means cured, for the drinking began on that day and gathered force through the week. This condition of things determined me to lead a movement for the reduction of saloon licenses, and we succeeded somewhat in our efforts. The result, however, did not diminish the drinking; it simply concentrated it in the remaining saloons and increased the gains of their proprietors.

Then Mr. Frost tried another plan. As a counter-attraction, he would have a reading room and a good library. Games and Sunday lectures were arranged for. The rooms were attractive, well stocked with books and papers, and he spent many an evening there to make things sociable. At first the workers came freely, but as time went on they seemed to lose interest. Finally, the rooms were deserted; but not so the public-houses.

The Sunday afternoon meetings were a fiasco (he came to see), partly because I gave lectures and not the Gospel. At last I abandoned the whole effort and turned the reading room into my private office. The experience was most discouraging, and made me hesitate about attempting anything further.

Much as he desired to help, it was a case of trying to give what he did not possess. As to the Sunday-school class, it was about the hardest work he had ever undertaken. And, worse still, his own inner life was more and more unsatisfactory. It was there that the real difficulty lay.

I had thought that joining the church, teaching a Sunday-school class, and doing what other good I might would bring most of my life-problems to an end. But this was far from the case. In fact, I discovered that inwardly I was just about what I had been—sometimes uplifted, sometimes depressed, sometimes fervent, sometimes cold, sometimes strong, sometimes weak.

At last he could bear it no longer. It was not so much a question, then, of helping others, as an overwhelming sense of personal need. He was not even sure about his own salvation. Shutting himself in his room one day, he faced the facts.

Dropping on my knees beside the bed, I told the Lord that I had come to Him for relief from deep distress; that I was such a poor Christian that I was not sure whether I was one at all; that my heart was as hard as a nether millstone and cold as a frozen stream. I went on to ask the Lord for a new heart, for tenderness, warmth, love, assurance, without which I could not live. And then I waited patiently and long. There was no sign of any kind, though I prayed fervently. At last, no new feeling having come, I arose more dissatisfied and disheartened than ever. Turning to my study table, I noticed my Bible lying there.

"What book is that?" my mind began to question.

"It is the Bible."

"Is it true?"

"Why, of course it's true."

"Is it true for me?"

"Yes, wholly and eternally true for me."

"Does it promise forgiveness of my sins?"

"Yes, it does; forgiveness for all my sins."

"Does feeling or lack of feeling have anything to do with the certainty of its promises?"

"Nothing whatever."

"Then why not accept its statements as to my salvation, irrespective of feeling, once and forever?"

And there I continued to stand, looking at the Bible, forgetting myself and my feelings, thinking only about the God of the Book. Presently I laid my hand on the inspired volume and reverently, gratefully, and very quietly accepted its testimony as to what Christ had done for my soul.

A definite transaction thus took place in which there were two participants. For God's side was no less real than the young man's side. Do we realize that every act of faith on our part is met by a corresponding act on the part of the Faithful One? That which we commit to Him, He undertakes. That which we accept in faith, He seals in fact. No outward sound or sign marked that memorable hour, but fifty years later Mr. Frost could write:

I have never since for a single instant, so far as I can remember, doubted the reality and certainty of my salvation. I began in that moment to realize the truth of the word used of God to bring Luther into the light, *"The just shall live by faith"*; and the blessedness of the faith-life has been increasingly prized as the days have lengthened out. And so it was that a new steadiness began to characterize my spiritual experience.

The feelings of Columbus as he sailed among the West Indies for the first time, discovering one island after another, may be imagined. But I much doubt if his discoveries gave him greater pleasure than the following days brought to me. It was truly a voyage of discovery, as I was led from one religious experience to another—new skies of heavenly blue, new seas of golden light, new isles of verdant green, new trees and fruit and flowers! In other words, the Lord was gradually disclosing Himself to me, and I was delighted with the view. Of course, as far as maturity is concerned, I was but among the isles with an unknown continent beyond. Nevertheless, my heart was glad as I rejoiced in God my Saviour, and I was grateful to Him for every fresh revelation made.

At first, the change in the young man's life was not as apparent to others as to himself. Some very devoted if rather austere Christian ladies, for example, were still concerned over his "worldly ways." For it took a little while to learn, as he wrote, that "conscience, which seems such a dependable guide, may lead its followers far astray in matters of divine truth."

In other words, this guide of our life needs enlightening. And just then, I was an example of this. From early years I had considered certain amusements harmless, and therefore justifiable. Theater-going, dancing, card-playing, and like indulgences, provided they were respectably carried on, were so favorably regarded that they never disturbed my conscience in the least. On the contrary, there in Attica, I honestly held them to be a means to a good end— for the promotion of social life, for the establishment of an influence over worldly people whom pious ways might repel, and for making known what seemed to me a very important fact, namely, that a Christian is not necessarily an old fogy. And so I went on in those days, happily enough, a bit religious and a good bit worldly, a true Laodicean in being "neither cold nor hot," and all to the damage of my own life and the lives of others.

But the new spiritual experience was awakening questions about many things, and the influence of the austere ladies kept the matter of "wordly amusements" before him.

When they spoke of one's privilege in this connection, I could understand their meaning; but when they dwelt upon one's duty, declaring that dancing and card-playing, for example, were inherently and diabolically wicked, I debated their statements. As a matter of fact, I felt certain that my thoughts and actions in these matters were not wicked and that it was right to regard pleasures of this sort as "innocent amusements"; hence I persisted in the opinion that what was harmless was lawful. Mrs. W—— and her sister at last abandoned me. I fear their final thought was, "Ephraim is joined to his idols; let him alone." God, however, is more patient than the most patient of men and women. Moreover, He is a better teacher. And what those dear women—I thank God for them—failed to accomplish, He succeeded in doing. And His method was simplicity itself.

I had come to have some suspicion concerning a club to which I belonged. It was called "The Shakespeare Club," for its original intention had been to have social gatherings where the master-writer's poems and plays would be read. But it had descended from such heights, though the name remained, to the lower level of card-playing. This had brought me into intimate companionship with some people whose reputation had been established in the town as antichristian. I still saw no harm in card-playing, but I came seriously to question the Christian consistency of being closely identified with such a class of persons. I was thus led to pray about the matter and also to keep my eyes open, as I read my Bible, for any passage that would be a help in my perplexity.

It was in this way that I came across 1 Corinthians 10, one day, and was arrested by the words: "Whether therefore ye eat, or drink, or whatsoever ye do, do all to the glory of God. Give none offence, neither to the Jews, nor to the Gentiles, nor to the church of God." If the sun had suddenly shone forth at midnight, darkness could not have been more illuminated! I saw at once that the Christian life is not to be a negative but a positive one, that the question is not, "What's the harm?" but rather, "What's the good?" And I discovered that we are to lead blameless and harmless lives, not putting stumbling-blocks in any person's way, including not only the strongest of mankind but also the weakest. I needed no more. It was no longer a question as to whether or not a thing was inherently wrong, but rather whether or not it was wrong in its relationships. It was also no longer a question of duty but of privilege. Willingly, therefore, I gave up all doubtful practices, and the amusements which had more or less gripped me lost their hold, once and for all.

If the young man, as a Christian, had to sacrifice some things at this time, he was certainly gaining in other ways, specially in the friendship of Dr. Ellinwood and his family. The elder daughter had been none too favorably disposed, at first, toward the guest of whom she heard in letters from home. But personal acquaintance awakened more than a passing interest; and they had much in common, as she discovered, when Mr. Frost's spiritual life began to deepen. And he, on his part was finding something very satisfying in the friendship.

Bright and sweet of face (as he wrote), alert in movement, ready for in- or out-door sports . . . widely read, a good English, Latin, and historical student, and an unusually proficient pianist, Abbie

Ellinwood was one to command the respect and admiration of any to whom grace and culture might appeal. And, far more than this, she was a high-minded and devoted Christian.

But it was evident that, while thinking of her as "the rarest young woman I had ever met," he was as yet unconscious of all that this appreciation meant. The thoughts of both were centered, not on themselves, but on Him to whom their lives were given, and upon service to others. Miss Ellinwood longed to make the most of her opportunities as a teacher, to win her girls to Christ. Stirred to fresh prayer and effort through her association with Mr. Frost, she had the joy of seeing several brought into spiritual blessing. For him, there seemed less outlet for his new-found joy in the Lord. But something he must do! And, happily, his connection with Dr. Ellinwood opened a way.

As surgeon-in-charge of a division of a busy railroad, the Doctor was often called to accident cases of a more or less serious nature. Mr. Frost found that he could be useful in attending to dressings and helping in operations. He became so interested in this work that he made time to take a special course in minor surgery in a New York hospital. This increased his welcome among Dr. Ellinwood's patients, not a few of whom he continued to visit after their recovery.

Many interesting experiences grew out of this voluntary service, and many sad ones. Mr. Frost's chief object was to point his suffering friends to Christ, but he was receiving, himself, fully as much as he was giving. Sometimes the work was heavy and exhausting. One Saturday evening, for instance, word was brought to the office that there had been a freight wreck on the railroad and that a young man, Frank Nelson, had been crushed between two cars.

The Doctor went immediately to see what could be done. He found young Nelson in a terrible state, gave an opiate, and came back to his office to prepare for the amputation of both legs. On returning, he took me with him. A further examination made it clear that no operation could for the present be undertaken, the heart's action being too weak to allow of it. Then began a long wait, through the evening, into the early night, past midnight, and onward. After a time delirium set in, with heavy moanings and wild movements of the arms. The opiate seemed to have little effect, and we had to hold the patient's wrists, a railroad man on one side and I on the other. Hours passed in this way, till morning began to dawn. By that time I was about exhausted. But my chief concern was to speak to the poor, dying fellow about his soul. I had known him and was well aware that he was not a Christian. So I prayed that reason might return, that the spirit might be calmed, that the eyes might open, and that I might be able to point him to Jesus. But no, it was not to be. Calm did come, but it was the calm of death. There was no longer any need of holding the arms; they were indeed still. The only sound was the faint breath, coming and going. Just as the sun rose on that beautiful Sabbath morning, there was a slight tremor, and the spirit took its flight.

I stayed with the family for some time, trying to comfort the broken-hearted mother and other relatives. Then I went out into the wonder of the spring morning, awed and bowed. As I passed the church, the bell rang for Sunday School. Though feeling unequal to it, I turned in and took my class. But the strain and sorrow of the night had been too much for me, so I excused myself and went to my then home, my father's house. As I stepped from the front hall into the library, everything suddenly went black before me and I reeled. My father, who was sitting there, leaped and caught me, and helped me to my bed in the adjoining room. Then everything earthly faded.

But, in his unconsciousness, Mr. Frost received impressions so memorable that they went with him through life. He seemed to be in a world of light and glory, passing up a great highway, with many other pilgrims, toward the Celestial City. He could see it in all its beauty before him, and hear the softest, sweetest music. The gate of the city stood open, and one by one the pilgrims were welcomed with songs of triumph. Hastening his footsteps, he had almost reached the portal—when the great gate swung to, before his face, and he found himself shut out. Then in his desolation, almost despair, the Voice which is as none other spoke clearly, tenderly to his heart:

"Not yet! I have work for you to do."

CHAPTER

IV

ENRICHMENT

NOTHING was farther from the thought of Henry W. Frost at this time than the life-work that really lay before him. He was absorbed in business, on the way to financial success, and was being drawn into political activities with a view to much-needed reforms in his county and state. But, all unconsciously to himself, an unseen Hand was restraining and guiding, and rich gifts were coming to him that prepared the way for further usefulness.

But first there was a time of disappointment, of painful awakening, which left a sense of failure. For with great eagerness he had thrown himself into the campaign for reform with Mr. Carl Shurz and Mr. Theodore Roosevelt, hoping in this way to serve the cause of righteousness. Local success had attended his efforts, for the young man had gifts and was wholly disinterested. But the result fell far short of his expectations. For, as time went on, it appeared that he had helped to defeat one set of evils only to admit another.

He found also that he had made enemies where before he had none, and that his influence for good in the community was not what it had been. All this was deeply perplexing and made him realize the need of further thought and study. He longed for a firmer grip on fundamental truth and some authoritative word on life's problems:

I had taken, it seemed to me, a plunge into the darkness, and needed to be led back into the light. Service for God, evidently, was more than activity; it was, as well, receiving wisdom from above and walking under divine control. It was plain to me, at last, that reform activities would never satisfy my soul, but it was not clear what service God would have me undertake. I saw, therefore, that what I needed was illumination, and I knew that this could only come from the Word of God. So I turned as never before to the Scriptures.

But how to discover the truth he sought was the question. In studying the Word of God, the field is so vast and the paths so many that the beginner is often at a loss to know how to proceed. In these days he may find direction from correspondence courses and a wealth of literature upon the subject, not to speak of Bible Schools with day and evening classes. But at that time there were almost no helps and the student, as Mr. Frost recalled, had to make his own way as best he could.

The very difficulty, however, turned out to be, in one sense, an advantage. It threw me back upon the Book itself and developed much dependence on the Holy Spirit. One of the greatest preachers Canada has produced once told me that he was obliged, when he had finished his seminary course, to begin the study of the Bible almost as if he had never seen it—"for I knew about the Book," he said, "but I did not know the Book itself." My circumstances made this preacher's after-course necessary for me from the beginning, and this meant relying upon God in a peculiar measure. I went on, therefore, with my reading in a blind sort of way, yet with no little confidence that the Holy Spirit would be my leader and teacher.

Feeling also the need of further education, he gladly embraced an opportunity of going to Europe for the summer. He was planning a course of study in Edinburgh; but God had in view something still more formative and far-reaching. The enrichment of a lifetime was at hand, and a touch of loneliness and even sorrow was needed to awaken him. At first he could see only sorrow, when a letter from Attica told of bereavement in the home of his friends. Great was the grief that had come to them in the unexpected death of Mrs. Ellinwood, who had filled a large place in his life as well as their own. But sorrow is a great revealer, and before long it disclosed that which happiness had hidden. His special friend, whom he had taken almost for granted, like sunshine on a summer day, stood before him in a new light. She was in trouble, perhaps needing him. How he longed to comfort her! Then the truth dawned—the overwhelming discovery that, for him, there was but one woman in the world and that his heart was "wholly and irrevocably hers"!

After this, he was glad rather than otherwise for the illness which put an end to his program of study. The attending physician insisted upon complete rest, and a quick return to America brought what he needed most, full rest of heart. For his great love was returned. An engagement followed,

and before long the marriage which made Abbie Ellinwood
the partner as well as the permanent joy and inspiration of
his life.*

Naturally preoccupied before their wedding, the young
couple seem hardly to have been affected that summer
(1883) by a new development which was profoundly to
influence their future. Only thirty miles from Attica, a conference was held at Niagara-on-the-Lake, near the great
Falls, in which Mr. Frost's parents were especially interested.
For its leaders represented the group that had gathered
around Mr. James Inglis, their beloved relative, in earlier
days in New York. The spiritual movement begun in his
book room and office had been continued through these like-
minded friends—ministers and Bible teachers of various denominations—until it had grown into an annual conference.

---

* In answer to the question, "Who is the most charming woman?" it has
been well said, "The one who can most enrich the everyday moments of life."
By natural and spiritual gifts, the bride of that September day (1883) ex-
celled in this very way. Her training had been rich and varied, as the one
nearest to her records:

"Mrs. Frost in early life graduated from Houghton Seminary, Clinton, New
York, taking high standing and being the salutatorian of her class. Later,
she taught Latin and music for seven years at the Ossining Institute, at
Ossining-on-the-Hudson, and was professor of music for one year at Elmira
College, Elmira, New York. Her musical ability had been cultivated at the
Buffalo Conservatory of Music and by private tutelage under Dr. William
Mason and Mr. Max Pinner, both of New York City. Her missionary
sympathies had been developed by her mother from childhood, also at
Houghton Seminary which was definitely missionary in character, and by
contact with her cousin, Dr. Edmund K. Alden, Secretary of the American
Board of Foreign Missions, and her uncle, Dr. Francis F. Ellinwood, Secretary of the Foreign Mission Board of the Presbyterian Church, U.S.A. She
was of pure Colonial stock, being the seventh in direct descent from John
and Priscilla Alden, of *Mayflower* fame. With such antecedents and such
educational, musical, and missionary training, it is evident that Mrs. Frost
had much to give to the China Inland Mission, when she became connected
with it. This was particularly true of her music, her playing of hymns at the
meetings of the Mission, both public and private, being something which
will long be remembered"—H. W. F.

That year, for the first time, it was convened at Niagara-on-the-Lake, and Mr. Frost's parents returned from the gathering full of thankfulness for the rich feast they had shared with many old friends.

So much was their son impressed by what he heard of the conference, and especially of its chairman, the Rev. W. J. Erdman, that he greatly desired to bring the latter to Attica for a series of devotional meetings. This took some time to arrange, and the bride and bridegroom were living with Dr. Ellinwood, who needed his daughter's help, when the visit took place which was to have such far-reaching results. For the Bible Readings, good as they were, only whetted Mr. Frost's appetite for more such teaching. It was just what he had longed for; and Dr. Erdman was persuaded to return, a little later, to give his young host a continuous week of Bible study. Those were memorable hours in the quiet of the familiar home. Rich treasures of divine truth were opened up and a friendship begun of which Mr. Frost could write in later years:

It was said that if Dr. Mark Hopkins, the great educator, sat on one end of a log and a student on the other, there was a university. It might have been said with equal truth of Dr. Erdman that, if he sat on one end of a log and a student on the other, there was a theological seminary. And I, through life, have been that student. There were four men, by the grace of God, who made me: my father, who set before me the pattern of a perfect Christian gentleman; my uncle, James Inglis, whose godliness and erudition were an inspiration; Hudson Taylor, who led me into the sacred depths of the devotional life; and W. J. Erdman, who planted my feet in enduring stability upon the impregnable rock of revealed truth.

One outcome of Dr. Erdman's teaching on that first occasion was that Mr. Frost was confirmed in his views as to the

personal and premillennial coming of Christ. Often, in early
life, he had heard discussions on this subject, in which his
father was absorbingly interested, but his own apprehension
of the truth had lacked conviction. Now, to his surprise, it
was the topic Dr. Erdman suggested for their conversations.
Mr. Frost had expected new light to shine upon the Word
as they considered it together, but hardly anything as epoch-
making as that study of the second chapter of Daniel.

I was in politics in those days (he recalled) and intent upon
reforming the United States, if not the world; but Dr. Erdman's
exposition of Nebuchadnezzar's vision, with its divinely given interpretation, smashed my ideas as truly as the great Stone in the dream
smashes the image. For here was God's prophetic utterance concerning the development of earth's kingdoms—to the effect that it
was to be, not from the bottom up, but from the top down; not
from feet of iron and clay to head of gold, but from head of gold
to feet of iron and clay. It was clear, therefore, that the divine
pronouncement was that there should be a gradual declension of
national life and strength; and also that God's ultimate purpose was
that of bringing forth the Stone, even Christ, whose glory should
fill the whole earth. This view of divine truth changed the current
of my life. There in the quiet of that upper hall, though I said nothing
about it to my teacher, I renounced politics and gave myself to the
furtherance of those things which would make for the salvation of
men and the coming of Christ as earth's Lord and King.

After this visit, Mr. Frost turned with new ardor to systematic Bible study. Dr. Erdman's comprehensive grasp of
Scripture had suggested to him the importance not only of
consecutive reading, book by book, but also of tracing out
leading subjects through all parts of the divine library.

This method (he found) made the Bible a new book, as I began
to obtain correlated views of its teachings. I cannot fully recall the
first Scriptural subject I undertook to master, but I think it was that
of Assurance. At any rate, this topic came early in my new pursuit of

knowledge. And it had a definite bearing upon all of my subsequent selection of subjects. I chose Assurance because I desired to be assured; that is, I chose the subject because of personal need. This led to the practice of selecting topics from my individual standpoint, and of studying the Word in order to supply some spiritual lack in my life. I traversed in this way large portions of Scripture, seeking to lay broad foundations. . . . Subsequently, I took up such great fundamental doctrines as the Inspiration of the Scriptures, the Trinity, the Deity of Christ, the Atonement, Justification by Faith, the Resurrection, finding in these subjects, as I had in others, a strong establishment of faith and a great uplift toward God and heaven.

The wealth thus gathered grew with the years, for Mr. Frost was careful to conserve the result of his studies. In this he was helped by noting, in an indexed book, all the passages he found bearing upon the subject in hand.

The result of this system has been to secure more exact views than I should otherwise have had and to help me to see truth full-orbed. Another result has been that of leading me to pay as much attention to the Old Testament as to the New, which increased and confirmed my confidence in the inspiration of the Bible as a whole. And further, I have been led to see, through pursuing subjects in straight lines from Genesis to Revelation, that what was infolded in the Old Testament was unfolded in the New, and that the great consummation of all themes is the exaltation and glorification of Christ. . . .

Two passages, even in those early days, stood out before me: the first was, "If ye love me, keep my commandments," and the second, "The testimony of Jesus is the spirit of prophecy." The first impressed upon me that all searching of Scripture would be valueless, unless its certain and positive result was the living out of the things learned; and the second convinced me that the person of Christ is the interpretation of both Old and New Testaments, and is to be the soul's one constant objective. In other words, it became plain to me from the beginning that to know and not to do could never mean anything but condemnation, while all true knowledge must be derived from Christ and would result in the revelation and reproduction of His character.

These last thoughts led me finally to study the Word from a devotional standpoint. In doing so, from that day to this I suppose that I have read the Bible through between fifty and sixty times. In this way I have sought the revelation of the Son of God. And it is a joy to add—such is the inspiration of the Word and the power of the Spirit—that I have never failed to find on every page, always clearly and often radiantly, His divine Person.

And all his searching was with the prayer that the Scriptures, as the very Word of God, should search him.

CHAPTER

V

SOUL-WINNING

ONE outcome of Mr. Frost's devotion to Bible study was that while he "was musing, the fire burned." God's estimate of the value of a soul began to lay hold upon him. Reformation, at which he had been aiming, was seen to fall far short of human need. "Ye must be born again," took on new meaning. Life can only come from life, whether natural or spiritual; thus Christ received into the heart by faith is the only possible way of regeneration. "He that hath the Son hath life; and he that hath not the Son of God hath not life." And what facts can be more practical and compelling?

To be used of God to bring others to Christ now became the young man's ambition. But how to go about it he did not know. The more he tried to witness for his Master, the more difficult he found it. Speaking on other subjects was easy enough, but to introduce spiritual matters, helpfully, seemed almost impossible. In spite of a growing sense of responsibility, his lips were too often sealed.

All this came home to him one Sunday evening, not long after his marriage.

Constrained, at last, by a sense of need, I went to my room, turned the key in the door, and fell on my knees to ask for divine illumination and power. With much earnestness I told the Lord that I wanted to be wholly His and to be used by Him; that I did not know where to begin nor how to proceed; that I had failed in my past efforts and was discouraged. If ever I was to be used, I pleaded, He would have to bring it to pass. All I could do was to put myself at His disposal, and this I did unreservedly. I then asked Him to point out the way, and give me work which would result in souls being brought to Christ, promising to undertake whatever He might set before me. I felt relieved in spirit after this prayer, though how it would be answered I could not imagine.

Little expecting to meet the answer to that prayer on his way to business, Mr. Frost set out next morning as usual. Passing the post office, he stopped to open his mail box, and stood for a moment on the sidewalk with a number of letters in his hand.

"Is this Mr. Frost?" questioned a voice he did not recognize.

Turning, he saw an elderly man, who went on to say that his name was Emerson, and that he came from the village of Attica Center. There was a church, he said, at the Center, but for some years it had been out of use. There were people there who wanted a Sunday service. "I could get the folk together," he added, "and we wondered whether you would come and speak to us."

"No, Mr. Emerson," was the prompt reply. "I could not do that. I never preached a sermon in my life."

"We are not asking for sermons. Just come and talk to us."

"But that would be just as impossible. I should not know what to say."

Again Mr. Emerson pressed his request. It was a critical moment. For again Mr. Frost was about to refuse, when his prayer of the previous evening came vividly before him. Was this the answer? But he could *never* speak in public like a minister. Surely God was not asking that of him! But the conviction came that He was. The struggle was indeed death to self before the young man could answer:

"Thank you, Mr. Emerson. I will be there next Sunday."

So the victory was gained, once for all.

There was much to do before the Sunday came. The little church had been long disused, and Mr. Frost, pressing "Nellie" into service, drove out several times to give it a thorough cleaning.

When we got through (he said) I knew how to dust, sweep, mop, and scrub. All this I found to my advantage, for the farmers were more ready to listen when they knew that "the rich young man from Attica" was not above working with his hands.

But the biggest task was the preparation of the address. Arming himself with sermon paper of regulation size, the preacher-to-be withdrew to seek a text. It was springtime, and Nature had flung her treasures abroad with a lavish hand. His heart was stirred with delight by all he saw, and his discourse took the form of an exhortation to return gratitude and worship to the heavenly Giver of all good.

The sermon was written out and carefully rehearsed. But, even so, reading it to his audience was a terrible ordeal. The little church on the hill was well filled with people, and Mr. Frost's mother, who had driven over with him, was bright and encouraging, but he came home wondering sadly whether God could make any use of such a poor instrument.

Happily, after that, the young preacher abandoned the set sermon. With a written manuscript before him, he felt like David in Saul's armor, but when he trusted the Lord to bless His own Word, and just gave it simply to the people, the effect was very different. Week by week the congregation increased. The Sunday School flourished, and Mr. Frost felt his heart more and more drawn out to these worthy people. But one thing troubled him. Summer would soon be at an end; cold weather, bad roads, and a chilly meeting-house meant that the services could not go on through the winter; it had come almost to the last Sunday, and he had never attempted to draw in the net. Might there not be some halting between two opinions? Ought he not to press the question of immediate acceptance of salvation? And yet, suppose there should be no response!

The last Sunday came and his decision had been reached. He would begin with the children. So, his address, with its earnest appeal over, he asked whether any of the boys and girls had accepted Christ that summer, or would then do so. To his surprise, twelve young people stood up. Then he turned to the adults. What reply would they give to his Master? Had any received Him during the meetings as their own personal Saviour? It was not easy for those steady-going country people—but to his joy and wonder, young men and others rose to their feet, until six or eight were confessing Christ for the first time. It was a never-to-be-forgotten scene in that little church on the hill. The young preacher was profoundly moved. Indeed, it was a crisis in his own life, as well as for the eighteen or twenty who stood before him.

I drank at that moment the sweet nectar of soul-winning. . . . The Lord had fulfilled my longings and answered my prayers. I returned to Attica solemnized in heart and with an unspoken resolution. Henceforth, I would give myself to God, as I might find it possible, to bring precious souls and lives to Him.

Back in Attica, that resolution was put to the test. The large majority of people in the town did not attend any place of worship, and were as needy, spiritually, as could well be imagined. But this was a very different proposition from the friendly, country group of the summer. There was no Mr. Emerson to open the way, and "church people" were all engaged in their own work. If anything were to be attempted for outsiders, it must be a new departure. But how and where to begin!

True, there was a roller-skating rink that could be hired for use on Sundays. It was centrally located and, though roughly built, was familiar to the very people Mr. Frost desired to reach. Could not the Lord give blessing there, as He had in the little church on the hill? So the rink was rented, thoroughly cleaned, provided with chairs, stoves, and hymn books, and the first service was announced for Sunday afternoon.

The speaker was there in fear and trembling, but he was not alone. At his side was the true "helpmeet" who never failed him. Her music and her brightness were invaluable in such work, and still more so her faith. For Mrs. Frost could write "tried and proved" over many a precious promise, and thus had much to give to those who gathered about them. And as to the audience, if Mr. Frost had been surprised that first Sunday at Attica Center, he was more so now.

There before me in the rink were fully two hundred people, and I knew that very few of them ever went inside a church except for marriages or funerals. A few weeks later we were obliged to leave the rink on account of the cold. But we went into Lemon's Hall, which was even more of a common meeting ground for all classes, and the change turned out to our advantage. Here my wife organized a boy and girl "Gospel Choir," and as it was composed of the children of laborers and some from the families of saloon-keepers, we soon had in our services the people we desired to reach. . . .

Being well known in town, I found it easy to go from house to house, inviting people to the meetings, and even to visit the saloons, to extend a welcome to proprietors and their patrons, which service the Lord much blessed. Thus the work went on all through the winter, the attendance remaining good throughout, and the interest increasing in depth and sincerity. To our joy, not a few of the boys and girls of the choir came out brightly for Christ, including the son and daughter of the most notorious saloon-keeper in the place. Several grown-up people also confessed the holy Name, and showed in their lives that a great inner change had taken place.

More than this—during that same winter, invitations began to come to Mr. Frost to speak in other places. One of these brought him into contact with Mr. George H. Hall, General Secretary of the Young Men's Christian Association for the State of New York. This new friend was evidently impressed with the way in which the Lord was using the young business man from Attica, for he spoke of him to others, and openings increased in number until Mr. Frost was faced with a perplexing situation.

What did these frequent requests for outside service mean? And especially, what answer must be given to three different proposals that had been made to him? The first was from the pastor of a Presbyterian Church in Rochester, Dr. William R. Taylor, who wanted Mr. Frost to act as his assistant; the second was from Dr. Lyman Abbott of Cornwall-on-the-Hudson, who asked him to undertake his mid-week meetings and pastoral work; and the third was from Dr. Merrill E. Gates, President of Rutgers College, New Brunswick, who suggested home missionary work in that New Jersey city, specially for the factory people.

It was with astonishment that I received these invitations, not only because I felt unworthy of the opportunities presented, but also because the idea had not so much as once crossed my mind that the Lord would ask me to leave my business and home. I was willing enough now to serve Him, but unconsciously I had taken it for granted that He had established me in Attica for the rest of my days.

To add to the perplexity of the young people, their hearts were touched by an unexpected happening. News had got abroad that Mr. and Mrs. Frost might be leaving town, and a group of business men who attended the Lemon Hall meetings determined that this must not happen. Thinking that a financial inducement might help to decide the matter, they privately raised a fund for carrying on the Sunday meetings. Armed with a long subscription list, they waited upon Mr. and Mrs. Frost, begging them to remain in Attica.

The document contained the names of some two hundred people, few of whom were church members. Most of those who had subscribed were working-folk, many were children, and several Mr. Frost knew to be saloon-keepers. Not a few of the gifts and promises were small, down to a few cents, but this unexpected token of appreciation amounted in all to nine hundred dollars. And it was an offering of love!

Prayer had indeed been answered, and doors of service were opening, beyond all they had asked or thought.

CHAPTER

VI

A HOME FIELD

IT was no easy decision that young Mr. and Mrs. Frost had to make. They had come to a parting of the ways. On the one hand were parents who fain would keep them, the claims of business, the joys of home, and now the love of many to whom God had made them a blessing. On the other hand was that deep sense of call which cannot be disregarded, and the need of souls for whom no man cared.

But they were not left long in doubt, for outward circumstances began to shape in harmony with the inward call. First, a purchaser appeared for the gas and water works, and Mr. Frost was relieved of his chief business responsibility. Then his father undertook to run the flour mill, greatly desiring to see his son wholly engaged in the Lord's work. Set free in this way from local claims, quite apart from their own seeking, what could the young people do but go forward?

Their longing to work among the needy took them to New Brunswick, N. J., rather than to the churches of great preachers.* On the outskirts of that large city was a district occupied almost entirely by factory workers of the poorer sort. It was neglected and unattractive, as such localities were apt to be in those days. Churches and ministers were not in evidence, though the emissaries of Satan were unusually busy. Evil houses abounded, and the only witness for Christ seemed to be a mission Sunday School in a store on Troope Avenue. Here, then, with the approval of the group which had invited him, Mr. Frost decided to commence operations, working out from the store and Sunday School as a mission center. He had often thought, while in Attica, of giving up his pleasant surroundings to live entirely among the people he was seeking to win for Christ. As a follower of Him who "though he was rich, yet for your sakes became poor," that sort of approach appealed to him, but he found it far from easy in practice.

Two rooms in the cottage of a market gardener, near the store, afforded a lodging for which he was thankful, for his Scotch hosts were clean and quiet people. Here Mrs. Frost joined him, with their baby of nine months and his German nurse. This meant that one of their small rooms had to be a day and night nursery, while the other served the purposes of bedroom and living room. A little experience took all the romance out of this sort of thing and so tried Mr. Frost's spirit that he wrote to his friend and adviser, Dr. Erdman:

---

* "Little did we realize, at the time, how firmly and lovingly the Lord's hand was laid upon us in this matter. If we had gone in either of the other directions, we should have become identified with men who afterwards forsook evangelical truth, and whose influence and teaching might have harmed us beyond describing. How blessed it is that God sees the end from the beginning, and that His guidance, when hearts are right toward Him, is given with that end in view"—H. W. F.

I find that "following Jesus" in easy chairs and in warm parlors is a little different from doing it in nasty streets, up lanes and byways, into dark rooms, beside sick beds, and among poor and dirty people. I have hated it all and longed to run away. The fare at the boarding house makes me sick, and our one room seems sometimes like a prison.

Not very heroic, perhaps! No, but what true missionary does not know the experience? And the point is, they *kept on*. The love of Christ is a wonderful anchor—love that goes out to the most unlovely and loves them into loveliness. He who had sent them was with them; and Mr. Frost found, as the days went on, that he had the companionship of a wife who did not know the meaning of the word falter. So they reorganized the Sunday School, started singing and sewing classes, visited from house to house, and made the weekly services attractive. With their friendly calls they combined cottage prayer meetings, which proved the most rewarding of all their efforts. People might look askance at regular meetings in a mission hall, but just dropping into a neighbor's house for an hour seemed different. And the strange thing was that even notoriously sinful people would open their homes for such gatherings.

Visiting in this way one day, Mr. Frost came to the abode of a tall, gaunt woman from Lancashire, England, who was a drunkard and the terror of the neighborhood.

I entered this virago's yard just as she was expressing her mind to a pig which had pulled from the clothesline and trampled under foot a large cloth which she had been dyeing blue. Her oaths were making the air as blue as her dye had made the cloth. I could but feel, under these circumstances, that I had chosen the worst time possible for a call. But the sight of the missionary brought to mind the woman's old-country training, and she immediately attempted to do deference to "the cloth." With many apologies, she led me into her rack of a home, where I was made welcome. Before leaving, I had a straight talk with her about her soul. This led to other calls and talks, to meetings in her house, and to her coming to the mission. At last she was converted, and that gloriously. It was not long before her life was completely changed, and finally her drunken husband and sons were wholly reformed, if not saved. More than once afterwards I was inclined to thank God for the pig, for it was this desperado which gave me my formal introduction to Mrs. Birch, and opened the way to lead her to Christ.

This sort of work drew people to the hall in increasing numbers. The fact that their missionary lived with them, not far away in a better part of town, was all to the good. He was always available and ready to step in wherever he could be a help or comfort. Gradually even the worst people came to realize that he was their friend, and he and Mrs. Frost were welcomed into the places they had scarcely hoped to reach. In one house of ill-fame a little child had died, its short life having been lived amid moral corruption. Mr. and Mrs. Frost were invited to the funeral:

The room was large, dark, and bare. Filth was everywhere. The mistress of the place, in spite of her brazen face, was ashamed to look at us, and the other women stood shrinkingly about or sat in shadowy corners. Evil-looking men loitered outside the open door and windows. Everything about the house and people suggested that it was no place for a reputable person, except for a divine purpose. And there sat my wife in the midst of it all, looking like an angel of light, while I stood by her side, shrinking from contact with such vileness, yet glad to bring the message of salvation to those who so greatly needed it. This place was wholly changed. The death of the little child and the funeral service were God's means of transforming lives. It was the love of the Holy Spirit which constrained us at such times. And it was this love which broke down barriers and opened the way for the conquering Christ.

Many who came to the mission had not been inside a place of worship for years. Naturally, at first, they looked and felt out of their element, but it was not long before they began to forget themselves and take part in the singing. From the time that some well-known characters were converted and began to witness for Christ, new life was felt in the meetings. Among these was an old colored woman who broke forth one evening in a testimony specially addressed to the preacher:

"Oh, honey, de Lord hab done great things for me! He hab taken all my sins away—clean away, honey. Dey all gone. And I tell you, Chile, when dey went—dey went off ob me, Hallelujah, just like a clap of tunder!"

Blessed reality lay behind the statement, surprising as it was—reality that was changing many a life in that dismal quarter of New Brunswick. As the mission became known, people from other districts found their way to Troope Avenue and shared the blessing. It was not that the preaching was anything wonderful. The missionary was learning that it is the Word itself, quite apart from human wisdom or eloquence, which is the power of God unto salvation. A young man, recently converted, was giving a Bible Reading one evening on the subject of Peace. Having looked up a number of texts in the concordance, he was full of matter, but as the talk proceeded, Mr. Frost discovered that he had not been quite sure of his spelling, for while some of the texts contained the word "peace," others had to do with "piece," such as the new cloth in the old garment.

The "Reading" proved to be a jumble. But, curiously enough, its blessing abides with myself and my wife to this day. We soon forgot the mixed metaphors, and the sweet earnestness of the young convert proved a permanent benediction. This fact has often suggested to me that learning is not, by any means, the chief factor in one's being used by the Lord in bringing blessing to souls, but rather surrender to God and dependence upon the Holy Spirit.

The missionary learned also to expect results, for when God is working, wonderful things happen. He had been speaking one evening from John 6:47: "Verily, verily, I say unto you, He that believeth on me hath everlasting life." As the meeting proceeded, he became interested in a fine-looking young man, a stranger, who evidently belonged to a more educated class than the people about him. At the conclusion, the visitor stepped into the aisle to wait for a lady who had come with him. Seeing his opportunity, Mr. Frost shook hands with him and asked:

"Are you a Christian?"

"Oh no, Sir," he replied, with perfect frankness.

"Would you not like to be?"

"Well, yes, I should."

"Why should you not become one now?"

"Oh, I did not come here to get saved. I only came to bring my sister."

"It does not matter what you came for. If you want to be a Christian, you can become one now, as you stand here in this aisle."

The young man looked at me incredulously. Then, as we still stood there, I pointed to the verse about which I had been speaking, and showed him that God only requires one thing, namely, simple faith in Christ as the One who bore our sins. He looked at me searchingly.

"Do you mean to say," he questioned, "that as I stand here in this aisle I may take Christ at His word and be saved?"

"That is exactly what I mean," I answered, "for it is exactly what Christ says."

The young fellow lowered his eyes, stood in silence for a moment or two, and then said suddenly, *"I'll do it."*

With this he bade me good night, and went out into the dark.

I was staggered. Theoretically, I was sure that I had spoken what was right; but practically, I wondered if I had. There had been no confession of sin, no prayer, no emotion, nothing that was usual in cases of conversion. But the next Sunday quieted my fears. The young man was in the evening meeting, his face shining, and at the first opportunity was on his feet witnessing for Christ. As the days went on, we had abundant evidence that his soul was in safe and blessed keeping. And, beyond a doubt, the change had come to pass, not as a result of my words or earnestness, but simply and only from the divine fact that the entrance of God's Word giveth light.

Month after month this happy work went on, until to their great regret Mr. and Mrs. Frost were compelled to return to Attica. Dr. Ellinwood urgently needed them, and Mr. Frost's mother was far from well, and in his father's frequent absences was very much alone. It was hard to part from the converts they loved. But the good work went on. The very neighborhood was changed. Houses of ill-fame disappeared, and once-degraded men and women were transformed outwardly as well as inwardly. For there is no social uplift to compare with Christ's own life in the soul.

WIDER VISION

W HILE still in New Brunswick, Mr. Frost had received a circular from Dr. W. J. Erdman announcing the second Bible Conference at Niagara-on-the-Lake. For various reasons the gathering had not been convened the previous summer (1884), so that he was the more anxious to attend this one. Mrs. Frost was not able to go with him, but taking a brief holiday from their mission district, he was soon at the summer hotel in whose grounds the conference was held. The place was beautiful and the Christian fellowship refreshing, but it was something deeper that made that Conference forever memorable. For it was there the young evangelist was first awakened to the spiritual need and claims of the great world beyond America.

Strange as it may seem, Mr. Frost had reached twenty-seven years of age without ever hearing a missionary sermon. While still at Princeton, he had passed through a phase of romantic interest in India, and had even offered to the Board of his church for that field, only to be declined because he had not had seminary training, after which the matter was forgotten.   But now, alive as never before to spiritual realities, he found himself listening to two of the most impressive missionary speakers of the day—W. E. Blackstone of Chicago and young Jonathan Goforth of Knox College, Toronto, who was looking forward to service in China. Those who know the power and inspiration that so long attended Dr. Goforth's ministry can well imagine the appeal of his consecrated youth.   He arrayed facts and figures in a way that was startling, overwhelming: more than eight hundred millions in the darkness and hopelessness of heathenism, living, dying, within our reach—no longer inaccessible, but left to perish, with no knowledge of the Redeemer's love!   And there is "none other name under heaven given among men, whereby we must be saved."

One heart, at any rate, met the challenge in the light of eternity.   For there, in the pavilion by the lake, Mr. Frost's conclusion was clear: Yes, life must be given *not* to those who needed him (like his people in New Brunswick, for whom others would care) but *to those who needed him most.*

And something happened to deepen this impression.   For, on leaving the meeting, the young man stopped at a bookstall and was arrested by a publication lying right in front of him.   It was an illustrated book, larger than most, with a picture on the cover of seven men, young and athletic-looking, but dressed in Chinese dress from head to foot. They were certainly not Chinese.   Those forceful attitudes and marked features were little in keeping with their oriental garb. Who could the odd-looking fellows be? Curiosity held him. The book was called "A Missionary Band." Mr. Frost bought it, went to his room at the hotel, and at once began to read.

First at Niagara and then in his New Brunswick lodgings, the book took hold of him in a way he little expected. An impassioned heart and practised hand had gathered into its pages not only the facts as to the men of culture and position whose going to China was deeply stirring the Christian world, but also much that was best and strongest in missionary appeal. The profound incentives which had moved these men could not but move the reader, and from pencil marks on the pages one can follow the trend of Mr. Frost's awakened thought.

God has shown that there is nothing He will not do, or give, or suffer, that men may be saved; and yet, in spite of the pouring out of all that infinite wealth of love, men are going down to death, because you and I do not tell them of the Gospel. . . .

Not one of these Christless millions is forgotten before God. . . . Not one of them goes down into the darkness but the very tears of Christ are falling, so to speak, upon his head. Shame on us when we look at the wonderful, inconceivable love of God toward those lost ones—and then look at our own hearts!*

More than this, the book presented opportunities for missionary service of which he had never heard. He read, particularly, of the "faith mission" in China (strange term to him), which by its simplicity and Scriptural principles had attracted those Cambridge graduates and army officers. He read of their going out with no promise of salary or support,

---

* True, there is much in Scripture about the wrath of God against sin, and the "day of wrath" awaiting the sinner; but let us never forget that it is the wrath of a father's heart, the terrible "wrath of *the Lamb*." Judgment, though it is "His work," is always "His strange work"—Isaiah 28:21.

save the promises of the Bible, to live in a simple, Chinese
way, and devote themselves to making known the Gospel
among the unreached millions of the vast interior. He read
of the faith of Hudson Taylor, founder and leader of the
work, and of the brave, persistent pioneering which had
gained a footing in ten out of the eleven provinces previously
without Protestant missionaries—provinces with an aggre-
gate population of a hundred and fifty millions. It was
Henry W. Frost's introduction to the China Inland Mission.

Five months only had elapsed since the sailing of the
Cambridge Band,* but already their whole-hearted consecration to the service of Christ was awakening world-wide reactions. American universities were feeling it. Robert
Wilder and John N. Foreman, both of Princeton, had lighted
the torch of missionary enthusiasm soon to flame into the Student Volunteer Movement, with its noble watchword, *The
Evangelization of the World in this Generation*. Revival
movements started in English and Scottish universities
through the visits of C. T. Studd and Stanley Smith were
increasing in power, and after years of quiet foundation-
laying the China Inland Mission had been brought into
prominence as surprising as it was unsought. It was still
the day of small things, for the Mission was not yet international, but Mr. Frost found himself strangely drawn to its
principles and objectives. No debt, no solicitation of funds,

---

* Leaving England on the fifth of February, 1885, the party consisted of
C. T. Studd of cricketing fame; Stanley P. Smith, stroke oar of the Cambridge boat (1882); Montagu Beauchamp, the present baronet; A. Polhill
Turner and W. W. Cassels, clergymen, the latter of whom became the first
Protestant Bishop in West China; C. Polhill Turner and D. E. Hoste, officers of the Dragoon Guards and the Royal Artillery, respectively. Fifteen
years later Mr. D. E. Hoste succeeded Mr. Hudson Taylor as General Director of the China Inland Mission.

dependence upon the faithfulness of God as all-sufficient for the needs of His own work, and the definite purpose of making known the Gospel to China's remotest bounds—how his heart went out to such a fellowship! Yes, the call was clear. He must give his life to China's evangelization, and, if possible, in the ranks of the China Inland Mission.

But the Mission headquarters were far away in Shanghai and London. New developments crowded the young man's life as he found himself again in Attica. There seemed no prospect for the present of leaving the parents for whose sake he and Mrs. Frost had resigned the work in New Brunswick. Other spheres of service were opening before him, and his father, seeing the need of the little family for a settled home, was generously providing one.

With ample means to draw upon, that roomy "cottage" next door to his own residence was made as attractive and convenient as could well be imagined. Young Mr. Frost was busy, meanwhile, with spiritual work in the town and neighborhood. And so the vision faded. It was not that the missionary purpose was given up; but nothing could be done about it at the time, and needs out of sight have a way of passing out of mind. The renovation and furnishing of the two-storied "cottage" were absorbing work, and not long after the young couple moved into it a second son was born to make their happiness complete. What a perfect home it was—beautiful in every appointment, surrounded by the lawns and gardens of the two houses thrown into one, and filled with light, love, and music!

And then the practical question had to be faced—what was the young father to do about the support of his family? The flour mill was still his property, and Mr. Frost, Senior, was expecting to hand it back to him, though he would far rather have had his son continue in whole-time Christian service. This the son also desired, though the duty of providing for his own pressed upon him. A choice had to be made, but he was not the only one pondering the problem.

"Harry, my boy," said his father one day, "listen to me. I want to make an arrangement with you. I cannot preach, but I can do business. You can preach, and I want you to do so. Suppose, therefore, that I make the money and you do the preaching. How will that work?"

Keenly as the young couple appreciated this generous suggestion, they could not but see that to accept it would involve a loss of independence. To sensitively proud spirits it was not easy to relinquish a self-supporting basis. But, after much prayer—

We finally reached the decision (he wrote) that God was leading us out, and that my father's offer was His provision for us. So we died to our pride, and I surrendered myself to the Lord for a service of soul-saving in a new relationship and by new processes. I then burned my bridges behind me by turning over my business interests to my father, leaving myself without a penny to my name.

The experiences that followed more than justified the course thus entered upon. One invitation after another took Mr. Frost to churches of various denominations, to tent missions, and to a collegiate preparatory school, where many of the boys and young men were led to faith in Christ. Places differed a good deal in their response, but at the close of the year he was able to write:

I had not visited a single locality where the power of the Spirit had not been displayed, and I was able to look back over it all with joy and deep thankfulness to God. I was not deceiving myself as to the

RESIDENCE OF MR. MAHLON S. FROST IN ATTICA

Intimately associated with the beginnings of the Mission in North America

cause of the blessing. I knew well that my speaking was simplicity itself and that what had been brought to pass had been wrought by God. So I was encouraged to go on. The One who had worked would work and could be trusted to the full.

But there was, underlying it all, a sense of uneasiness. It was not the long separations from wife and children that troubled Mr. Frost, though the loneliness at times had been almost unbearable, nor was it the conflict for souls in which he was engaged day by day. There was another conflict, unknown to any but himself. For the call which had come to him at Niagara-on-the-Lake was real and would not leave him. The Conference came again (1886) and he attended it, very much on his guard against "emotionalism." Niagara had become his school of theology, and the Bible teaching was as vital that year as ever. But, alas for his peace of mind, it was Dr. A. T. Pierson's missionary address that impressed him most, with its startling arraignment of a compassionless and disobedient Church. It was not easy, after this, to compromise with his aroused convictions. The joys of home and the claims of his spiritually fruitful work absorbed him, however. And again the vision faded.

But facts had not changed. The passing of the sense of responsibility did not mean that the need had ceased to exist. God's purpose for his life had not changed, though the young evangelist came so near missing it. In the midst of his labors, important as they were, he was increasingly convicted. The very blessing given spoke loudly to his inner consciousness:

"If the need here is so great, what must it be in China? If God can use me here, could He not use me there? And what about the souls that would be saved?"

Finally Mr. Frost was brought to see that this state of things could not continue. It was making his inward life unreal and sapping spiritual strength. He must test his conflicting thoughts and feelings by the one unchanging standard—that of the Word of God. This he had not really done. He had been moved by stirring appeals and by the example of others, but his sense of call had no grip or joy, because it was not grounded upon the will of God.

All this brought me to the conclusion that I ought to face the whole subject of foreign missions from an entirely different point of view—that is, from the Scriptural. It was thus I was led to undertake a Bible study of a searching kind. This was in reference to two subjects: first, *what was the spiritual condition of the heathen?* and second, *what was the duty of the church concerning the heathen?* Through the whole winter, therefore, I carefully read the Scriptures to obtain God's answers to these two questions, the quiet between my evangelistic meetings being largely given to this undertaking. This is not the place to present the reasons for the conclusions to which I was led, but I would say that I came out of my earnest and prayerful study with two fixed beliefs: first, that the heathen are lost and can be saved only by faith in Christ; and second, that it is the duty of the church to do all that is possible to give them the saving Gospel.* I may say that little emotion resulted from this study. But I would add that it brought me to the deep conviction that it was my unmistakable and unalterable duty to give myself to the task of proclaiming God's good tidings to the ends of the earth.

It was not till summer brought again the ministries of the Niagara Conference that these convictions became illuminated with deep and wonderful joy. And, strange to say, no direct reference was made that year (1887) to the work of

---

* Dr. Frost's brief pamphlet on *The Spiritual Condition of the Heathen,* giving the result of these studies, can be obtained from the book room of the China Inland Mission, Philadelphia.

foreign missions. But all that was said seemed to the young evangelist to point in that direction.

My study during the winter had brought me to new ground, namely that of the Word; and I now found that it contained sign-posts everywhere, indicating that all Scriptural roads ran in one direction and to one consummation. That consummation was not foreign missions. It was, rather, the coming of the King and the establishment of His kingdom. At the same time, it was clear that the witness of the missionary among Jews and Gentiles was the divinely ordained means of bringing to pass that promised end. . . .

Under this influence I saw that the work of foreign missions was no "forlorn hope." It was the stately steppings of God Himself among the nations, to result in a glorious conquest, turning the kingdoms of the world into the kingdom of His Lord and Christ. There could be no place in such service for the thought of self-sacrifice. If God would accept me to be in some measure used for the hastening of Christ's kingdom, mine would be nothing less than the highest possible privilege and honor.

On this occasion, there was no arousement, no emotionalism. On the part of the teachers at the Conference it was quiet demonstration, and on my part, quiet conviction. At the same time, a beautiful vista opened up before me of a blessed service leading to the infinite and eternal exaltation of Christ. I had now not simply the view of the heathen, but also and particularly that of the coming kingdom of God. This was satisfying and inspiring. Thus the premillennial view of missions, as related to the Lord's return in glory, took the word "duty" out of my missionary vocabulary and put the word "privilege" in its place. The result was that it turned pessimism into optimism and the ephemeral into the enduring.

CHAPTER

VIII

THE QUEST

A STEAMER facing wintry storms on the Atlantic, bearing a solitary traveler on his way to England, his heart
full of a great quest—thus closed for Henry W. Frost the
year that had brought his clear and final call to missionary
service. But the way was far from open before him.

After the Niagara Conference he had returned to Attica,
to share with Mrs. Frost the new light that had come to him.
They were so truly one that no step could be taken in which
they were not fully agreed. Hitherto they had had no difficulty in being of one mind, but now Mr. Frost found to his
sorrow that they were far from seeing eye to eye. Mrs.
Frost, though otherwise in sympathy, took a serious view of
the home situation. She could not feel it right to forsake
the parents who were dependent upon them for loving care.
This made a difficult situation.

That I could not go forward to China until my wife saw that it
would be right for us to do so was perfectly plain. On the other
hand, to stand still in such an important matter seemed disloyal to

58

Christ and His definite command. I pondered the problem, therefore, until head and heart were weary, and prayed until I could not
but wonder if God were not more weary than I.

At last light came, and he was led to a step which Mrs.
Frost could approve. This was to write and consult the
China Inland Mission in London. If the way gradually
opened, he would be thankful. If not, he would at least have
done what he could. So the letter was sent off in the confidence that the reply would be guided of God. And it was,
but not as Mr. Frost had hoped. Further correspondence
elicited the facts that he was twenty-nine years of age, had
two children, and that Mrs. Frost was caring for her invalid
father.

The Secretary, Mr. Benjamin Broomhall, was kind enough to
allow me to fill out my application papers, which were filed in the
regular way in London, where they still lie. A polite and gracious
answer was given, encouraging me to wait upon God for further
guidance, and there the matter ended.

But in God's plan, this was only the beginning.

Summer had passed into fall when the young evangelist
accepted an invitation to Lindenville, in northern New York,
for a mission in which three churches were uniting.

The moon was at its full (he recalled). The air was crisp, yet
not cold; there was much interest on the part of ministers and
people, and I was glad to be in service once more, in spite of longings
to be in far-away China. As the days went on, the attendance became
more than was anticipated, the church being crowded, and the impressions produced by the Spirit proved deep and convicting. Previously indifferent Christians were revived, and God brought some
wanderers home to Himself.

For two weeks the meetings continued daily, with increasing blessing, but more and more Mr. Frost was conscious

that the Lord was speaking to him as well as through him.
Quartered in a comfortable farm home on the outskirts of
the town, he had a good deal of leisure. His host was preoccupied, as were other farmers around them, and but little
visiting could be done between the meetings. With more
time than usual at his disposal, the perplexity as to his future
service drove the young evangelist to special waiting upon
God. And then things began to happen. Question after
question came up in his mind as he reviewed recent happen-
ings. True, there were serious obstacles in the way of what
he believed to be his life-work, but was there nothing more
that he could do toward their removal? London was far
from Attica, but might it not be possible to go there in person
and talk over matters with Mr. Hudson Taylor and the Secretary of the Mission? What a help it would be to meet them
and have their counsel, and—it was there light broke! If
he could not go himself to China, might he not be used of
God to bring the China Inland Mission to America and thus
open the way for others?

Well do I recall the moment when, on my knees in my little
bedroom, this thought first came to me—to propose to Mr. Taylor to
establish a branch of the Mission in North America, that it might be
to Christians on this continent what it had been to many across
the sea, and that young people here might have a new inspiration and
opportunity which would result in putting additional laborers in
China. From that moment I could not get away from it. Clearly,
the thing to do was to go to England! I would write to my wife and
father to this effect. I did so, and soon received favorable replies,
my generous father offering to meet my expenses across the ocean, to
and fro.

Shortly after this, the meetings came to an end. I immediately
returned to Attica. Preparations for departure were quickly made,
and the afternoon of November 12 (1887) found me on the steamer

in New York harbor, my face turned toward the broad Atlantic and the port of Glasgow on the other side.

The "cloud" moved rapidly, but I had followed it with ready heart and willing feet. I began to see light ahead, and the cheer of a new hope took possession of my spirit. Even if our way to China should remain closed, we should certainly have the joy of seeing the China Inland Mission established in North America, with all the new inspiration and blessing which this would bring to our people. How wonderful were the ways of God! It was indeed worth while both to wait upon and to wait for such an One as He.

So the eager traveler paced the deck of the ocean liner, fairly started on his quest. He was full of expectation, full of thankfulness. God, he was sure, was leading on.

CHAPTER

IX

HOPES THAT FAILED

LONDON in November is not the most cheery of places, and its northern districts offer little that is attractive. Well was it for the American visitor that his heart was warm with the joy of having led a fellow-traveler to Christ before landing, and with the anticipation of meeting friends who already meant much to him.

But Mr. Hudson Taylor was away from home when the young man found his way to Mildmay. As like as peas in a pod, the houses of Pyrland Road faced each other across the quiet street, each with a strip of garden at the back, but none in front to break the monotony. Fog and damp chilled the air, and the small open fire in his lodging at Number Forty-two was a poor substitute for the warmth of an American home. But he was near the Mission headquarters, which occupied several of the Pyrland Road houses, and Mr. Taylor would soon be back from his meetings in Ireland and Scotland.

Meanwhile, Mr. Frost did not lack occupation. Welcomed by Mr. and Mrs. Broomhall, he was free to come and go as he pleased and to look into all the details of the home side of the organization. An absorbing study he found it, for in those modest surroundings a remarkable work of God was centered.

It was the year of "The Hundred," the high-water mark of the tide of blessing that accompanied the outgoing of the Cambridge party. The Mission had been led to ask in believing prayer for no fewer than a hundred new workers for China in 1887, and when Mr. Frost reached Pyrland Road the last of the number were about to sail. Simple and humble as the Mission Home was, its atmosphere glowed with spiritual life and power. Party after party had gone forth from its doors, every need met in answer to prayer, no appeal for funds having been made nor any debt incurred. The daily prayer meeting went far to explain these facts to the American visitor, who wrote:

> This noon meeting deeply impressed me, its simplicity, earnestness, comprehensiveness, and spirituality being beyond anything I had ever known.

Usually only members of the household and staff were present, but, whoever might come or go, one little woman was always there whose prayers brought a peculiar sense of access to God Himself. Mrs. Broomhall, the mother of that busy household, was Mr. Hudson Taylor's sister and very like him in the simplicity and reality of her faith. In a quiet, loving way she brought into every detail of life a confidence in God as practical as it was uplifting. She was always ready for prayer, and impressed Mr. Frost no less than her genial and gifted husband. Of these new friends he wrote long after:

Mrs. Broomhall was a remarkable woman, quiet, calm, prayerful, believing, ruling her large family of ten children by love, imparting spiritual impressions wherever she was—a worthy sister of Mr. Taylor. Mr. Broomhall was a noble specimen of British religious life, with an English face and voice. He was a handsome man, with a snow-white head of hair and beard. Also he was keenly observant, simple of mind, earnest and informing in conversation, and devoted to the interests of the Mission and the spiritual welfare of China. The children were full of vibrant life. In spite of their youth they showed signs of real consecration to God, which bore fruit in later years in deep devotion to Christ and China. It was a unique and uplifting experience to be in the midst of such a group . . . and when I came away from London I felt that God had taken me there to meet, not only Mr. Taylor, but also Mr. Broomhall and his re-markable family.*

An early and eager letter to Mr. Taylor set forth the object of the young man's coming. While making the most of his opportunity for studying the methods of the Mission and its financial and business arrangements, he was longing for the time when his quest would be justified and his hopes fulfilled.

I am now at Pyrland Road (the letter read) and have been here long enough to satisfy myself concerning the spiritual standing of the China Inland Mission, and to confirm my desire to connect myself with it. . . . But I came to London with a larger purpose in view. . . . It has been laid on my heart for months past to talk with you and Mr. Broomhall about the establishment of an American Council that might work as a feeder of men and money for China, on the same principles of faith that have made the China Inland

---

* Five of the ten children were called of God to China, while all the others have been active in Christian work at home. Several of the grand-children are now missionaries or have their faces set toward the foreign field.

Mission so favorably known. Meeting Mr. Forman in Glasgow, I found that he too had been praying for something of the same kind for a long time, and that Mr. Wilder, his companion, has also had the matter laid on his heart.

Never having met Mr. Taylor, the young American was the more touched by the frankness and warmth of his reply. He had pictured this man of faith as probably rather austere and apart from ordinary mortals. But the small, clear handwriting, the thoughtful arrangements for an early interview, and the subscription, "Yours affectionately in Christ—though personally unknown," encouraged more friendly feelings. Here was someone approachable and considerate, someone to be loved as well as trusted. And when the interview came these impressions were only deepened.

In some strange way, I had visualized Mr. Taylor as tall and rather portly, with black hair and beard and a full, deep voice. And there stood before me just the opposite of all this. This great man, who had risen from his desk and was coming to meet me, was shorter than I expected, and had fair hair, blue eyes, and the pleasantest and gentlest of voices. But what impressed me most was his greeting. Taking my outstretched hand in both of his, he bade me welcome to England, to the Mission, and to his home, telling me of his deep interest in the matter of which I had written and assuring me that he had already prayed much about it. I had, then and there, what amounted to a revelation—first of a man and then of his God. Never before had I seen one so humbly tender or so divinely noble. From that moment my heart was fully his . . . and also, in a new and deeper sense, his Lord's.

After an hour's conversation, Mr. Taylor had to turn to other matters, but he arranged for a further interview that evening when Mr. Broomhall could be present, which sent his visitor away full of hopeful anticipation.

I then sped back to my lodgings (he continued), light of foot and still lighter of heart. Dropping on my knees, I poured out my thanksgiving before the Lord. How good He was! How blessedly and unmistakably He had guided me! The cloud had indeed gone before, and it would yet lead into the promised land of my heart's desire. Mr. Taylor had not advised my going to China, but had seemed to encourage the hope that the Mission would be extended to America. This, after all, was the larger and more important matter. My way, therefore, was very bright, and our future talk, no doubt, would serve to brighten it still more.

But by evening a change made itself felt. It was not that Mr. Taylor's attitude was less kindly. By the glow of a cheerful fire the study was just as welcoming, when the three drew up their chairs for talk and prayer. It was not until they entered seriously upon the question of establishing the Mission in America, that Mr. Frost began to be apprehensive.

Presently I learned that Mr. Taylor and Mr. Broomhall had had a conference upon the subject that afternoon. A little later it appeared that Mr. Broomhall was opposed to my proposal, feeling that it involved too much and that American missionary societies would not welcome the transfer of a British organization to American soil. . . .

At this point Mr. Taylor began a dissertation, interesting in theory but discouraging in application, upon the difference between planting and transplanting trees. In the one case they were liable to perish, but in the other—as in the planting of an acorn and the growing up of an oak—they were likely to thrive and become so firmly rooted that they would stand the severest storms of wind and rain. No, it would not be best to accept my suggestion. His answer must be a refusal. What was to be hoped for was the upspringing in America of a purely American society on the lines of the China Inland Mission, but indigenous in every way.

And this decision, it appeared, was final. Surprise and disappointment held the listener almost silent. Then he remembered that Mr. Taylor had spoken of returning to

China the following spring. Would he be willing, Mr. Frost inquired, to travel by way of America, if invited to speak at Niagara-on-the-Lake and Mr. Moody's Conference at Northfield? Yes, Mr. Taylor thought such invitations might be accepted. And there the interview ended.

It was then after ten o'clock at night, so I bade Mr. Taylor and Mr. Broomhall farewell. Yes, truly, night had come! I went to my lodgings, physically and spiritually in the deepest darkness, and back into the room where, that very afternoon, I had poured out my praise to God. On that same spot I fell upon my knees, simply dumb in the bitterness of my disappointment. So then, instead of following the cloud, I had pressed my way across land and sea after an *ignis fatuus*, which had led me into a veritable bog of blasted hopes. What then was that experience in the farmhouse at Lindenville? How then could I ever again believe in divine guidance? I knew not what to think. There was no occasion for praise now. The best I could do was to hold on grimly and, as far as possible, still trust in God.

It was hard to part from Mr. Taylor. There was so much of the presence of the Lord about him that it held one's heart. He had no further light, however, on the American question. That subject was definitely closed. Three days later Mr. Frost sailed from Liverpool in deep perplexity. And the saddest part of it all was the oft-recurring question—how could he ever again be sure of the guidance of God?

CHAPTER

X

"DWELL DEEP"

THE winter that followed was one of silent, inward growth, through much exercise of heart. All that Mr. Frost could do with regard to his missionary call was to leave it with God. He continued to pray about Mr. Taylor's coming to America, knowing that the Lord could bring it to pass, and meanwhile threw himself with renewed earnestness into missionary work close at home.

Not far from his father's Madison Avenue apartment in New York, conditions existed which, for sin and misery, could hardly be exceeded. There, on Bleecker Street and in the Bowery, friends of Mr. Frost's were urgently needing help in a Rescue Mission, help which he was in a position to afford. For his wife and children had come from Attica to meet him on his return from England, and his parents were eager to keep the little family with them for the winter. It was something of a Chinese arrangement, three generations under one roof; but the apartment was spacious, and young Mrs. Frost with two little sons was an ideal daughter-in-law.

The Florence Mission on Bleecker Street, with which Mr. Frost now connected himself, proved even more costly in labor and sacrifice than the work in New Brunswick had been. But it was fully as rewarding. Mr. and Mrs. Henry Gibbud were congenial associates. Both were Niagara Conference friends, and as leaders of the Mission set an example of Christlike devotion. Beginning with the nine o'clock evangelistic service every night, they and their fellow-workers were hard at it until six in the morning, either on the bleak, wintry streets, or in saloons, dance halls, and disreputable houses.

Our method on the street was that of distributing tracts and having personal talks with men and women. To reach the thinly clad, shivering, fallen women, Mr. Gibbud and I carried between us a huge coffee urn, with a light burning below and with strong, hot coffee above—a means of grace amply used of God in bringing many a poor prostitute to Himself. In the houses of ill-fame and dance halls we also distributed tracts, holding meetings and having conversations with those who were interested. . . .

Night after night that winter, Mr. Gibbud and I went to places which even the police would not have dared to enter. In those sections police officers went in pairs, never leaving the well-lighted streets except in serious need, and then only with revolver in hand. But we young men, unarmed and unafraid, went into alleys so dark that we had to feel our way, and into dens of iniquity more awful than I had ever imagined to exist this side of hell. In the pursuit of lost souls we went down into dives three stories below the ground, where men and women were crowded together in heaps, where they bought whisky at half a cent a pint (the place where it was made they called "The Morgue," and the whisky itself "Death"), and where women sold their virtue for a few cents. And the marvel of it was that we were welcome. Somehow they knew, particularly the women, that they needed us, that we had come to do them good.

So they would ask us to sing and would listen as we spoke; and many a man and woman was led from those abysmal depths up to glorious heights of salvation.

A besotted, trembling drunkard was sitting in the hall one night when Mr. Frost was speaking. He was tall, but bent and filthy, a poor, battered wreck of humanity. As soon as the meeting was over, Mr. Frost went over and took a seat beside him, for in his bleared and shifty eyes he had caught a look that was appealing. After speaking of his need of the Saviour, Mr. Frost turned to Romans 6:23, "The wages of sin is death"—

"You needn't read that," his listener interrupted, "I know it already."

"All right, then we may go on."

So I continued, "But the gift of God is eternal life through Jesus Christ our Lord."

I then asked him what we have to do in order to get a gift.

"Take it," he answered, clearly.

At this, I urged him to take the gift of God. But he refused, telling me that he was drunk. In vain I urged that this was just the reason why he should accept the salvation Christ offered. No, he would not. He would go to his room, he said, get out his Bible, read it, kneel down and pray, get sobered up, and come the next night and get saved.

"Poor fellow!" I replied. "You mean well. But let me tell you—you will do nothing of the kind. You will turn into the first saloon you come to."

He assured me that he would not. He would go down a back street and do exactly as he had promised. So he went out into the dark, unsaved.

I was not able to be at the Mission the next evening, but the following night I was there. As I took my place on the platform, I looked for my tall friend. Sure enough, there he was, just where he had sat two nights previously. After the meeting, I went to him immediately.   Seating myself beside him, I asked if he had come the night before.   He said he had.   I saw, however, that he was even more drunk than when I last met him.

"Did you go into the first saloon you came to?" I questioned.

"No," he answered, "it was closed.   I went into the second."

"Well now," I replied, "what about tonight?"

Looking at me earnestly, he said, "Mister, I'll never go out of this place till I am saved."

"Thank God!" I exclaimed.   "Then it will be easy."

Turning to our verse, I read again: "The gift of God is eternal life through Jesus Christ our Lord."   The dear fellow was ready to close with the offer.   We knelt together and I prayed.   Then he prayed simply, like a little child, accepting "the gift" and thanking God for it.

Upon this a strange thing happened.   He got up, still trembling from head to foot, but perfectly sober.   Then he turned from me as if I were no longer of any consequence, looked over at another wreck of humanity who had been in a fight and had his head bandaged, walked across the hall to this man, put his arm over his shoulder, and began to preach the Gospel to him—telling him that he could have the gift of Christ for the taking: and when, later, my friend went out into the night, it was as seeing a great light.

Among the women saved from the depths of sin was one who was a special joy to her missionary friends.   She was so changed that when Mr. Frost went back to Bleecker Street a year or two later, he did not recognize her in the sweet-looking, nicely dressed lady who was playing the organ for the hymns.   But it was indeed Nellie Gilmore, and the gentlemanly man at her side was a former companion in her degraded life.   Not long after her conversion they had been married, and Nellie never rested until her husband came with her to the Mission and was saved.   Once every week, from that time onward, they were there together, helping with the singing. They kept in touch with Mr. Frost by regular letters and were esteemed by all who knew them, until called to the Home above.

The joy of such experiences cannot be told, and as for the cost—is it not fellowship with Him who "poured out His soul unto death" that He might seek and save "that which was lost"?

> "I know how hardly souls are wooed and won;
>   My choicest wreaths are always wet with tears."

Worn with the winter's work, Mr. Frost was glad when spring came to return with his family to Attica. Life was deepening in those days, and his heart went out more than ever in longing for God's best, both in personal experience and in service. This brought up not a few practical questions, such as what a Christian's attitude should be with regard to debt and costly living. The beauty, even luxury, of their Attica home began to trouble both Mr. and Mrs. Frost, especially in view of a series of trenchant articles from the pen of Mr. E. M. Baldwin, then a missionary in Morocco. But first, the question of purchasing on credit had to be settled and, as Mr. Frost recalled, it proved no simple matter.

We were never greatly in debt, but from time to time, as remittances from my father reached us somewhat irregularly, we had accounts at the stores, which we paid as soon as the money was in hand, but which, while waiting for a remittance, we could not pay. Coming in contact with the China Inland Mission and learning that it never went into debt, I began to search the Scriptures for instruction upon the subject. I did not find that the Word says much about the matter. I did discover two texts, however, which said: "Provide things honest in the sight of all men," and "Owe no man anything."

It is strange the way the Lord has of making verses which you have often looked at, suddenly to look at you, and that with piercing, searching eyes. It was certainly so now. I had frequently seen those words, but had passed them by; now they gazed at me and held me arrested, almost fascinated. What could they mean? After much thought, I came to the conclusion Mr. Spurgeon reached on one occasion. A young minister wrote: "Dear Mr. Spurgeon: What does such-and-such a verse mean?" and signed his name. Mr. Spurgeon replied: "Dear Mr. So-and-so: It means what it says. Charles H. Spurgeon."

Yes, manifestly, the texts meant what they said; so far, it was fairly simple. But now, what was the application to be? Were we to buy no meat, no groceries, no food of any sort, at any time and under any circumstances, until we had money to pay for it? In other words, were we to obey and starve, rather than disobey and live? Letters flew back and forth, thick and fast, between Mrs. Frost and myself in those days, as we tried to help each other. (Mr. Frost had resumed his evangelistic missions.) But, as usual, she helped me rather than I her. With a woman's sanctified common sense, she wrote in substance:

"If God has said it, there is but one thing to do—to obey. I don't believe we shall starve; but if we do, as compared with disobeying, it will be a small matter."

King Solomon, who knew something about wives, spoke most truly when he said: "Whoso findeth a wife findeth a good thing." I agreed with him on this occasion, as on many another.

So Mrs. Frost and I determined never again to go into debt, even to the fraction of a penny. And then came the testing time, as testing times always come when one decides to do God's will. More than once, later, we were without funds. At Lockport, on one occasion I had not enough money to buy a postage stamp for a letter to my wife, and well do I remember the day when for the first time I shaved myself, because I did not have enough to permit of my going to a barber. It amuses me now to think of the spiritual panic into which these trivial events threw me; but in all honesty, they seemed so great that I felt as if the end of the world had come. However, we held our ground and, needless to say, we did not see the stars fall nor the moon turn into blood.

The position to which Mr. Frost was led at this time was of such importance in after years that it calls for fuller statement.

Having reviewed this whole subject of indebtedness after the above experiences, I came to certain conclusions which have remained fixed in my mind; first, that "a debt" is not a debt if one has funds in hand to cover it; second, that "a debt" is only a debt when one owes for something for which he finds it impossible to pay; and third, that a debt of this kind is wholly and forever forbidden by the Word of God, whether in individual or collective life, whether in respect to a Christian or to the church, whether as related to a missionary or a mission. It is a joy to add that God's command in this case has proved His enabling, for we have never since 1888—except in one or two cases of unintentional miscalculation—owed anything for which we could not at any time pay.

Mr. Baldwin's articles on Matthew 10 were causing great exercise of mind to Mr. Frost as to many others. They were ably written; their appeal was to Scripture; and their spirit of devotion was unmistakable. Yet they were based upon false premises which he was led to see in time. One benefit, however, remained. Mr. Baldwin's convicting plea for simplicity and self-sacrifice in missionary methods led the young people in Attica to a revision of their whole manner of life. This resulted in many quiet changes, in view of the principles underlying the passage in question, and undoubtedly made room for larger blessing. Thus Mr. Frost could write:

We came to see quite clearly that it would be a great privilege, for the Lord's sake, to live much more simply than we had been doing. So we looked about our house, and finally stripped it of things specially ornamental and valuable. We parted with our best pictures. We gave back to our parents the costly solid silver service which they had given to my wife when we were married. I sold or burned most of my secular books, and I sold my beloved violon-cello.

And we have never regretted what we did. The things we put away from us had more or less come to stand between us and Christ. We gave them up in order to prove to Himself and to ourselves that we loved Him supremely. We have always felt, therefore, that this was gain, not loss; and if it was fanaticism, we do not think that the Lord was altogether displeased with it, since it was our heart-offering to Him who had given His all for us.

Often the greatest heights are best seen from the lowest depths. It was so just then with us. We were wanting to see 'way up—so we had to go 'way down.

CHAPTER

XI

A MAN AND HIS GOD

THE coming of Mr. Hudson Taylor to America, in the summer of 1888, was certainly brought about by prayer. Here and there, unknown friends were longing for him, or longing rather for the uplift of his faith and certainty in things unseen. The two who were praying in Attica little thought of the petitions going up from other hearts and of letters crossing the sea to the same end. But at this very time, Dr. Arthur T. Pierson, one of America's foremost preachers and editor of *The Missionary Review of the World*, was writing from Philadelphia:

No man on earth whom I have not seen in the flesh has so much of my heart's best love as you. I am in profound sympathy with your aims, methods, mission, and spirit. . . . But what I took pen to write is that I wish to propose to you at least a short visit to America. You cannot measure the good that would come of it.

Just before this letter reached Mr. Taylor, he had received an urgent invitation from Mr. Moody to the Northfield Conference, and already he had the assurance from Dr. Erdman and others of the welcome that awaited him at Niagara-on-the-Lake.

To Mr. Frost it must have seemed that God's answer was above all he asked or thought when he learned, not only that Mr. Taylor was coming that summer, but that he was to be accompanied by his son, Howard, and also by Mr. and Mrs. Reginald Radcliffe of Liverpool, widely known and loved for their evangelistic labors. More than this, ten or twelve students from British and Continental universities were coming with Mr. George Studd (brother of C. T. Studd of the Cambridge Band) as delegates to the Northfield Student Conference. This was stirring news, and called Mr. Frost to New York in good time to welcome them.

For it was in the home of his parents that Mr. Taylor's party was entertained for several days—"long enough to endear them to us all, from my father to the servants."

It was a large party, and one pardonable *faux pas* which the visitors made put an unusual tax upon American hospitality. Following the old-country custom, they placed their shoes outside the bedroom doors at night, for attention. There young Mr. Frost found them, after a long, tiring day. It required courage, under the circumstances, to gather up eight pairs of muddy shoes and set to work upon them in the bathroom. Midnight found him still polishing. Deciding, at last, to take a little rest, he overslept—and in the morning, what was his surprise to find the task completed!

"Father," he asked, "who shined those shoes?"

"Well," was the smiling reply, "I did."

Though nothing was said about the matter, one of the party had misgivings which led to the purchase of individual polishing outfits, and prevented the recurrence of the mistake. But Mr. Taylor, made wise to the situation, had some real enjoyment as a result. For after that, whenever he and Mr. Radcliffe—who remained unenlightened—were off alone for meetings, he would watch for his friend's nightly act and would quietly slip out of his room, annex the shoes, polish them to perfection, and put them back ready for the morning. To his satisfaction, Mr. Radcliffe never identified him with the competent bootblack.

Four hundred college men, enjoying Mr. Moody's beautiful campus and school-buildings at Northfield, proved an impressive audience for the Conference speakers, especially as the earnestness of their spirit was very evident. Many of their leaders were still undergraduates, and the whole movement, with its wonderful response to the claims of Christ and of the waiting world, was just what Dr. Pierson called it, "the epiphany of youth." Such a company could not but move a missionary, and Hudson Taylor gave richly day by day to meet their problems and spiritual needs.

With the exception of my own father (Robert Wilder said, years later), Mr. Taylor was the man who was the greatest spiritual help to me. When he came to Northfield and spoke at the Student Conference, the hearts of the delegates burned within them. And he not only made the needs of the mission field very real, he showed us the possibilities of the Christian life. The students loved to hear him expound the Word of God. He had a masterly knowledge of the Bible, and his sympathy and naturalness attracted men to him. His addresses were so much appreciated that Mr. Moody had to arrange for extra meetings to be held at sundown (shortening the time reserved for recreation), so many of the students wanted to hear more from the veteran missionary. . . .

It was not, however, the words only of Mr. Taylor that helped us, it was the life of the man. He bore about with him the fragrance of Jesus Christ. . . . Eternity alone will reveal the results of that life and the effects of his words upon our Student Movement.

This was the impression made also at Niagara-on-the-Lake, though Mr. Taylor was able to be there for only two days of the Conference. Mr. Moody had urged his giving a Sunday to Chicago, so after speaking twice at Niagara, he had to leave. And as it happened, Mr. Taylor said little or nothing about China in either of those addresses. He was not there, he felt, to speak about the Mission. He was simply passing through the States on his way to Shanghai, and his desire was to give, not to get—to be a channel of the best of all gifts, spiritual blessing. The friends who thronged the pavilion by the lake were disappointed at first to find that the "great missionary" was not appealing for his field. He had only one theme, it appeared, that of the beauty and glory of Christ. Once he spoke on the spiritual meaning of the Song of Solomon and once on the words that meant so much in his own experience, "Have faith in God," or according to a more literal translation, "Hold fast God's faithfulness."*

And how our hearts did burn within us (Mr. Frost recalled) as he spoke of Christ, and as Christ spoke to us! If at Northfield they were days of heaven upon earth, these at Niagara proved to be days in heaven itself. For we were certainly lifted into "the heavenlies" and into the very presence of God.

For it was not with this speaker as it may so easily be, when the heart is not fully in touch with the Lord, "the words sound all right, but *He* is not there; there is no communication of His life through the words." Wherever Mr. Taylor was, and however simply he might speak, the man was lost sight of in his God. He loved to refer to him-

* Mark 11:22. "It is not so much *great faith* that we need," Mr. Taylor would say, commenting on this passage, "as faith in *a great God*."

self as "the little servant of a great Master." The faithfulness of God was his constant theme and the love of Christ his daily strength and delight. When he spoke of abiding in His love as the secret of fruitfulness (John 15:5) he spoke out of the joy of his own experience. And it was this reality that made hearts hungry wherever he went, and stirred so many, young and old, to seek and find the heavenly Bridegroom.

It was perhaps natural to feel that when Mr. Taylor left the Niagara Conference, "the best wine" was no more. But Mr. Radcliffe and Robert Wilder remained, with other speakers, and, as it proved, God was only beginning to pour out blessing.

CHAPTER

XII

THE UNEXPECTED

IT was in the closing days at Niagara, after Mr. Taylor had left, that the unexpected and truly wonderful movement began which altered all his plans, took the situation out of his hands, quickened missionary devotion near and far, and launched the China Inland Mission in North America. All this was so unlooked-for that those of the party who remained at the Conference could hardly believe what was happening before their eyes. It was only gradually that Mr. Taylor learned the facts of which Mr. Frost wrote as follows:

The Friday evening session was appointed as a missionary meeting, and Mr. Radcliffe and Mr. Wilder were the speakers. And how they did speak! Mr. Radcliffe's utterance was a polemic and Robert Wilder's a plea. So far as I was concerned, I did not mind how strongly they put things, for at last my heart was fixed, trusting in the Lord. But others there spent a very uncomfortable two hours and hardly knew which way to turn when the meeting was over. There was one man, however, who did. He went up to the side of the platform and asked Mr. Radcliffe how much it would take to support a missionary for a year in connection with the China Inland Mission. Good Mr. Radcliffe, who talked British to the end of his

time in America, replied, "Fifty pounds," leaving it to the American
to multiply the amount by five. The man did this, and determined
to support a missionary. Dr. Erdman then had the annual missionary offering taken. It was usual to divide this among various missionary societies. This year, however, the committee had decided
to give the full amount to the China Inland Mission. At the close of
the meeting, therefore, the offering was handed to me, with the
request that I would pass it on to Mr. Taylor, and with the suggestion that it should be used for North American workers in connection
with the Mission. The friends who had given the money were
mostly poor, so I did not expect that the offering would be a large
one. Imagine my surprise when I found that it amounted to over
five hundred dollars, or enough to provide for two missionaries in
China for a year.

This was surprising, but it was not all. Mr. Frost entered
the pavilion a little late next morning, having been occupied
in dealing with the money put into his hands.

When I reached the meeting it was in full force, and this in more
ways than one. A large audience was assembled and a spirit of
enthusiasm seemed to possess it. As I came into the room, an individual was on his feet saying he wanted to work twenty-four hours
a day for missions, and he was followed by another affirming the
same thing. In putting the matter thus, these persons were referring
to a story which Robert Wilder had told about a lady who said that
she had solved the problem of working twenty-four hours a day. She
herself worked twelve hours, and then had a representative in India
who worked the other twelve, while she slept. These friends, therefore, meant that they desired to have representatives of their own in
China, and they were offering to support the same at the rate of two
hundred and fifty dollars a year.

Following these offers, ten young women called me to the veranda
and asked if they could combine in the support of a missionary by
giving twenty-five dollars each. I replied that there could be no
objection to this and that there would be much advantage in such
a combination. This offer, as it was mentioned in the Conference,
greatly stirred the friends present, and immediately other combina-
tions were set on foot. Then someone insisted that another offering

be taken—and this was done. Then someone asked if I would be willing to act as treasurer of these various funds. I replied, of course, that I would be willing to do anything I could. At the end of the morning session, the money gathered, together with checks and written promises, was brought to me. My pockets on the day before had bulged with the gifts put into my possession, but now they were nigh to bursting. I got to the hotel at last and began to gather up the spoils, in the sense of finding out what had been given. When my figuring was finished, I found that the Conference had put into my hands sufficient money to support, not simply two but actually eight missionaries. The whole movement, from first to last, had been wholly spontaneous. Evidently, then, it was of God. By no man's appointment, I suddenly found myself an informal treasurer of the China Inland Mission.

After all, it looked very much as if the leading I had followed in going to England was no *ignis fatuus*. I do not hesitate to say that I was as happy as a child. That very evening I should see Mr. Taylor. He was waiting for me at Attica, and I was purposing to hurry home. Meanwhile, I had a good many private praise meetings. It was blessed to resume thanksgiving after the long months wherein God had seemed hidden and I rejected. He had at last manifested Himself and had accepted me for service in China's behalf. So now I found it easy to give Him adoring praise.

Support for eight missionaries! What would Mr. Taylor say to such news? Later, it proved that Mr. Radcliffe had underestimated the cost of each worker, for while the sum mentioned was sufficient to meet the personal needs of a single man or woman, it made no allowance for house rent, traveling expenses, and other necessary items. These had to be provided from the General Fund until the matter was adjusted, but meanwhile the call to advance was unmistakable.

There are times when fast trains travel very slowly (Mr. Frost continued), and this was one of them. I was the bearer of good tidings, and if I could have connected with a hundred-miles-an-hour airplane I certainly should have been tempted to take it. And to make matters worse for my impatient spirit, I missed at Buffalo the earlier train connection for Attica, which meant that I should not be able to reach home before midnight. I concluded that under such circumstances I should not have the privilege of talking with Mr. Taylor until the following morning, and must keep "bottled up" for another ten or twelve hours. I paced the station floor till the time of the train, then settled down in the car for the hour's ride. At midnight the train crawled into the station, but I did not crawl out of it. Bag in hand, I leaped to the platform. Even if I could not tell the good news that night to Mr. Taylor, I could to Mrs. Frost, and this put wings to my feet.

Mr. Taylor was an unusual man. First, he did unusual things; and second, he did them in an unusual way. As I alighted from the train, to my surprise I saw him standing before me.

"How do you do, dear brother?" was his quiet greeting.

"Very well, Mr. Taylor," I could have replied, "and all the better for seeing you here tonight."

But I did not overflow. My secret was sacred, and I wanted the privacy of home before imparting it. So we walked quietly to my father's house, where Mr. Taylor was staying, went upstairs to his room—and then, I could wait no longer!

Turning to my friend as soon as the door was closed, I said:

"Mr. Taylor, I have good news for you. The Niagara Conference has put into my hands money enough to support eight missionaries in the China Inland Mission."

Mr. Taylor usually had a responsive face and equally responsive lips, especially when the Lord's mercies were in mind. But this time, his face fell and his lips remained silent. For once, I was deeply disappointed in him, for I had expected something quite different. Presently he said:

"I think we had better pray."

With these words, he fell on his knees beside the bed and began to ask God what it all meant. I, of course, knelt beside him and when he had finished praying put in my little word of thanksgiving, which sounded like the dying strain of a half-forgotten song. When we had risen, Mr. Taylor, still with the serious look on his face, inquired:

"Was anything said by the donors of the money about its being used for North American workers?"

"Yes," I replied, "it was requested that it should be put to that use."

"This is serious," was all he said, more to himself than to me.

In other words, Mr. Taylor had had an immediate perception of the meaning of what had taken place. I had seen the divine love, he had seen the divine plan as well, and this had deeply solemnized him. Previously, he had refused to extend the Mission to North America. Was God forcing him to reverse that decision? He said afterwards:

"To have had missionaries and no money would not have caused me any anxiety; but to have money and no missionaries was a very serious matter."

For he realized that now he would have to appeal for North American workers, which so far he had carefully refrained from doing; and this, in the nature of the case, would mean that the Mission would be established on this side of the ocean.

However, Mr. Taylor was not a man unprepared to give up prejudice and let God have right of way. His only concern at any time was to discover the Lord's will. After this, he was ready to obey and follow, whatever the cost to himself or others. And it was so now. We parted that night about one o'clock. Both of us were happy. But the larger and more mature man was holding peculiar communion with his God, and to him, under such circumstances, the "secret place" meant solemnity of mind and heart.

CHAPTER

XIII

LET GOD HAVE
RIGHT OF WAY

THE quiet town of Attica in that beautiful Wyoming Valley became to Mr. Taylor at this time a place of faith and vision, much as Brighton Beach had been long years before. As a young man, he had faced at Brighton the call of God to go forward in the superhuman task of the evangelization of inland China. Now, twenty-three years later, with a widely open door in that great interior, he saw the hand of the Lord leading to developments so unexpected that they called for new faith and courage. Dared he embark upon an adventure, however promising, that would involve no one could tell what added burdens? America was to him almost an unknown quantity. What would come of launching out in faith so soon after his arrival, and without the backing of trusted colleagues at home? Yet, how could he hold back? God was manifestly working. If His time had come for a new departure in the interest of His kingdom, would He not be responsible for the results? So the days at Attica were largely spent in prayer. And it was from the "secret place," where his soul had been strengthened, that the man who was "small enough and weak enough for God to use" went to another crowded Conference at Northfield.

And they were expectant crowds, for the fame of the English visitors had to some extent gone before them. Ministers were there, representing not a few denominations, and Christian workers from many parts of the States and Canada. Mr. Moody was chairman of the Conference, infusing into all its proceedings his own evangelical convictions and warmth of spirit. And Mr. Frost, among those of the inner circle, was waiting upon God in prayer.

There were great teachers there (he wrote in retrospect), but Mr. Radcliffe and particularly Mr. Taylor stood at the center of these and preëminent among them. There were many leaders who brought blessings to souls; but about the ministry of these two strangers there was an indefinable something other-worldly and awesome, which made us question our spiritual positions and actually tremble before God. While the idea of present-day divine revelation of truth is untenable, it is not so with regard to present-day divine illumination of truth already revealed. And this is just what these men of God brought to us. They threw light upon the revelation completed in Scripture and showed us how to live it out. I am speaking not only of their teaching. Strong and winsome as this was, it was their lives which impressed us most.

In those as in other days, Mr. Taylor's life constantly reminded me of that transcendently beautiful verse: "Thy gentleness hath made me great." As I saw him, he was never childish, but he was ever childlike. His humility before God and meekness before men had a transforming influence upon many of us, for character, as has been well said, is not taught but caught. As to his utterances, they were truly great. They were not scholastic, though our friend was more of a scholar than most people knew, but they were clear analyses of human life and experience. Moreover, they were always fundamentally true, the evangelical ring being in every coin of speech. And lastly, this preacher magnified Christ above all the sons of men. And so it was that these two friends from across the sea came to be greatly loved, by young and old alike, and by no one more than myself. I had felt sure that there was something in Christ for the Christian which I had not before seen. Now I had found it, in men of flesh and blood, and I could but adore the One who made the experience possible.

But it was in the missionary meeting that Mr. Taylor came to the fullness of his message. He had a wonderful story to tell of God's faithfulness in the experience of the China Inland Mission, and of the power of the Living Christ to save in China as at home. Small in stature, simple and natural in speech, he disarmed criticism and brought that great audience into the Presence of which he himself was supremely conscious. Behind him sat Mr. Moody, "large and upright," as Mr. Frost tells us, "in his central chair on the platform," with many speakers gathered about him. Mr. Taylor stood in silent prayer a moment, conscious of his utter dependence upon God.

Then he led in audible prayer; and then he spoke, as a little child might speak, as a prophet might speak, as one who sees a vision of a needy land and a dying people might speak. And when, after an hour, he finished, there was a great sigh from the listening throng, followed by a silence which was profound.

From that hour, the cloud moved forward so definitely that there could be no further misgiving. A trained nurse and two Northfield students volunteered for China at that Conference, and "God's surprises," as Mr. Frost recorded, "were beyond counting or measuring." For people's hearts were opened as they had been at Niagara. Gifts were so generously given that Mr. Taylor was placed in an unusual dilemma. He had counted upon using the money already in hand for the support of North American workers; but when as many as eight had been accepted, the original fund was still untouched. And the farther they went, the less chance there seemed to be of using it up. Consecrated money, he found, was something like consecrated loaves and fishes, there was no coming to an end of it.

But all this took time. Northfield was the starting point only. Offers of service began to come in there, and clear indications as to who was to hold the ropes at home, taking over the details Mr. Taylor could not himself carry. For, after years of training in God's own school, the one to assume responsibility was ready at his side. Of these experiences Mr. Frost continued:

Mr. Taylor was one who always had a morrow in his heart. He was born of the Spirit with his face forward and belonged to God's advance guard. Thus it was that he was no sooner committed to his new course of action than he became most eager to press forward. The look of solemnity which had rested on his face passed away. Why should he be anxious, now that God's path had been made so clear before him? He had heard the calling voice, felt the guiding hand, seen the directing eye. His part from this time on was simply to follow his advancing Lord.

So, as soon as we got back from Northfield to Attica, he began to plan more meetings at which he could speak of China. We had stopped at Clifton Springs and Rochester on our return journey, where great blessing had been granted and additional donations given. But this only incited him to fresh effort. . . . The money must be used. How could we best secure the men and women to be supported by it?

I was always watching Mr. Taylor in those days out of the corner of my eye. To tell the truth, he was in some ways a mystery to me. . . . It was not that he was unnatural. Indeed, I had never seen anyone so natural as himself. Nor was it that he was spiritually fantastic. He was the sanest man I ever had to do with. Nevertheless, there was a spiritual quality about him which gave me surprises at every turn and kept me on the lookout for new and strange experiences. When he came, therefore, to my study in Attica and asked me to help him plan for the time at our disposal before his sailing for China, I was filled with curiosity and interest. Now I should discover just how a godly man got guidance from the Lord when important issues were at stake and the path was not clear. And I confess that I expected something dramatic. The way it worked out was this:

Mr. Taylor sat down beside my desk. Then he said, "Before we begin to plan, don't you think we had better pray?"

With folded hands and bent head, he told the Lord that we were little children and it was not in us to direct our steps, but that He, the Lord, knew everything—and would He not give us the wisdom we needed. All this was in itself most startling, just because it was so simple. But the next episode was still more so. Turning to me after his prayer was done, he said:

"Have you any time-tables?"

"Time-tables!" I said in my inmost heart. "Time-tables! How utterly commonplace!"

I had been dealing with time-tables all my life and had never connected them with getting guidance from on high. But the man of God had actually asked for time-tables! When would wonders cease? Yes, I had time-tables in the desk at which we sat and I got them out. Then Mr. Taylor said:

"Do you suppose there is a general map in one of these?" Yes, there was a general map. I found it for him.

"Now," he said, "here is Attica, and I must start west from Toronto when I leave for China. What lies between?"

I had more or less recovered myself by this time and could give attention to the subject in hand. So we worked out an itinerary, date by date and city by city, until Toronto might be reached at an appropriate time. And this ended our task. Meanwhile I had learned a big lesson. Getting guidance, then, was not a sort of "snapshot" arrangement. It was first prayer, then common sense, and it was childlike trust all the way through. And from that commonplace figuring out of a route in my study at Attica sprang things so big that they were not less than infinite and eternal. Evidently, it is worth while being simple, provided one puts his trust in the living God. For God is anything but simple. He is majestic and wonderful in all His ways, His going forth being prepared as the morning.

CHAPTER

XIV

THE FIRST AMERICAN PARTY

THE meetings that followed were memorable. Everywhere people were found with prepared hearts, ready to respond to the spiritual appeal of Mr. Taylor's addresses. It was love to the Lord Jesus that he sought to quicken, and practical fellowship with Him in His redeeming work. He put no emphasis on the need for money, but urged the far deeper, greater thing—consecration of the whole heart and life to the Master Himself. And in this spirit, more than forty young men and women were led to offer themselves for service in China.

Unusual incidents happened in connection with some of the meetings, the fact that no collections were taken being almost incredible in certain quarters. In Chicago, on one occasion, there was a great opportunity in the auditorium of the Y. M. C. A. Mr. J. V. Farwell, who had given the building, was present and Moody was in the chair. The packed audience was deeply moved by Mr. Taylor's message.

"The need of China—how he brought it out!" said one who was called at that time to the work of the Mission, and who could never forget the unexpected turn that meeting took.

For as Mr. Taylor finished speaking, the Chairman came forward and, taking advantage of the manifest interest of the gathering, called for ushers and baskets and proceeded to take an offering. In a moment Mr. Taylor was at his side.

"Did I not make it clear, beforehand," he said quietly, "that the China Inland Mission does not take collections?"

"Yes, but we must not lose such an opportunity," Moody exclaimed in the kindness of his heart, motioning the ushers to go on.

Mr. Taylor asked permission to explain his position to the audience, which he did briefly, thanking them and the Chairman for their generous impulse, but saying that the Mission he represented had always refrained from taking collections, lest money that might be given to the older Boards should be diverted from its regular channels.

"It is our desire," he said, "to help and not to hinder the work of the denominational societies, quite properly maintained through such offerings. If any one wishes, over and above their accustomed gifts, to have fellowship with the China Inland Mission, they can communicate with us through the mail."

"Well," said Moody at last, with manifest reluctance, "you are the first man I ever met who refused a good collection!"

But there were tears in his eyes, for the address had come home to him with power. No offering was taken, and the great meeting closed with prayer.

A year later, a well-known Christian merchant, speaking to the students of the Moody Bible Institute, mentioned this incident. He had been present at the meeting, he said, and as he left the hall congratulated himself on being twenty dollars to the good. He had a bill with him for that amount, and would have given it had the offering been taken. But Mr. Taylor's action left him so much the richer. That night, however, he could not sleep, and lay thinking over it all. Mr. Taylor had refused the collection, but could it be that money was not required? God spoke to his conscience, and he had no rest until he decided to send by post, next morning, not the bill in question, but a check for five hundred dollars to forward the evangelization of inland China.

This was, confessedly, an unusual occurrence, but many were the lesser instances of God's watchful care. A train missed in Lockport, when the missionary party was leaving for an important meeting, would have meant failure to keep the engagement, had not an extra train, not on the schedule, arrived just in time to take them to Toronto for that evening. Mr. Taylor's perfect calmness in their dilemma, and his assurance that the Lord could still get them to the meeting if He wanted them there, made a lasting impression upon his young companions.

For as they moved from place to place the party was growing in numbers. Careful investigation was being made into the cases of many young men and women who were offering for China. Some were disqualified physically, others needed further training, and several who were accepted were not able to go at once. But six men and eight women proved ready to avail themselves of Mr. Taylor's escort, and of these he wrote to Mrs. Taylor:

We are so happy and united! You would enjoy knowing the dear young workers God has given us, in the fresh bloom of consecration and love. May it never wear off! Every day I feel more thankful for each member of our band. Little difficulties of travel only bring out character and show more clearly how good God's choice has been.

You can have little idea how mightily the Spirit of God has been and is working.

Too soon, the full-freighted days of that North American visit were numbered. The power of the meetings seemed, if anything, to increase as the time of departure drew near. In the city of Hamilton, Ontario, this was especially the case. Through a young Mr. Rough, Secretary of the Y. M. C. A., Mr. Taylor was brought into contact with a remarkable group whose response to his message, one can well believe, stirred the churches. Converts from an evangelistic campaign, they had banded themselves together in a Young People's Christian Union.

We represented all the evangelical churches in the city, I think (wrote Mr. Rough). Intense love and devotion to the Lord Jesus characterized this group and also the active members of the Y.M.C.A. Meetings for Bible study were well attended, and our eagerness to serve the Lord found vent in open-air work, cottage-meetings, and co-operation with others, as opportunity afforded.

Into the midst of this group came Hudson Taylor, in the course of his first visit to North America. Result—some dozen of our circle ultimately landed in China. Six of them sailed in the first party with Mr. Taylor—the Misses Cassie Fitzsimmons, Hattie Turner, and Jeannie Munro (my fiancée), and Messrs. George Duff, J. H. Racey, and W. M. Souter. I followed later.

Little wonder the churches were moved as all these bright, purposeful young men and women responded to the chal-

lenge of "a million a month, in China, dying without God."
It was the love of Christ that constrained them, and the lure,
perhaps, of the difficult in His service. For the Mission
offered anything but an easy billet. No promise of salary;
Chinese dress and ways of living; pioneering journeys; loneliness in the far interior; no marriage for at least two years;
yes, and the privilege of preaching and living Christ where
He had never yet been named—this was the attraction. As
to material benefits, the Hamilton Press made it specially
clear that nothing was to be expected. For it was in that
city that a leading daily, with every desire to be sympathetic,
gave much of its front page to a report of one of Mr. Taylor's addresses, which caused him some dismay as well as
amusement:

> The venerable gentleman (it said) concluded a long and most
> interesting address by informing the audience that the members of
> the China Inland Mission depended upon chance providences for a
> scanty subsistence.

If this was the reporter's reaction to the faith principles
of which he had heard, it certainly was not the experience
of the young people from Hamilton who joined Mr. Taylor's
party. To them, God was an utterly reliable heavenly
Father; nor did they find His provision "a scanty subsistence"
in far-off China. For the promise still holds good to those
who follow fully: "Seek ye first the kingdom of God, and
His righteousness; and all these things shall be added unto
you."

The Frost residences in Attica had become by this time
almost a home and business center for the China Inland
Mission. The hospitality of the parents as well as the
younger people knew no bounds as, at their invitation, the

outgoing party assembled and final arrangements were made for departure. In the community also no little interest was stirred by the joy with which these young people left all to enter upon a missionary life. The farewell meeting which crowded the Presbyterian church was long to be remembered.

Mr. F. S. Parker, father of one of the party, had accompanied his daughter from Pittsfield, Mass., and was seated near the platform. Touched by the light on his face, Mr. Taylor invited him to come up and follow the testimonies of the young people with a few words as to his own experience. He did so; and the unveiling of that heart, simple and unpremeditated as it was, filled the house, like Mary's spikenard, with imperishable fragrance.

He spoke with a father's tenderness (Mr. Taylor loved to recall) of all that his daughter, an only child, had been to him and to her mother. He told of her helpfulness in the home and in his mission hall, and something of what it meant to part from her now.

"But I can only feel," he said, "that I have nothing too precious for my Lord Jesus. He has asked for my very best, and I give with all my heart my very best to Him."

That sentence (Mr. Taylor added) was the richest thing I got in America, and has been an untold blessing to me ever since. Sometimes, when pressed with correspondence, the hour has come for united prayer, and the thought has arisen, ought I not to go on with this or that matter? Then it has come back to me—"Nothing too precious for my Lord Jesus." The correspondence has been left to be cared for later, and one has had the joy of fellowship unhindered. Sometimes, waking in the morning, very weary, the hour has come for hallowed communion with the Lord alone; and there is no time like the early morning for getting the harp in tune for the music of the day. Then it has come again—"Nothing too precious for my Lord Jesus," and one has risen to find that there is no being tired with Him. That thought has also been a help when leaving home and loved ones. Indeed, I could never tell how many hundreds of times God has given me a blessing through those words.

CHAPTER

XV

NO TURNING BACK

TORONTO, that September, was moved as it rarely had been by any event of religious significance. A city of wide Christian sympathies, it had welcomed the coming of Reginald Radcliffe and Hudson Taylor for their own sake, but when it became known that they had with them no fewer than fourteen young people on their way to China, whose expenses for a year ahead had all been met without collections or appeals for funds, except to God in prayer, interest deepened, and a mass-meeting had to be held from which hundreds were turned away, unable to gain admission. The spiritual power of Mr. Radcliffe's addresses, the quiet certainties of Hudson Taylor's faith, and the happy testimonies of the outgoing-missionaries made an impression deeper than they themselves could realize at the time.

When the last day came, all this interest found unique expression, for it was from Toronto the party set out on their long journey westward. Mr. Taylor had already left with Mr. Frost for engagements in Montreal, but it was arranged

for the young missionaries and their friends to meet in Knox
Church and take the Lord's Supper together, going from
the church to the station, where hundreds gathered to see
them off. To Mr. and Mrs. Radcliffe who accompanied
them, the whole occasion was profoundly moving.

You have often seen (the latter wrote to Mrs. Taylor) how God
has sustained His children when leaving home and loved ones, but
I hardly suppose that even you have witnessed such joy as beamed
on the faces of the thirteen who left for China on the 25th of September (another joining the party farther on). . . . Never, perhaps,
has Toronto witnessed such a scene! When the travelers were all
on board the train, Mr. Radcliffe lifted up his strong voice in prayer
for blessing and protection for them, the great concourse repeating
the words aloud after him. Then the old Union Station rang with
farewell songs, until the train disappeared, after which the members
of the Y.M.C.A., joined by many others, walked four abreast along
Front Street and up Yonge Street to Association Hall, singing
hymns of triumphant praise.

This was what appeared on the surface, but hidden out
of sight were the deeper things of which Mr. Frost was
thinking, when he wrote a few weeks later:

In Canada there was a great awakening. Mr. Taylor himself
was not in a position to see what was being done through him. . . .
The minds of hundreds have been radically changed. Men see
things in a new light. The Bible is more real in its commands and
promises. God has become nearer and dearer. His Fatherhood is
better understood, with all its blessed consequences. . . .

I would not say too much, but remaining on the field and looking
at results from the standpoint of an American, I can only think that
forces have been set in motion which will effect very deeply the
minds of our people in respect to missionary methods. I do not think
that the results will all center in the China Inland Mission; but
somehow, somewhere, they will be manifest in due season, and the
Mission will have its share of the blessing.

In an upper room of The Christian Institute, Mr. Alfred Sandham, its able and devoted Secretary, was engaged with Mr. Taylor and Mr. Frost in final consultation and prayer. It had come to the very day when Mr. Taylor had to leave Toronto (September 24), and there still remained matters of importance to settle. Mr. Sandham had generously undertaken to represent the Mission as Secretary-Treasurer in Canada, Mr. Frost occupying the same position in the United States. It was the question of an Advisory Council that occupied them; how to bring together a group of representative men to share the responsibility of dealing with funds and with the many candidates offering for work in China. Mr. Taylor would have been glad to make arrangements in person, to be confirmed after consultation with the Council in London, but many engagements prevented his going into the matter with those whose names had been suggested, and now, at the last moment, it seemed that he must act through others. But sometimes, "mountains" that have been much prayed over are removed very quickly.

Three names were under consideration, those of the Rev. H. M. Parsons of Knox Church, Mr. William Gooderham, and Mr. J. D. Nasmith. All were key men in Toronto, in the religious, philanthropic, and business world, respectively. There was no question as to their attitude toward the Mission, or their fitness to represent it before the public. Mr. Taylor regretted that he could not see them to talk over the matter, and had just asked Mr. Sandham to convey his request for their co-operation, when a knock came at the door. Somewhat reluctantly, for moments were precious, it was opened, when who should appear to the surprise of the friends in consultation but Dr. Parsons himself. He soon understood the warmth of his welcome, and Mr. Taylor had the satisfaction of receiving in person his hearty consent to act upon the Council.

Hardly was this settled before another step was heard in the passage and someone else was at the door. Rather more willingly, this time, it was opened—to reveal none other than Mr. Nasmith with his cheery smile! Full of thankfulness, Mr. Taylor explained why they were so glad to see him, and found that he too was ready to take up the proposed work as a call from God. And then, five eager people almost held their breath as another step came to the door of that upper room. Quickly it was opened, and—for truth can be stranger than fiction—there stood Mr. William Gooderham. No wonder Mr. Frost wrote that his presence was almost like an apparition!

It was more than delightful; it was startling. Once more Mr. Taylor gave his invitation in person, and once more it was accepted. The arrival of these three friends in quick succession seemed all the more remarkable when we learned that not one of them knew that Mr. Taylor was in the building, that all of them were seeking Mr. Sandham, and that two of the three had not entered The Institute for several months past.

What a sacredness there must have been about the hour that followed!

Gathered thus by the Spirit of the Lord, we held on Monday, September 24, 1888, what was practically the first Council meeting of the Mission in North America. We decided before separating to enlarge our membership, and the names of Mr. J. S. Helmer of Lockport, New York, the Rev. Robert Wallace of Belleville, Ontario, and the Honorable S. H. Blake of Toronto were added to the five already on the list. . . .

Thus our little barque was thrust out into the deep. As to whether the voyage was to be short or long, smooth or rough, prosperous or adverse, God only knew. But we all believed that we had the best Pilot on board, and were content to leave the issue with Him.

The words read simply, but the renewal of faith through this remarkable experience was very real. Evidently, God was watching over the new developments to which He had led that summer. Mr. Taylor could now go to Montreal, rejoining his party a little later, in the "quietness and confidence" inspired by more than human resources.

To Mr. Frost, the sense of responsibility was almost overwhelming as he turned his face homeward after parting from Mr. Taylor in Montreal.

I had been basking in the glory of a great man, and this experience was suddenly ended. Now I was alone and just myself, which meant that I was nothing. It was little wonder that I looked about me with fear and into the future with dread. So, after a few hours in Toronto, I took my unnoticed and lonely way, first to Buffalo and then to Attica. Arrived under my own roof, courage somewhat revived. It is a comforting thing, when conscious that you are nothing, to have a home to which to turn and a heart there that feels, however great the hallucination, that you are—something.

Then it was that the young American fell back with thankfulness upon experiences gained the previous year at the headquarters of the Mission in London. For he had the papers of some twenty-eight candidates to consider, and the number still increased. Very often he called to mind Mr. Taylor's quiet reply when he had urged:

"But I don't know anything about dealing with candidates and Mission matters!"

"Quite true," the man of larger faith responded, "but *the Lord will help you.*"

That help was very real in the days that followed Mr. Taylor's departure, and it was increasingly needed. For trials began to close in upon the young couple such as they had never known before. Beginning with family affairs, these soon extended to the interests of the Mission, and were so serious as to imperil what God had wrought. But the faith of His own giving stood the test and came out strengthened.

Up to that time, Mr. Frost, Senior, had been in easy circumstances. He was prospering in his business undertakings, especially in connection with a railroad which he had taken over and was building up with marked success. This attracted the attention of financiers who determined to absorb the improved line in a larger system of their own. Pressure was brought upon Mr. Frost to sell, and at such a loss that financial ruin could not be averted. He might have had recourse to legal proceedings, but decided to take his son's attitude and leave their interests to a Higher care. This meant large enrichment spiritually, though he could no longer have the joy of maintaining that loved son and his family. Coming just when it did, this change of circumstances was a great shock. It had been the joy of the younger people to give their services freely to the cause in which God was using them; but now came the question, how were daily needs to be met?

And, to add to the testing of those days, another trial was permitted compared with which personal difficulties were light. Complications had arisen in London with regard to the extension of the Mission to North America, and so strong were the objections raised in certain quarters that all advance had to be suspended and correspondence with candidates held up. No explanation could be made, and it was difficult even to answer donors' letters. It is not necessary now to go into detail with regard to this serious situation. Suffice it to say that for a time it looked as though to continue the work begun in the States and Canada would lead to the disruption of the Mission. It was a question not at all of personalities, but of the principles upon which the work was to proceed, then and in days to come. A development of unknown significance had taken place, and it is not to be wondered at that it should cause apprehension to responsible leaders in the Mission who only heard of it from a distance. In China, meanwhile, troubles were coming thick and fast.

•   •   •   •   •

> "Jesus, Saviour, pilot me
>   Over life's tempestuous sea;
> Unknown waves before me roll,
>   Hiding rock and treach'rous shoal;
> Chart and compass come from Thee:
> Jesus, Saviour, pilot me!"

It was the song of the North American party as they crossed the ocean and landed in Shanghai, that tragic fall of 1888. For strange to say, even before they could arrive, a storm broke which was to be devastating and long continued. But through it all the trustful voices sang on:

> "As a mother stills her child,
>   Thou canst hush the ocean wild;
> Boist'rous waves obey Thy will
>   When Thou say'st to them, 'Be still!'
> Wondrous Sov'reign of the sea,
> Jesus, Saviour, pilot me!"

Wonderful indeed was the sustaining love of God to His servants, as month succeeded month and sorrows seemed only to increase. Truly, He is never nearer than when we need Him most. "It does not matter how great the pressure is," Mr. Taylor used to say in after days; "it only matters where the pressure lies—whether it comes between you and God, or whether it presses you closer to His heart."

"It would fill a volume," wrote the leader of the Mission at the time, "to tell in any detail of the trials that seem to come from every quarter." In Japanese ports the first mails from China were received, burdened with the loss of two experienced men, sorely needed in their respective fields. Adam Dorward, pioneer evangelist in Hunan, had fallen at his lonely post among the thirty millions of that anti-foreign province. Even he had not been able to gain a permanent footing, and who could be found with the devotion and ability to fill his place? Herbert Norris, Headmaster of the school for missionaries' children at Chefoo, seemed just as indispensable. In protecting his boys from a mad dog he had been badly bitten—and had died of hydrophobia. Loving the members of the Mission as his own children, Mr. Taylor's heart was bowed with grief, only increased when he reached Shanghai to find that a younger man of much promise had succumbed to serious illness in Chekiang, and that in the Mission House to which they were going, a woman of Christlike spirit was even then passing over.

Stranger still was the death from black smallpox, a little later, of a bright, beautiful girl in charge of a newly opened station, and the arrival in Shanghai of the saddest party ever received from England. For on the way out, one of the number had contracted a chill in bathing which, though it seemed unimportant at the time, had serious results. She arrived in a condition of acute mania. At the same time a telegram was received from Hongkong saying that a member of the China Council, whose return from furlough was eagerly awaited, was seriously ill with double pneumonia and it was doubtful whether he could live to reach Shanghai.

We are passing through wave after wave of trial (Mr. Taylor wrote in January). Each day has its full quota. God seems daily to be saying: "Can you say, 'Even so, Father,' to that?" But He sustains and will sustain the spirit, however much the flesh may fail. Our house has been a hospital; now it is an asylum. All that this means, the Lord only knows. . . . The day and night strain is almost unbearable. . . . But I know the Lord's ways are all right, and I would not have them otherwise. . . . He makes no mistakes. He can make none. Even now, we accept with thankfulness His dealings, and soon with joy shall see the deep purposes of wisdom and love wrought out by all that is so mysterious at present.

The mystery only deepened when correspondence with England and Mr. Frost's perplexed letters told of the disfavor with which North American developments were regarded by beloved colleagues at home. It was all part of the discipline needed, that the Mission which was growing so rapidly might be "stablished, strengthened, settled" on the only sure foundation—trust in God, not man.

The Lord is sending a very flood of trials (Mr. Taylor continued). No doubt they are all necessary. We might be lifted up, perhaps, or lose spiritual life and power, if success were unaccompanied by discipline. . . .

Satan is simply raging. He sees his kingdom attacked all over the land, and the conflict is awful. But that our Commander is All-mighty, I should faint. I think I never knew anything like it, though we have passed through some trying times before.

Satan often says: "All these things are against you." But God's Word is true and says the opposite.

I am more and more desirous to do God's will; to be pleasing to Him, and that at all costs.

Personal sickness and loneliness added to Mr. Taylor's burdens, for he was keenly missing wife and children. But this was the winter when his daily prayer became:

> "Lord Jesus, make Thyself to me
> A living, bright Reality;
> More present to faith's vision keen
> Than any outward object seen;
> More dear, more intimately nigh
> Than e'en the sweetest earthly tie."

A prayer richly and tenderly answered.

"Dwell deep," cried the prophet to Edom in a time of danger, and the child of God, whatever comes, has but to "dwell deep" in his abiding Refuge. Other leaders of the Mission, as well as Mr. Taylor, were blessed through these afflictions. Days of fasting and prayer brought them very near to God and enabled Him to cleanse and strengthen the work and in the end to give "power over all the power of the enemy." For they proved that the greatest trials they had ever had resulted in the greatest blessings. And there was no turning back.

Before spring came again, an added note of strength and confidence appeared in Mr. Taylor's letters. One that was specially helpful to his tried friends in Attica was dated March 5, 1889.

It seems to me, dear brother, that our great foe is leaving no stone unturned to hinder the progress and development of the China Inland Mission at the present time. We must not be surprised should even greater troubles arise than have as yet. The one thing we have to do is to look off unto Jesus and obey His command. That command, as I understand it, is to do all that we can to save souls in China and to assist missionaries into the field. And if we do this faithfully, wisely, and well, will He not give the wisdom we need? We may count upon His sustaining grace and blessing.

The Mission is nothing, if it is not His work. If it is not this, let it go to pieces tomorrow, the sooner the better. If it is His work, all the world cannot hinder it, and the mistakes of God's dear children will be overruled for blessing.

CHAPTER

XVI

PART OF THE PRICE

A S soon as Mr. Taylor could be spared from China,. he set out for England, in the hope of being enabled to remove by personal intercourse misunderstandings which correspondence had failed to adjust. The journey was a lonely one and none too pleasant, third-class by French mail, but he was glad of the leisure it afforded for waiting upon God in view of all that lay ahead.

I have been greatly distressed (he wrote to Mrs. Taylor before leaving), but all that is past now. God has spoken, and my heart is at rest. . . . I see no light as to the future of home arrangements; but I see God, the living God, and I love Him all the more for this trial, and simply *trust.* . . .

As for the Mission, it never was so truly the Lord's own work; and He alone is all-sufficient—sufficient for the heartache and the sorrow as well as for the service. . . .

Our hope must be in God; He is equal to all emergencies.

Traveling via Suez, the heat was oppressive, and a large detachment of soldiers taken on board at Saigon did not add to the comfort or quiet of the third-class quarters. Yet the burdened heart was enabled to prevail in prayer; and from the day of his arrival in London Mr. Taylor found that God had been working to make a continuance of happy relations possible.

I reached England on my birthday, May 21 (he wrote some weeks later), and found the stone already rolled away.

A great deliverance was indeed wrought by the Lord Himself. Old ties were strengthened as differing points of view were adjusted. Mutual understanding was restored. And God's hand came to be so clearly seen in the North American situation that the London Council made Mr. Taylor the bearer of a letter of fraternal greetings to the Council in Toronto, when he went over again to the Niagara Conference. This was in July (1889), just the time of his first visit the previous summer. That he was full of joy in the Lord and expectation of blessing is evident from a letter to Mrs. Taylor, sent back from Queenstown Harbor. Faith already envisaged the rich fruitage of coming years.

Darling, I do want our whole life to be an ascending plane—not resting in anything we have learned or felt or attained, but a pressing on and up. . . . God has been faithful to us, as far as we have gone out on His promises and have trusted His faithfulness; but how little we have done so! How small, after all, have been our prayers and expectations, seeing we have such a God to do with. . . . We must get on to a higher plane of thought altogether, and of prayer, if we are to walk worthily of God and deal in any sensible way with the world's crying need. Let us ask in faith for such workers for every department as shall be fit and able to deal worthily with their work at home, in America, in China, and for such an enduement of power as shall make the feeblest mighty and the strong as the angels (messengers) of God. Is it too much to expect of Him, too much to ask for His glory? May God save us from limiting the Holy One of Israel. May He open our eyes to see *Himself*, and help us to go forward on the strength of His "Have not I sent thee?"

Thus, renewed in spirit after months of unprecedented trial, Mr. Taylor came again to the conferences at Northfield and Niagara-on-the-Lake. Friends of the previous year felt the quickening impulse. Great as had been the blessing of his previous visit, there was something now that drew hearts to him and to the work in a yet deeper way. To Mr. Frost, who had shared his sorrows, it seemed like a dream to see him again in Attica, "with the old-time peace in his heart and a new-time joy on his face."

I soon found (he wrote) that there was reason for the one and the other. For Mr. Taylor was not slow to inform me that all of the difficulties in London had been removed; that the one most concerned had shown a beautiful spirit and had withdrawn his resignation; that the London Council had become entirely favorable to the work in North America being a part of the China Inland Mission, and that now we could proceed as we had originally hoped and intended. There were many praise meetings in our home in Attica during the days that followed. God, whose face had seemed hidden for a while, again smiled upon us, and the aspect of things was like the clear shining of a morning after rain. How we did rejoice! And how fervently we gave thanks to God.

In all this, Mrs. Frost was most truly one with her husband. Mr. Taylor was entertained in the larger home of the parents, next door, but his room looked out on The Cottage, and its overflowing life, love, and music were a great refreshment to him. Two little boys and a baby girl kept the young mother busy, but did not hinder her from being a help in prayer and in many other ways.

Mr. Taylor's time on this visit was all too short for his speaking engagements. Mr. Frost was his traveling companion as before, and wrote of "the trail left behind him of light, love, and newness of life, of deepened missionary interest and dedication to holy living." But it was at the Niagara Conference that his special ministry was fulfilled, for there the members of the North American Council came together to meet him. The cordial letter from London had opened the way for advance and many matters of importance had to be considered. Chief among these was the need, which had become urgent, for a full-time Secretary to represent the Mission. Mr. Sandham, with his many claims in Toronto, including the editorship of *The Faithful Witness,* had to be relieved, and the situation called for a man hard to find—one who could deal helpfully with candidates for the work in China; who could continue the spiritual ministry which had drawn friends to the Mission; who could handle correspondence, bookkeeping, and office details, and, above all, bear the interests of the work continually on his heart in prayer. This need had not been unforeseen, nor, in the providence of God, was it unprepared for. It was with Mr. Taylor's full concurrence that the Council invited Mr. Frost to assume the official position of Secretary and Treasurer to the Mission in North America, although it would involve making his headquarters in Toronto.

Never had Attica looked more attractive than it did that summer to the young people faced with this proposal. Their loss of income, some months previously, had brought them into experiences which had been far from easy. They understood now the meaning of "a life of faith" as never before, and the story of those months goes far to explain their growing fitness for spiritual leadership. It explains also the hesitation they felt in giving up the home which was all they had left to call their own. But in spiritual work, as they were coming to see, it is not so much great gifts or resources that are needed as great certainty of God. And how can that be gained apart from experiences that test and strengthen faith? The choice lay before them—whether to shrink back, holding on to human sources of supply, or to leave all and go forward in dependence on God alone. These are "the holy places in life, the places of power"; and if at first there were undercurrents of questioning, does not that bring the record more within the range of our too-little faith? About the months that led up to that summer, Mr. Frost recalled a little later:

Hitherto, my wife and I, both before and after our marriage, had always had abundance of this world's goods. First in business life and then through my father, all our wants had been supplied. Now, we were suddenly faced with the possibility of scarcity and suffering. What to do we did not know. I could not take up my business again, for it had passed into other hands. Besides, we had reason to think that the Lord had led me out of business that we might be free for His immediate service. We could only conclude, therefore, that He was testing and training us. Indeed, He seemed to be saying:

"Now, which Father have you been trusting? If you have been trusting your earthly father, you see that, with all his love, he has failed you. If you have been trusting Me, your heavenly Father, and will still trust, I will never fail you."

These words rang in our hearts and demanded an answer. It was clear to us what answer we desired to give. We wished to trust God to the full; and before long decided just to stand still and see what He would do for us.

The words of Matthew 6:33, "Seek ye first the kingdom of God, and His righteousness; and all these things shall be added unto you," became very precious to us in those days, and to the utmost of our ability we sought to fulfil the conditions, in the hope that the promise would also be fulfilled.

In spite of all our prayers and desires, however, we failed to realize, at times, the peace which "passeth all understanding." We were in the midst of an entirely new experience. Peter walking on the water was a true picture of the condition in which we found ourselves, and to us, as to him, the waves seemed high. We hoped that God would supply our needs in some way or other, but we feared that He might not—which led to much heart-sinking and distress.

Feeling, at last, that we must take steps at least partly to provide for ourselves, by reducing our expenses, we decided to part with our two faithful servants. We greatly regretted this afterwards, not only because we needed them, and they needed the home we had given them, but also because we found that the Lord could provide for the servants just as well as for the heads of a household. We felt at the time, however, that if we were going to starve—which I fear we half expected—we could not ask them to starve with us. So we let them go.

And now, alone in our cottage home, with no one except my parents aware of our situation, we set ourselves to wait upon God, to see whether He would indeed fulfil His Word and supply our needs; and a strange time we had of it—a very solemn time too—before we got through with our experiences. We had been left with ten dollars in cash. We had also a cow in the pasture, some flour in the barrel, and potatoes in the bin. What food we could obtain from these sources was all we had to eat. My dear wife went into the kitchen for the first time in her life and did the cooking; and I for the first time in my life did the best I could at the housework. Thus, with the utmost care, we made our ten dollars last somewhat over a month, but it finally came to an end and we were left with still a little food but no money for the further necessaries of life.

Our prayers, under these circumstances, were earnest indeed— each one being more of a cry, I fear, than anything else. We pleaded with God, again and again, to have mercy upon us and meet our need. We pleaded with Him, above all, to show us in our extremity whether His children who, through the claims of His service, were unable to work for themselves, could indeed trust Him to provide every needful thing. And did He fail to answer? That was four years ago, and I rejoice to testify that He cared for us then, as a faithful Father, and has cared for us ever since.

Deliverance, at that time, came from a most unlikely quarter.

An unexpected visitor came to the door one day and rang the bell. The man-servant (which was myself) opened it. The friend came in and seating himself said, rather abruptly:

"I want to leave you some money. You did me a kindness not long ago, and I would like to make some acknowledgment of it."

This was surprising, for the speaker was known to me as a very close man, and I was a good deal touched by his kind thought. It was the first time, however, that money had been offered to me in this way, and pride would not allow me to accept it. Besides this, I did not want the man to suppose that I had served him with any thought of reward. So while earnestly thanking him for his offer, I as earnestly declined.

"But I want to give the money," he persisted, "and will feel much better if you will allow me to do so."

"No," I replied again; "I am very sorry, but I cannot take it."

Again it was urged upon me, and for the third time I was about to refuse, when the Lord seemed to say to me ——

"Is this what you are going to do with My gifts? You have been asking Me for funds. I send this money, and now you refuse it!"

Silenced, I stood there, and the moments seemed like ages as I felt my pride and myself passing down into the grave of the Lord Jesus. The third "No" never came out. When I spoke, it was to say with an emotion of which my friend had little knowledge:

"Yes, I will take the money, and I am very thankful for it."

Upon this, he stepped to the central table, clicked the silver pieces down upon the hardwood top in little piles, and left them there. He was an unconverted man, and I had an opportunity of speaking to him earnestly about his soul. This I found I could do with freedom, for a great quiet had taken possession of my own spirit.

The conversation ended, my kind friend left, and I turned from the door to the kitchen in search of my wife. It did not take long to bring her to the parlor to see the piles of money which I had left untouched.   There we stood, she and I, quite alive now to the tender love of our heavenly Father.   With faith in the promises of God renewed and strengthened, we bowed our heads in prayer, and then and there gave ourselves afresh to our adorable Lord and His much-loved service.

Nor was this all.   Our Father's understanding is infinite. He saw that spiritual fellowship was needed just then, by these true hearts, so eagerly following on in His way.   So He sent right into their home in Attica one whom He could trust to work with Him.   And He sent her all the way from China.   But Mr. Frost, himself, must tell the beautiful completion of the story.

Not long after this, when our supplies were again running low, we received a letter from one of the members of our Mission, Miss Florence Campbell, who was on her way home to England.   She wrote that Mr. Taylor had suggested that she might be of help to us in deputation work in North America, and that she would be glad to come and stay with us for a while before entering upon such service.   Under other circumstances, we should have been much pleased to receive anyone sent to us by Mr. Taylor, and representing the Mission, but we had no help with the household work, and our funds did not admit of properly entertaining such a guest as we knew our friend to be.   It was impossible, however, to request Miss Campbell not to come to us, so I wrote inviting her to make the visit at any time convenient to herself.

In a few days our friend arrived, and we could not but see how greatly she was surprised to find us in such circumstances.   She was a lady, however, and never intimated that she thought there was anything strange or unusual in our position, and with a practical sympathy we much appreciated set to work at once to share our unaccustomed tasks.

With this increase to our household, supplies did not last as long as they would have otherwise, and our fears in this respect were fully realized.   Then it was that we found why our friend had been sent to us.   From first to last she was not only a comfort, but a strength to our souls. Her spiritual life was of a cheerful, hopeful kind, and day by day she helped us learn the lesson of trust in God and joyful dependence upon Him. While she was with us the Lord further answered prayer by sending the second gift which had ever been made directly to us, in supply of temporal needs, and when she left us we were more than ever assured that we were in the line of His purposes for us, and should be blessedly cared for to the end.

Some time after this we were emboldened to invite one of our servants to return, and it was with gladness we found that the Lord could as easily provide for a larger as for a smaller family.

And this was just the time of Mr. Taylor's return from China, and the proposal of the Council that Mr. Frost should undertake the leadership of the Mission in North America. One hardly knows which to think had the greater faith in going forward—Mr. Taylor, to turn away from the fruitful ministry before him in North America and leave the new and promising work in comparatively inexperienced hands, or Mr. Frost, after recent experiences, to assume such responsibilities. There was certainly no financial inducement to encourage him. Mr. Taylor set apart a check given for his personal use, toward the expenses of the move to Toronto, and as they traveled together for meetings, he was much in prayer with Mr. Frost that further provision might be made. But he did not attempt to disguise the facts as they were.

"You know," he said frankly, "that the Mission can guarantee no salary. Beyond this check for two hundred and fifty dollars, and some small sums in hand, I can promise you nothing. You will have to look to the Lord for all supplies."

And what was the reaction?

I confess that Mr. Taylor's words did not, at first, suggest an inviting prospect. To move my family and belongings to a strange city, to take a house and invite into it a number of candidates, to supply their daily needs as well as our own, and carry on the work of the Mission with little more than two hundred and fifty dollars in hand was far from a promising arrangement from a worldly standpoint. But recent experiences had given me to understand that there was a factor in the case which was not to be left out, and which made all the difference—that factor being the Lord Himself. Two hundred and fifty dollars might seem a small sum with which to begin such an undertaking; but two hundred and fifty dollars *and the Lord* was all that we could need. So, as far as finances were concerned, I was ready to move to Toronto as soon as possible.

But there was another aspect of the matter which was causing exercise of mind and heart to Mrs. Frost especially. It was not that she lacked faith or devotion. Far from it! But there were others to be considered—chiefly the parents, who seemed increasingly to need them in Attica, and the children, to whom their country home meant so much of health and happiness. Could it be right to turn away from it all and take those little ones to a city life in crowded quarters? How longingly she waited on the Lord for light!

Home, as it happened, was specially attractive that summer. Some imperfection in the ceilings of the downstairs rooms had led to considerable alterations. Wooden ceilings had been put in place of the plaster ones which had fallen. Paneled in beautiful patterns and stained to harmonize with the coloring of the rooms, they added to the charm of the whole. And, unexpectedly, those wooden ceilings, attractive as they were, settled the question for that mother-heart.

It was a Sunday early in August. Mr. and Mrs. Frost had returned from the morning service and had gone to separate rooms to be alone for prayer. Both were feeling that a decision must be reached, and both longed for definite guidance from the Lord Himself. No voice is like His voice, speaking from the pages of His Word. Presently, a light footfall crossed the library to Mr. Frost's side, and his attention was arrested by an open Bible laid upon his knee. Mrs. Frost said nothing, but pointed to the passage she had been reading:

"Is it a time for you, O ye, to dwell in your ceiled houses, and this house lie waste?"

"*Your ceiled houses*"—the words seemed to stand out from the page. He glanced up. Yes, the ceilings had taken on new meaning! Beyond the comfort of their much-loved home lay that waiting world of China, with its vast, neglected opportunities for building the spiritual house of God. His Voice had spoken. To hearts so true in their response, nothing more was needed.

I looked into the face of my wife, and saw a new light there. From that moment onward, in spite of all possible sacrifice, there never was a doubt in her heart or in mine as to what God would have us do. For the sake of His spiritual house in China, we would respond to the call that had come to us and go to Toronto and undertake the work of the Mission in North America.

PART II

FAITH'S OBTAINING

"Through faith . . . obtained promises."
HEBREWS 11:33.

"Nothing before, nothing behind:
The steps of faith
Fall on the seeming void and find
The rock beneath."
WHITTIER.

CHAPTER

XVII

"THE WORK" AND "THE CUP"

IT was never the Master's way to disguise the difficulties or requirements of His service. Any thoughtful reader of the Gospels must be impressed with this. He did not make things easy, even at the first step. To all His followers He promised the cross. But the tenderest heart was behind the stern requirements. "And Jesus, looking upon him, loved him," was said of one from whom he was asking all.

More than this, our Lord accepted for Himself the same mystery in the will of God. He spoke not only of "the work which my Father hath given me to accomplish," but of "the cup my Father hath given me" to drink. That dreaded cup, from which He might have turned away! Yet, surely, the divine tenderness was never more closely wrapped about Him, than as He accepted that cup. "*Therefore* doth my Father love me . . . because I lay down my life for the sheep."

It is almost startling to find how great were the sorrows that were allowed to bar the way, so to speak, of the young leaders setting out with such true devotion upon the new enterprise of faith, until one remembers this unalterable principle. They had risen up to follow, anywhere, at the Master's call, and even before they could leave Attica for Toronto trial came that might well have given them pause.

It was early in August when the decision was reached to go forward. Mr. Hudson Taylor left for England on the 17th of that month, and a few days later Mr. Frost was in Toronto, looking for a house. He was greatly encouraged by Mr. Sandham's offer of the whole top floor of The Christian Institute for the purposes of the Mission. This provided dormitory space for the young men candidates, and good office accommodation. It also brought the new Secretary into close touch with Mr. Sandham and other members of the Council, including Mr. William Gooderham, who had given the beautiful building and took great interest in the many-sided work of which it was the center.

The search for a house was circumscribed by these developments, for it had to be in the neighborhood of The Christian Institute, so that candidates who roomed there might keep in touch with the Mission Home where they were to take their meals. That downtown district offered few residences, and the only house that proved suitable was one on Shuter Street which, to Mr. Frost's disappointment, the landlord refused to rent for less than a year. He was willing to sell, but monthly rental he emphatically declined.

This attitude was the more trying as it proved to be pretty general. Houses could be had for purchase or lease, but Mr. Frost had no money for such transactions. Indeed, he had reason to be concerned over the inroads already made into the two hundred and fifty dollars, which was all he had at his disposal. Prayer was the only resource—and even while the gracious answer was on its way, that little praying company was overwhelmed with a baptism of sorrow.

For it was in those August days that tidings reached them which had been seven weeks on the way from an inland province in China. There one of the most promising and beloved of all the young workers from North America had died of malignant fever. Susie Parker—gone! the only child of the father who had said in giving her up, "I have nothing too precious for my Lord Jesus."

One of the hardest things Mr. Frost ever had to do was to write, out of his own distress, to the parents in that Pittsfield home. How could he tell them that the daughter whose life had seemed so full of promise had been called to meet suffering and death, far from home and loved ones? What would be the anguish of their hearts? What was the reaction of his own to such a mystery? Plunged in grief and silence of spirit he waited—but comfort came with the reply he had dreaded to receive. For Mr. Parker was able to write, by the grace of God:

"I can still say, 'I have nothing too precious for my Lord Jesus.'"

Light broke as thought was lifted from their pain and loss to the joy of Him who, in face of His own utmost sacrifice, had prayed, "Father, I will that those whom Thou hast given me be with me where I am."

Heavy as has been the blow (Mr. Taylor wrote from England), and I cannot express the sorrow it has brought, I thank God for His help to recognize His right to deal as He wills with His own, in wisdom and love. . . .

Oh, how great her joy—and how much greater her Lord's! May His joy ever be first in our estimation.

But the mystery was still poignantly felt by the young leader in North America, faced thus for the first time with the cost to life itself of the work in which he was engaged. Difficulty and trial he had expected, and no doubt sickness, but not such early and tragic bereavement!

Our service for China (he wrote, five years later) took on in that hour of darkness a more solemn hue. We saw more fully what going into "all the world" includes, and what it might yet mean for others as well as ourselves. The Lord seemed to ask us then, as He asks us still,

"Can ye drink of the cup that I drink, or be baptized with the baptism wherewith I am baptized?"

Thank God! He gave us strength in that hour to say, "We can." The Holy Spirit taught us to look at all things through God Himself, and so to call even adversity "blessed." And this is still our victory, whether looking backward or forward—to see Christ on the throne, *"all things"* under His feet; to remember that *"all things"* are ours in Him, whether life or death, things present or things to come; and firmly to believe that *"all things"* work together for good, under His control.

But how much there is in the thought Mr. Taylor expressed:

Our partings from loved ones will soon be past; but unless we are faithful, how many there are who will never hear of Him to whom we owe our earthly joys as well as heavenly hopes!

And in the plea that came from burdened hearts in China:

We have the hope of seeing her again; but the thirty thousand who die here daily, are "without hope." Oh for workers! Shall Christians sit with folded arms and let these people *perish*? Oh Lord, hear our cry, and thrust forth laborers into this field!

CHAPTER

XVIII

WAITING FOR GOD

TESTED with sorrow even before they could leave Attica, the young Secretary and his wife were also encouraged by fresh tokens of the love and care of God. Needs at home as well as in China had a way of multiplying, and sometimes supplies seemed meager in comparison. Any deficiency for the North American missionaries in China was made up from the General Fund, which ministers to all alike, but the ideal was that each home country should contribute enough to to cover completely the cost of its own representatives. The unity of the Mission on the field being one of its chief characteristics, there was no fear that North American members would not be cared for, as far as the General Fund would allow, but Mr. Frost was keenly alive to the privilege of supplying not only personal remittances to all his young workers—many of whom were specially supported—but also a proportionate share of other Mission expenses, such as house rent, cost of journeys, hospital care in sickness, and the education of missionaries' children. Even in these early days he was burdened about shortage in this connection, and was giving himself to prayer that more undesignated gifts might be received which could be applied to general purposes. He was also faced with needs at home that, sometimes, generous friends of the work seemed to over-look. It may not have been the wisest plan, to keep the funds for China and for the home department entirely sepa-rate. But all gifts to the Mission were sent on to Shanghai in those days, unless specially designated for use at home in whole or in part, so that it was possible to be very short on the home side while there was abundance on the other. It was only gradually that experience made wiser adjustments possible, and meanwhile the willing learners were finding our infinite God to be a very understanding Father.

Soon after the tidings had been received of Susie Parker's Homegoing, the burden of this situation was pressing heavily on Mr. Frost who was much alone, house-hunting in Toronto. It was none too cheering an occupation, and he turned into his office in The Christian Institute one morning sorely needing encouragement.

I was beginning the day with a season of prayer which was earnest indeed (he records), when a new thought came to me. I had not failed to notice, in praying with Mr. Hudson Taylor, that while utterly simple in his petitions he was also very definite. He would go into details, asking for blessing not only in a general way but also in particulars. My own prayer-life had been of the more usual order, but now it seemed as if a voice beside me said,

"Just what is it, young man, that you want? Be specific."

So clear was the suggestion, that I rose from my knees, went over to my desk, took pencil and paper, and made a careful list of our immediate needs. I then added up the sums and found that they came to no less than six hundred dollars, about half for China and half for home requirements. This was staggering—to ask for *six hundred dollars*, when by far the largest sum we had hitherto received was the two hundred and fifty which Mr. Taylor had left with us!

Still, I took the paper, knelt down again, spread it out on the chair before me, and definitely asked the Lord for that six hundred dollars. So real was the transaction that when I rose from my knees the second time it was without a burden of any kind. With complete rest of heart, I went through my correspondence and other work for the day, though as hour by hour passed, nothing happened.

Even then, however, a letter from Cleveland was on its way, which reached me the following morning. It was from a friend whose previous gifts had been for the special support of workers in China. In this case he made no such designation. The check was to be used as we thought best, and when I looked at it—it was for *six hundred dollars*. There it lay, just where I had written that list only the day before.

At first I was so taken aback that I could hardly believe the evidence of my senses. Could Mr. Livingstone Taylor really mean that we might use the money for home needs as well as for China? I did not deposit the check but, putting it in a place of safety, wrote to ask whether I understood his wishes aright. The reply came by return mail:

"It is in your hands, for your disposal."

That this experience formed an episode in my life will readily be believed. It gave me an altogether new impression of what prayer means and of what God is. I entered into the realization, then, that we have in our heavenly Father One who is ready to act for our good in every detail of life; One whose ear is open to our cry in all lesser as well as greater matters. I seemed to see Him, up there on the Throne, listening with loving care to the prayer I had prayed.

"My servant said, 'six hundred dollars.' That is what they need, and that is what I shall send."

And there it lay before me! Did I pray in more detail after that? I certainly did! I remember that I used to breathe prayers at that time that I should have laughed at before, as childish. Something came back to me then that Mr. Taylor had said when we were together at Northfield.

"Have you ever thought," he asked, "of the difference between a father and a mother? The father goes to business and works hard to provide for his family, but it takes a mother to mend the childrens' stockings! And in a very real sense, God is a Mother to His children, as well as a Father."

And truly I have found it so, in all the years since then.

It was a great discovery—that definite petitions bring definite answers, and that nothing is too small and nothing is too great to bring to God in prayer. And such quickening of faith was needed. For all unknowingly, the young leader stood between two sore bereavements. The last days of August had brought the sorrowful news from China, followed by the above, fresh assurance of the Father's watchful care. In the strength of it, Mr. Frost continued the search for a home in Toronto which had proved so discouraging. The place that would have met their needs, it will be remembered, was not available, because the landlord refused the only terms that Mr. Frost felt he could offer. He proved to be the city bailiff, which perhaps explained the disconcerting shortness of his manner. But the disappointment was turned to thankfulness when, early in September, Mr. William Gooderham heard of the situation through Mr. Sandham, and undertook to purchase the property himself, as a gift to the Mission. All now seemed plain sailing. This generous friend was prepared to pay seven thousand dollars for the house, and Mr. Frost was able to go forward with his plans for receiving candidates.

What was the shock, within a few days of this happy arrangement, to learn that Mr. Gooderham, while conducting a meeting in Toronto, had suddenly been called to be with the Lord he so faithfully loved and served! A little later it appeared that his expressed desires with regard to the Mission and other Christian enterprises would fail of fulfilment, because his legal arrangements were incomplete and his latest Will unsigned.

The loss to the Mission was great, both materially and in the sympathy of one of its best friends. But was not the watchful care of God over His own work even in this? So warm was Mr. Gooderham's interest that it would have been easy to come to depend upon him, unconsciously, rather than on the Lord. Referring to both these bereavements, Mr. Taylor wrote in September:

> God does not rob His people: He raises our treasures that our hearts may be raised also. Miss Susie Parker's removal has been a deep blessing as well as a deep trial—a deep blessing to me because a deep trial. . . .
> How kind of Mr. Gooderham to think of buying the house you mention; and how remarkable his removal just at this time! I wonder how The Institute will stand now? His death is another warning to lean not on man, but on the living God alone.

So the unrewarding search began that made the month of September one of no little trial. The house on Shuter Street had to be given up, and no other could be found in the desired neighborhood. This meant a weary hunt all over the city, and at last a choice that was manifestly second best. However, the alternative house on Sherbourne Street was to be had on reasonable terms, and the owner having undertaken to prepare the lease for signing, Mr. Frost went back to Attica to pack and send off his household belongings. This accomplished, he returned to Toronto to take possession.

Meanwhile, the owner of the Sherbourne Street premises had met with a would-be purchaser. Being in financial difficulty, he was anxious to sell rather than rent—as he had explained from the first—and Mr. Frost found himself confronted by a trying situation.

Would I be good enough to relieve him of his obligation to rent the place to me?

Would I be good enough? I hardly knew! Our furniture was steadily nearing Toronto and would have to be disposed of as soon as it arrived. Never did I so long to hold a man to his bargain. But the Lord in His great grace won the battle for me. In a few moments the hesitation passed and I was able to tell the landlord that he was free to sell his house. I would look for another. . . .

It was noon when I left him, and the sun was shining, but so great was my feeling of disappointment and helplessness that it seemed as if I were going out into the dark. I knew not what to do or which way to turn. With a heavy heart I sought my office, and there told the Lord in prayer about the serious difficulty I was facing.

Was Mr. Frost reminded then of the lesson he had already had occasion to learn, that there is no little difference between waiting on God and waiting for God? Making a study of this subject, he was impressed to find that there are fully as many passages in Scripture referring to the one as to the other.

As I meditated upon the verses, it did not take me long to decide which, as between the two, was harder. Waiting *on* God is comparatively easy; waiting *for* God is decidedly hard. Just now it was a case of waiting for Him; and I fear I did not make much of a success of it.

We are all slow at learning that God's time is as important as His way. But we have a very understanding Father —"the Father of our spirits." He knows just what the discipline means to the one He is dealing with in love, and does not let the "chastening" be too long or too severe.

It was next day, I think, when I went to call once more on the owner of the Shuter Street house. I took this course after much prayer, not knowing what else to do, and in the hope that, possibly, he might change his mind and consent to rent the place to us. The interview was decidedly unsatisfactory. Mr. G— was an abrupt man, with a stern expression, and a hoarse voice. With this combination in full force, I was told I could have the house if I would buy it, but not otherwise. To buy the house, I explained, would now be impossible, as we only had sufficient funds in hand to take a lease, and that a short one; and we could not, under any circumstances, go beyond the cash in hand. . . . At this, the landlord turned upon his heel and without another word walked away, down the street, leaving me looking after him and wondering what the issue was to be. Back I went to my office to cry once more to God to undertake for us before that carload of furniture should arrive.

The following day, I was going up the stairs of The Institute to my office on the top floor, when one of the staff told me that my household goods had come and the car was waiting to be unloaded. For once, a freight shipment had been promptly made, when delay would have been appreciated! I answered that I had no place to put the goods, adding—too faintly, I fear, for anyone to hear:

"The Lord will provide."

Next moment, as I went on up the stairs, another young man came after me. There was someone below, he said, who wanted to see me about a house.

"Oh," I exclaimed, and this time aloud, "perhaps the Lord has provided!"

I immediately went down and found in The Institute library the landlord with whom I had had the trying interview the day before.

"Well, Mr. Frost," he said, "I have decided to let you have the house on your own terms."

"Thank you," I said; "and thank God!"

"When will you want to move in?"

It was Saturday, and I said, "On Monday, please."

An amused look came over his face, as much as to say "That is quick work." But I explained our position, and found that under the rough exterior there was a heart that could feel for another's difficulty. Through Mr. G—'s kindness, we were able to remove our goods from the car and take possession of the house the following Tuesday.

The Home thus given in answer to prayer proved to be all we thought it would be. It became to us a very Bethel, where from opened heavens we received many fresh blessings. Not least of these was the ever-increasing kindness of our landlord who, though far from being what he would have called "religious," seemed never to tire of helping us in every way he could.

CHAPTER

XIX

"SOMETHING DIFFERENT"

THE Home was ready none too soon. Mrs. Frost arrived from Attica on the 22nd of October (1889), and by the end of the month, number Thirty Shuter Street was full to overflowing with young people in training for the work in China. During the long weeks when Mr. Frost was alone in Toronto, looking for a house, he had written to Mr. Taylor:

For a little, the Lord is testing my love to Him, and my wife's also, by separating us. I feel it is His work because of the wonderful keeping of which we are conscious through it all. He holds us close to Himself, making us still and calm and constant in waiting upon Him, so that we may know that the Lord, He is God—there is none other.

And now that the new life opened before them, he added:

These things give me much encouragement to believe that the Lord is really with us, and that to bless, and that He is but waiting for us to ask, in order that He may hear and answer prayer. . . .

Please remember with special supplications my dear wife, that she may be strengthened both physically and spiritually for her untried service. We both feel very much our weakness and our ignorance, and pray that our lack may be supplied by Him who is "rich unto all."

"Something different," was the impression made upon many of the candidates who came into that Home—"an atmosphere of something different, and of trust." Mr. Frost's Bible teaching was unusual in its helpfulness and the spirit of prayer pervaded everything. Needs were constantly arising in so large a family, but, "They had a prayer meeting," seemed to meet the case, whatever it might be.

Even before the Home was opened, Mr. Frost had started the weekly prayer meeting, which now, for almost half a century, has been a center of blessing in Toronto as well as for China. Open to the public, it attracted and held a wide circle of praying friends. But no advantage was ever taken of those gatherings to make known the financial needs of the work. Prayer was made for China with its unevangelized millions, and for the North American members of the Mission, known to many present. Letters were read, telling of progress or of difficulties; and, in brief but memorable Bible readings, Mr. Frost ministered richly from the Word. There was not a little thanksgiving for continued manifestations of the presence and blessing of God. But there was no mention of money matters. Those were not the occasions for detailed prayer about funds.

Daily, in the inner circle at Shuter Street, these matters were brought to the Lord in quietness and confidence.

"You are candidates," Mr. Frost would say to the young people with him. "These needs are yours as well as ours."

It was simply miraculous (said one who was a candidate in those days) how supplies came in, and how openings were given us among the churches. For we were looked upon with suspicion in many quarters as "a free-lance Mission," with no regular means of support. But there was a depth and beauty in it all that made it well worth while. As we grow wider, we tend to get more shallow. We need to pray that that early spirit of enthusiasm, reality, and devotion may remain among us.*

And there were wonderful answers to prayer, not only in money matters, to be enthusiastic about. Mr. Frost had early become conscious of the need of helpers. At first, he did everything himself, acting as Secretary, Treasurer, book-keeper, and all else that was required. But when the care and training of candidates was added, it was evident that he must be relieved of the detail of office work. To adver-tize for a stenographer would have been easy. Mr. Frost had always been accustomed, in business matters, to follow business methods, "partly in a spirit of prayer, but more in a spirit of self-help," as he himself records. But now the case was different. He could offer no salary in the regular way, and needed, moreover, a special combination—Christian character and missionary interest, as well as business effi-ciency. Clearly, such a helper must be sought from God.

Besides this, I was slowly learning that it was my privilege to bring all needs to God, and look for a help as practical as it was

---

* It is interesting to recall that the first group of candidates at Shuter Street (1889-90) included four who were each to spend more than forty-six years in the fellowship of the Mission: Miss Isabella Ross, of Guelph, On-tario, now *Mrs. Isaac Page;* Miss Maud Fairbank, also of Guelph, Ont., now *Mrs. Percy Knight;* Mr. *William Taylor,* of Toronto; and *Dr. A. W. Lager-quist,* from the Moody Bible Institute, Chicago, recently deceased. Together, they have already given one hundred and eighty-nine years of loving, faithful service to the Lord, in and for China.

Miss Rebe McKenzie and *Mrs. William Taylor* (Miss Jessie Gardiner), members of the previous party (1888), who still take a helpful part in the work in China, add another ninety-eight years to this total. So that six of the first North American workers, who went out in 1888-90, have given a total of two hundred and eighty-seven years of service in connection with the Mission, an average of almost forty-eight years each.

great. Thus I was led to make definite petition for a lady helper, one familiar with shorthand and typewriting, who would be willing to serve without guarantee of salary, and one who would be a devoted Christian, with a spirit of consecration not only toward Christ but toward China.

Reverently, though somewhat falteringly, I fear, this demand was made upon the Lord. And seldom was prayer more quickly answered! Within a day of the time I made known my need, a young lady presented herself at the office and asked the privilege of serving God and China in connection with us, saying that she would expect no remuneration save as funds would allow, and then only according to her needs. Thus was given us, in blessed answer to prayer, one who has now for ten years identified herself with the work in faithful, loving service. And thus I was given a glimpse of what I have been delighted to see more and more fully, that the Lord is indeed, by His Spirit, the administrator of His work, and that no need can arise in a service that is His but that He himself will be its supplier.

This was further proved in the coming of helpers fitted to take part in testing and training the candidates. With eight or ten of the latter to care for in addition to her own family, Mrs. Frost was far too busy to take more than a general oversight of the work of the young women; and, even had he known Chinese, Mr. Frost could not have given time to teaching the language. Someone of spiritual influence was needed, experienced in winning people to Christ, and someone—most unlikely of all—who could teach Chinese! Again, prayer was the only resource.

Thus it was that we made a new venture of faith, and gave ourselves to prayer for both a man and a woman. Where the money to support them was to come from, we did not know. The need was manifest. We would pray for the persons; and if God gave them, He would no doubt provide for them. This seemed good spiritual logic, and we afterwards found that it had a good spiritual sequence.

For it was not long before the venture of faith was fully rewarded. And what good gifts were given in the young Japanese nobleman, Tozo Ohno, who was well able to teach Chinese, and in the little Scotch nurse, Agnes McIntyre, who was honored and loved in Toronto for her devoted work as a Bible teacher! Tozo was a beautiful character as well as a consecrated Christian. Banished from the home of his ancestors, because of faith in Christ, he had found in the United States a second father and mother in Mr. Frost's parents, and was glad to be of service to their son. The whole story was a remarkable instance of the providential care of God, and Tozo proved to be a joy and blessing in the Shuter Street circle. His Christlike life opened the eyes of the young people to the precious contribution the Orient has to make to the glory and kingdom of God. He helped them in their study of Chinese and still more so in their confidence in the Message they were to carry to "those that sit in darkness and in the shadow of death."

The same was true of Agnes McIntyre, for the quiet power of her life was due to a close and constant walk with God.

Morning after morning she went out to her work of nursing and Bible teaching, taking one and another of the young women with her, and evening by evening they came back to tell of poor and sick ones succored and of lost souls saved. She created thus, and in other ways, an atmosphere in our Home which was heavenly in quality, and it was a continual joy to have her with us. To our candidates she was a revelation of God's grace and power, and those who went to China from under her influence carried with them a knowledge of the divine will and way in saving souls which was an inspiration to them among the heathen.

Miss McIntyre lived with us for several years, and from first to last was a great and increasing blessing.

"Above all that ye ask or think" is the generous way in which the Lord loves to answer prayer, and to these helpers was added yet another specially qualified to train the young men in practical evangelism. For the leader, under Mr. Sandham, of the regular meetings and classes at The Christian Institute came to live in the Shuter Street Home, bringing fresh inspiration and guidance in personal work. Thus the Mission Home became a center of blessed activity in preparing "fishers of men"—a most important part of missionary training, for, as Mr. Hudson Taylor puts it, "a voyage across the ocean does not make anyone a soul-winner."

Naturally, the enlarged household at Shuter Street meant an increased tax upon supplies, until one day Mr. and Mrs. Frost were faced with a situation that seemed desperate. Larder and purse were alike empty; and with six hungry men coming over for breakfast there was nothing of which to make a meal. The table was laid, but when the first bell rang there was actually no food in the house. Would breakfast that day turn into a prayer meeting? What was the lesson the Lord was teaching? And what about the faith of the young people under their care?

The second bell rang ten minutes after the first, and when the household gathered it was to find a table more bountifully spread than usual! Something had happened in those anxious moments, and from the way in which Mr. Frost gave thanks it was evident that he was much moved. Wonderingly the young people waited for the explanation—and could they ever forget the realizing sense it brought of the love and care of God? For just in time, as if their anonymous friend had known the breakfast hour, a large hamper arrived at the door, packed full of bread, butter, eggs, bacon, groceries, and other supplies! No amount of theory could have convinced those young people as that breakfast did that God, our heavenly Father, cannot fail or forget His trusting children.

Usually, as Mr. Frost gladly testified, the needs of that considerable household were abundantly supplied. But it must not be supposed that walking upon the water as Peter did—as all who are called to a life of faith must still do, in one way or another—is easy.

For the most part (Mr. Frost could write) we enjoyed long reaches of prosperous days, when every need was fully met. . . . But days of adversity were put in between, just to keep us reminded Who is at the head of the Mission, and upon Whom we are dependent.

And, at those times, it was upon the young Secretary that the burden pressed most heavily. As Treasurer also, Mr. Frost watched the ebb and flow of funds from day to day, and his office witnessed many an hour of prayer in which the heart cried out to God—as Moses at the Red Sea—when no one knew it. Of one such time he tells us:

Our money was now almost exhausted, and I have to add with sorrow, that my faith was entirely so. We were willingly pledged not to ask anyone for funds and we were given grace to hold to the position which we had taken, but we did plead with the Lord that He would remind some of His servants of our approaching need; and yet, in spite of prayer, while gifts still came in for the work abroad, few were received for the home department.

One day, about this time, I knelt in my office to make special supplication for the funds so earnestly desired, when the Lord evidently took me in hand to teach me a much-needed lesson. I was painfully conscious, as I began to pray, that what little faith I had had was gone, and I began to think of the contrast between myself and Mr. Taylor, whose faith was always bright and triumphant. Out of this thought grew the longing:

"I wish Mr. Taylor were here."

I had frequently heard our brother pray while he was with us, and had seen the Lord answer his prayers, over and over again, and in most remarkable ways. I could not help the feeling that, if only he were with us now, the Lord would again hear and answer, and all our needs would be supplied. But it was no use wishing, for Mr. Taylor was far from us, on his way to China. Then came another thought:

"I wish I had Mr. Taylor's faith."

But immediately I realized that this too was impossible. Then, while still kneeling, I asked myself the question:

"Why is it that Mr. Taylor's prayers are answered?"

In a moment I recalled that more than once our beloved friend had told us that faith is *reckoning upon God's faithfulness*, and also that in his own prayers he always asked the Father for that which was needed *in the name of Jesus Christ*. At once, almost as if by revelation, I was led to see one of the chief secrets of the life of faith and answered prayer. I saw that faith did not occupy itself with itself, but with the promises of God and the God of the promises; and that one could receive answers to prayer only as one sheltered under the Name of names, the precious Name of Jesus.

This, then, was the twofold lesson Mr. Taylor had learned; and I began to see that, unworthy as I was, I had the same right to reckon upon the faithfulness of God and to plead before Him the ever-prevailing Name of Jesus. Thus, with new boldness, I ventured to look up, then and there, to the throne of grace, and to ask with altogether new confidence for the funds of which we stood in need.

Happy to relate, the Lord heard and answered, according to His abundant mercy in Christ Jesus. We came to an end of the money originally given to us, and of smaller sums subsequently received, but we did not come to an end of the Lord or of His supplies. Gifts were more frequently made to us designated for the general account, and even the faith which had failed so completely, as it now occupied itself more and more with the faithfulness of God and the worthiness of Christ, was renewed and strengthened.

But care has a persistent way, as we all know, of coming
back again and again. "Dismissed by the front door," as
Mr. Frost puts it with reference to those days, "it is very
apt to sneak in at the back." The lesson so graciously
taught had to be learned afresh with every trying situation.
But in such matters, heart answers to heart, and we cannot
but value the record of other searching experiences.

Well do I remember a day, when funds were lowest, going up
the long flight of stairs at The Christian Institute, with heavy feet
and a heavier heart.

"Who am I," I was thinking, "that the eyes of all in the Home
are turned to me in expectation? How can I provide for so large
a family, and for an ever-increasing work? I cannot! Nor can I
even try to do so. Will the Lord undertake? Or are we to pass
through deep trial and be in want?"

Reaching my office with such thoughts in mind, I turned as my
custom was to the Scripture calendar upon the wall, to tear off the
slip for the previous day. As I did so, the text for that morning
met my eye. There were only three words:

"Your Father knoweth."

At once, my thought was fastened upon the word "Father." It
seemed to stand out in letters of light! And my burden? Ah, my
burden, in a moment, was millions of miles away—in the glory, on
One upon whose shoulders the government has been laid! And
the money? Yes, the Father supplied all our need, "according to
His riches in glory in Christ Jesus."

At another time, matters looked so serious that a day of
fasting and prayer was arranged for, in accordance with
a custom which has proved a great blessing to the Mission.
Under a burden of anxiety the household and candidates
met in the living room at Shuter Street to lay their needs
before the Lord. Before uniting in prayer, Mr. Frost opened

his Bible, turned to the Gospel of John, and began to read a series of marked passages containing the great words, "I AM."

I could not have chosen a more unfortunate subject, if we had wanted to continue in doubt and fear. . . .

"Verily, verily, I say unto you, before Abraham was, I am."

As I read these words and spoke of what they meant—how they set forth Christ as the great, eternally existing, ever-present God; the One who had called forth Abraham, his family, his flocks, and herds, and had cared for them; the One who had called forth Moses and all the tribes of Israel and cared for them in the wilderness— I began to feel not a little ashamed of ever having doubted this Lord Jehovah, even though our money was all gone.

Nor did further reading improve matters, as far as shame was concerned. For the great "I am" promises were reiterated one by one:

"I am the living bread which came down from heaven"; "I am the bread of life"; "I am the living bread . . . my flesh . . . for the life of the world."

More and more overwhelmed, as the voice of the Lord came home to us, I was ready to cry out in confession before God for having grieved His great and tender heart by failing to trust Him wholly, who had ever been wholly true. And I was not alone in this experience. For all of us, as we sat there, were given to see something of the greatness of our Jehovah God; and all of us were given to feel that we had sinned against Him in not trusting to the full.

It will be understood that the time of prayer that followed was on other lines than we had first intended. Bowing down before the great "I AM" in humility and confession, we told the Lord that we could not doubt either His power or His love. Then we unitedly gave praise to God for having allowed us to be brought to a place where we were shut off from all other means of supply—just shut up to Himself alone. After this we sang another hymn, and, thank God, this one was not pitched in a minor key.

I may add that our fasting did not continue long after that meeting. Before the day closed we sat down to a table full of supplies which His loving hand had provided for us. Again the principle of trust in God for daily bread held good, and we were not put to shame.

Amid all this, Mrs. Frost moved with untroubled heart. From childhood she had known the Lord, and proved His readiness to hear and answer prayer. Many were the lessons learned by those about her from her natural, spontaneous reactions of faith under all conditions—lessons for which no one was more grateful than her husband, who writes, "for the sake of any who may be passing through similar experiences":

One day, about this time (1889-90), we came to our last five dollars. Feeling that we ought to be very careful in its use, I went to Mrs. Frost with the suggestion:

"We have only five dollars left. I hope you will make it go as far as possible."

For a moment my wife looked down, then quietly said:

"I don't call that faith."

"The Lord has given us clear enough guidance in the matter," I replied. "We have only this small amount left, and our family is large. Surely we must make the money last as long as we can."

The dear wife did not see it. Again she said, with a shake of her head:

"I don't call that faith." Then she added, "If we have been extravagant, we should economize at once; but if we have not been spending more than was necessary, I think we should go right along as if we had plenty in the bank."

I was not entirely satisfied, even with this explanation before me; but afterward I found that my wife was right, not I. When that five dollars came to an end, the Lord sent further supplies. And ever since, we have found it most blessed to go right along as if we had abundance for all real needs, simply because we are going along *with the Lord*. We have never come to an end of His resources.

CHAPTER

XX

GREAT ASSURANCES

IT was Saturday afternoon, and Mr. Nasmith, a specially helpful member of the Toronto Council, had called at the office to see Mr. Frost. He found him facing a big problem. Six of the Shuter Street candidates had been accepted for service in China, and the time was drawing near when they should go out. But there was no money in hand for passages and outfits; and after going into the matter it appeared that, to meet this and other impending claims, no less than five thousand dollars would be needed. No wonder that Mr. Frost was serious and preoccupied. But, as one of the inner circle, Mr. Nasmith knew of the situation, and soon they were discussing the matter freely.

It was no new thing in the Mission to accept young workers who seemed to be truly called of God, even if there were no funds available for passages to China and subsequent needs. The principle which had guided the conduct of the work from the beginning was that, if the "Lord of the harvest" called laborers into His vineyard, He would also provide for them; and behind it was His definite promise, "Seek ye first the kingdom of God, and his righteousness; and all these things shall be added unto you." For twenty-five years that promise had been fulfilled in the experience of every member of the Mission; but it was the first time that so large a demand had been made upon the faith of the Toronto group, and it certainly gave them pause. Five thousand dollars, in addition to all that was needed for current expenses—where was it to come from? And how long would they have to wait before the party could go out?

Mr. Nasmith was a business man, practical, direct and, like those who "served tables" in apostolic days, "full of the Spirit and of wisdom." He knew something of the great need in China, and could see for himself the suitability of the young workers who were ready to go. Gladly would he have given his check for the whole amount, had that been possible. As it was, he did something better. He encouraged his friend in God, until their hearts were in the attitude, "And now, Lord, what wait I for? My hope is in thee."

Having talked over the situation (Mr. Frost writes of that memorable hour), we both felt constrained to kneel in prayer and at once ask for the full five thousand dollars. This we did, and I led in prayer for that amount. Mr. Nasmith followed.

Never shall I forget his prayer. It was one of those Spirit-given petitions that go like an arrow to their mark. Humble yet confident, reverent yet bold, it laid hold upon the promises of God and made them, for the time being, blank checks to be filled in according to the need. As our brother went on reminding the Lord of His promised care, my faith was more and more strengthened. At last, I could doubt no longer. The faithfulness of our Lord was so present, the consciousness of His love and power so real, that my heart was rested in Him, and I felt we had the petitions we desired of

Him. As soon as Mr. Nasmith had finished, I could not but thank the Lord for His marvelous grace in listening to us, and praise Him for the funds for which we had asked and which we felt were now given.

The next thing was to act upon this faith, which Mrs. Frost did by using the little money they had to spare to begin outfitting the party.

We could not go far in our preparations without increased supplies, but what we could do we did. Meanwhile, the Lord enabled us to keep on praising, and this proved to be the open door for blessing. Indeed, praise ever opens the windows of heaven. It was so in the days gone by. "When the trumpeters and singers were as one, to make one sound to be heard in praising and thanking the Lord . . . *then* the house was filled with a cloud, even the house of the Lord." And so it was for us. God did not manifest Himself to us in shining Shekinah cloud, but He did show us His glory; for His goodness is His glory, and this He made to pass before our eyes.

Very soon after that, spontaneous gifts began to be received for the outgoing-missionaries. Nothing was said about the need for five thousand dollars, but interesting things happened that showed that the Lord was speaking to one and another, though His children kept silence. Mr. Frost was puzzled, one afternoon, by the embarrassed manner of a lady who called at Shuter Street to see him. He knew her only slightly, and waited to see in what way he might be of service. But it appeared that she had not come for help of any kind. Almost timidly, at length she drew from a cloth bag a long envelope containing money. This, she said, was to be used for the outfits and passages of the sisters, Maggie and Tina Scott, two of the party not yet provided for. To Mr. Frost's surprise, the envelope contained *four hundred dollars*; and before leaving, the visitor,

in her gentle, retiring way, said that she was sending an
additional hundred for the same purpose.

What a quick and large answer to our prayer and praise! And
what a beautiful answer too! For I saw that the embarrassment
which perplexed me was nothing else than the humility of Christ,
which seeks not to let the left hand know what the right hand does.

Two or three weeks passed, after this visit, without any
indication that the remainder of the five thousand dollars
was on its way.

Our hearts, which aside from grace would have been very un-
believing, through grace went on praising. And happy days they
were . . . for a praising heart means a happy heart, and a happy
heart makes happy days. At the end of this half month, however,
the Lord revealed Himself, showing us once more that the work
was entirely His, and so also all the responsibility. How blessed
it is to be taught, and really to *learn* this lesson! . . .

> "Bear not a single care thyself;
>   One is too much for thee:
> The work is Mine and Mine alone;
>   Thy work is, rest in Me"

One day about this time, I was in my office when two ladies called
to see me, one of whom I recognized. This friend introduced the
other lady as the mother of one of our missionaries. I then remembered having met her on a previous occasion, at a Toronto meeting
when her daughter was about to leave for China. But then, the
mother's face had been pale, her eyes full of tears, and her lips
trembling. Now, what a change! Her face was bright, and her
heart, evidently, very happy. No wonder I had not recognized her!
Then the dear mother began to tell me how the change had come
about. She spoke of how much her daughter had meant to her, and
how hard it had been to let her go to China. But from the time
she had given her consent, for Christ's sake and by His enabling,
she had begun to receive blessing from the Lord—blessing which
had gone on increasing, until now her cup was running over. She

had come to feel, she said, that she could keep back nothing from her Saviour. If He wanted her other daughter, she would willingly give her also.

"And, Mr. Frost," she added, "I have brought a little gift for the Mission as a thank-offering to the Lord for taking my Hattie to China, and for all the blessing that has come to me in consequence."

The speaker was not a wealthy woman. Ten or fifteen dollars from her, a farmer's wife, I should have considered a generous gift. But when I looked at the check she handed me, I was amazed to find that it was for five hundred and fifty dollars. She had given her *all*. A mother's thank-offering to the Lord for His goodness to her in taking her daughter to China! . . .

Nor was this all: for when I asked whether she wished the money, in whole or in part, to be set aside for her daughter's use—"No," she replied. "I want it all to go toward sending more missionaries to China."

And she knew nothing of our special need at the time.

With such a manifest token of the love and care of God, I could not wait until the friends had left before giving Him adoring praise —and it was with thankfulness to the Lord they realized that they had been the messengers of Him who hears and answers prayer.

Thus in two donations, coming within a month's time, nearly one-fifth of the five thousand dollars had been provided. The remainder that was lacking toward the expenses of the outgoing-party was soon given, and the whole sum prayed for was in hand within three months.

One can well believe that the six young women thus provided for "carried blessing with them," when they set out from Toronto in January, 1890, "and left blessing behind them." This was specially the case at Shuter Street, where hearts were being stirred to larger vision. The little front room, which was their place of prayer, became "a place of great yearning and strong pleading."

For God is always the God of enlargement. He was urging us by the constraint of His Spirit to lift our eyes from our petty cares

of food, house-rental, and a few outgoing-missionaries to the field
white unto harvest, to pray for *many* laborers to do the reaping.
. . . We were realizing in a new way the greatness of China's need,
and longing to be used of God in the fulfilment of His compas-
sionate purposes there. So we did what we could. Day after day,
we gave much time to prayer. How the Lord would answer and
enlarge our coasts we did not know. That had to be left with Him.
Our business was to ask, and then eagerly look for His working.

But that working did not come at first in the way that
might have been expected. Not more candidates, more gifts,
more blessing, but more serious trial than ever before was
the immediate experience. Out in China another aspect
of the matter might have been traced, for Mr. Taylor was
led to give special thought and prayer to the enlargement of
the North American work. But while he was planning to
strengthen Mr. Frost's hands, it seemed as if the Lord were
permitting His young servant to be brought to the place
of Habakkuk, long ago:

"Although the fig tree shall not blossom, neither shall fruit be in
the vines; the labour of the olive shall fail, and the field shall yield
no meat . . . yet I will rejoice in the Lord, I will joy in the God
of my salvation."

Yet, to Habakkuk, on his watch-tower, had been given
that great vision, "The earth shall be filled with the knowledge of the glory of the Lord, as the waters cover the sea."
How we need to be strengthened to receive the answer to
our own prayers!

"Shadow as well as sunshine is needed in the life that
would be fruitful," as Mr. Frost wrote of the summer that
followed. Fragments of letters remain that show how heavy
the shadows were—words penned to intimate friends "out
of a sorely tried soul, struggling to maintain its trust and

praise before God." Perhaps only those who have passed through like depths can fully appreciate the following:

June 10.

Just now our hearts are being made glad in much trial. The tokens of our Father's love are coming thick and fast and—blessed be God who causeth us to triumph—His all-grace is all-sufficient. We know now that we are "sons." Besides this, we believe that God is preparing us for mighty blessing. We have been asking great things; is it any wonder that our Father tests us with unusual trial, in preparation for great and greater blessing? May the Lord have His own perfect way with us. We want to be used of Him, and are willing, if need be, to be made "perfect through suffering." Please ask that the Father may portion out our lot, and may be able to give us His best.

June 11

We are finding the trial of our faith far more precious than gold which perisheth. In spite of the fact that we have only about eight dollars in hand, we are kept by the grace of God in perfect peace, knowing that "no good thing will he withhold." Pray for us, that we may bring joy to the Master's heart by being all-submissive before Him.

June 13

Our family here is being purged by fire and, I trust, is being prepared for a mighty work of grace. The Lord has allowed our supplies to run lower and lower. Yesterday we spent in fasting and prayer. . . . Jesus was in our midst, and we were taught to remember that it is never a question of what we are, but ever one as to what He is. This thought satisfies us, and we have no anxiety, but perfect peace. We do thank God from the depth of our hearts for allowing us to be tried by Himself. The result will be to His glory. Pray that we may be kept occupied with Himself—not second causes.

To add to Mr. Frost's concern at this time was the consciousness that, at the end of the month, a payment would be due on the Shuter Street house. The short lease had already run out, and monthly rentals of thirty-five dollars had now to be met. It was of the landlord, gruff Mr. G——, that he was thinking.

Our friendship for him had made him a friend to us. I did not want this friendship marred. Nor did I want him to think that the assurances we had passed on to him concerning the God who answers prayer had been just words and not facts. So I prayed with increasing earnestness, and watched the mails with some anxiety.

And then it was that a beautiful answer to prayer confirmed and strengthened faith in a way that could never be forgotten. The gift of a lady's ring had provided for immediate needs, and as to the rent, Mr. Frost continued:

We had come to Saturday, the last mail day of the month. On that day not a penny was received. I did not expect to receive any money on Sunday, and I got what I expected—that is, nothing. Then Monday came, when the rent was due. With the first rays of light I was up and on my knees. I had found that we had twenty dollars in hand which we could use for the rental, and hence, we needed fifteen more. For this I prayed and pled. And I soon found that someone else was up and around. For Satan seemed to stand just behind me, sneeringly saying,

"Oh, yes, you'll get your money; but not today, on the very day you need and ask for it."

What a wretch he is! He has no compassion of any kind, even when souls are in the distress of a bitter need! But there was One who did have compassion, even Jesus, and He drew near. And that One gave rest, drove away fear, and assured me that He would undertake for us. In a little, I was able to thank Him for Himself, His love and power and the answer which He would most surely give.

After breakfast we had prayers which, in my heart, was largely praise. A little later, I bade Mrs. Frost good-bye and went down the stairs on my way to the office. As I passed through the hall, the maid told me that a letter had been handed in and was lying on the piano. I turned back, got the letter, put it in my pocket, and hurried along the street office-ward. I had gone about two blocks when

I began to wonder about the letter. It was from one of our Council members who knew nothing of our financial need. After reading it, I looked at the check enclosed. This brought me to a standstill. For there was the figure *one,* of our fifteen dollars, and also the *five.* Only the Lord had added a naught to it and had made it, not fifteen dollars, but *one hundred and fifty!*

I walked fast after this, not to the office, but back to the Home. Getting into the hall, I rushed upstairs to the room where I had left Mrs. Frost. She was not feeling well, and I found her upon the sofa, reading. In a moment I was at her side, telling my wonderful story of how God had answered prayer. She smiled at me and quietly answered:

"Yes, I knew He would."

She had not been excited when we were without funds and was not now that we had them. I felt just a little crestfallen, not quite understanding the calm of a heart at rest in God.

My thought was, now, that the Lord had finished answering our prayer for the fifteen dollars, but I soon found that it was not so. When I reached the vestibule of The Christian Institute, I looked through the glass front of the letter box to see if there was any mail for the Mission. I found just one letter. It had not come through the mail, for it had no stamp on it; and it was from a stranger, for it was addressed to the "Inland China Mission." On my way upstairs I opened the envelope and immediately was brought to another standstill. Inside was a piece of white paper with no writing on it, and inside that were three, new five-dollar bills—our fifteen dollars over again!

This time I did not rush back to Mrs. Frost; she was too far away, and besides, I was half afraid that she might say again, "Yes, I knew He would." But I did hurry up to the office, where my overcharged heart found relief in praising the God of all grace. Since then, I have often thought that the gift of a hundred and fifty dollars was to show how ample the love of God is, and the gift of fifteen dollars to show the exactness of His understanding and care.

With August days came welcome evidence that God had also heard and was answering the larger prayer with which

the year had opened. For then, Mr. Taylor's helpful plans
ripened in the coming of two young couples—experienced
and devoted workers, much used of God in China—to forward as best they could the interests of the Mission in
Canada and the States.

Never was better gift given, in the form of colleagues,
than when the Rev. and Mrs. F. A. Steven joined Mr. Frost
in Toronto. Already their hearts had been drawn out in
love for the North American missionaries, of whom they
had seen a good deal in China. Mrs. Steven, before her
recent marriage, had escorted the group that had included
Susie Parker when they went from the Women's Language
School to the inland province of Kiangsi. Mr. Steven, a year
later, had introduced the men of the first American parties
to their pioneering work on the Kan River—a distant part
of the same province—and in sharing their many hardships
had learned to appreciate their endurance and devotion. His
heart burned with longing for more such men for the great
unevangelized interior of China and for the long-waiting
aboriginal tribes of the far west and the Burma border—his
familiar territory.

He was a man of far horizons (as Mr. Frost discovered), and his
prayers were addressed to the God of the Infinite. Moreover, both
he and Mrs. Steven were enthusiastic as touching the principles and
methods of the Mission. They were deeply spiritual, loving the
Lord with ardent faith and devotion, and were persuaded that God
Himself had planted the Mission in North America. Thus they
were fitted to serve its interests in every possible way.

The other friends who came to Mr. Frost's help at this
time were, as a matter of fact, on their wedding journey—
going home on furlough by way of the United States. Known

throughout a large district in North China as "Mr. Glory-face," Archibald Orr-Ewing had exercised there just as loving and fruitful a ministry as had endeared him to so many in Scotland. Though their stay in America was only for a few weeks, they visited many centers, speaking on behalf of China and quickening many hearts to larger faith in God.

Their service was so intense (Dr. Frost wrote long after) as to be remembered to this day. Their lives, continually, and in every place were "a sweet savor of Christ," and such fragrance does not pass away. If Mr. Orr-Ewing had done nothing else but look at his audience he would have blessed them, his face was so full of light. . . . And Mrs. Orr-Ewing was like him—about the only difference being that she was a gracious woman and he very much a man.

All too short was the stay of this delightful couple, but they accomplished, before leaving for England, the most helpful thing that could have taken place, just then, for the enlargement of the North American work. For they were used of God to lift Mr. Frost himself out of his engrossing life at Shuter Street and make possible, financially, his first visit to China.

Long had his heart drawn him to that great land. The sorrows as well as successes of the young workers he had been used to send out were ever with him. Several had passed through deep waters. Sickness and death had thinned their ranks. Pioneering labors in the interior necessarily made great demands upon courage and endurance. He could not but long to see them, to comfort them, to strengthen their hands in God. There had seemed no way by which he could be spared from Toronto, no light as to the question of expense. And now these mountains of difficulty were removed "and cast into the sea"! The way was open. The call was clear. But ——

It was not easy for Mrs. Frost to let him go. But hers was a devotion never daunted at the cost of obedience to what she believed to be the will of God. His guidance seemed plain. Mr. and Mrs. Steven were there to share both work and responsibility. Mr. Frost needed the closer touch with China. Their children on the field needed him. She would not hold him back.

And, while the parting was a hard one, Mr. Frost went forward with good courage. The close of their first full year in Toronto (1890) completed a wonderful record of God's faithfulness. Simply in answer to prayer, without solicitation or collections, more than sixteen thousand dollars had been contributed for the work of the Mission, most of it coming in small gifts through the mail.

When God is one's only confidant (the Secretary wrote from a full heart) such gifts are no longer small but large, their quality augmenting their quantity. And the thing that gave them quality was, first, that they had come in answer to prayer, and second, that they established the fact beyond questioning that the Lord, when a work was carried on in His Name and for His sake, was prepared to provide for it, whether it was large or small, whether made up of few persons or many.

These were great assurances for us to receive (he continued), as we went forward with outstretched-hands, in unknown-ways, making our ventures of faith with wondering and trembling hearts.

CHAPTER

XXI

MEANWHILE—IN CHINA

WHEN Mr. Frost arrived in China in February, 1891, it was to set in motion currents of joy and blessing that before long reached brave hearts in distant, lonely places. He knew something, through correspondence, of the experiences of the young workers bound to him by special ties, but could have little realization of the greatness of their tasks, their joys and sorrows, and the responsibilities that cast them as never before on God. He hoped to see them, every one, but most of those who had accompanied Mr. Hudson Taylor to China were already far away and scattered, the men especially seeming out of reach.

For the coming of that first party from North America had been providentially planned to fit in with a great need. Among the inland provinces still barely touched by pioneer evangelists was one that lay heavily on Mr. Taylor's heart. Years before, Mr. J. E. Cardwell had taken advantage of its endless waterways to visit more than a hundred towns and cities, living in a house boat, as he could get no footing anywhere ashore. He had faithfully preached the Gospel and scattered Scripture portions and tracts on many lonely, dangerous journeys. But other parts of the interior were opening up so fast that it had not been possible to continue these itinerations, and the report was sadly true, year after year:

"We have had no men to spare for the fifteen millions of Kiangsi."

But, in unexpected ways, God was working. He is ever the God of the "new thing," not limited to our poor plans and resources. He can use even "a worm" to "thresh mountains." He chooses to work through weak instrumentalities. How often we have proved this true in China! His thoughts are not our thoughts; and gradually Mr. Taylor was coming to see that, if there were no men to spare for the millions of Kiangsi, the "Lord of the harvest" might use women as pioneers—even quite young, unmarried women.

It was a tremendous innovation even to think of such a development in those days. The first women to go to the interior had all been married missionaries, or were under the protection of married couples. To trust young women alone in inland cities, far from other foreigners, would not have been considered for a moment, had not the Lord intervened. And it all came about so naturally, and in this very province.

For on the eastern border of Kiangsi a little plant had struck root which proved to be of God's own planting. A converted Buddhist leader from the neighboring province had crossed the beautiful watershed, and on the upper reaches of the Kwangsin River had gone from village to village preaching Christ. After a few weeks he returned to

Dr. Douthwaite in Chekiang, bringing with him one of his former Buddhist disciples, an old man who was simply bubbling over with joy. For more than forty years, Farmer Yü had been seeking peace of heart. So earnest was he as a vegetarian and worshiper of idols that he had become a sort of high priest in his district and had many followers. But the terrible fear of death and the future punishment of sin never left him. Do what he would, all was dark before him, until—oh, the wonder of it! From his old friend and leader he heard of a Saviour—One, Jesus—and at the foot of His Cross all the burden rolled away. Little wonder that the old farmer was happy! Words could not tell his joy and thankfulness. And he had come right away, across the mountainous borderland, to find the missionary and *be baptized*.

"But," said the doctor, kindly, "it will be better to wait a little, until you understand more fully what it means to be a Christian."

"No," urged Farmer Yü, "do not ask me to wait. I am old and may die any day! I want to confess Christ as my Saviour. Why not receive me now?"

He stayed in the city a few days, eagerly learning more of the truth, and the Kiuchau believers were so convinced of his sincerity that Dr. Douthwaite baptized him and sent him on his way rejoicing. Only a few weeks later he appeared again, happier than ever, bringing with him six others—men who had found Christ through his witness. These too were baptized, and in the old farmer's home they met together, Sunday by Sunday, to praise and worship God.

But that was not all. Through Farmer Yü and others, the Glad Tidings spread until in that Yüshan district there came to be a little church of thirty-six baptized believers. Eagerly they desired a missionary of their own, to lead them on in the things of God. But there were still "no men to spare for the fifteen millions of Kiangsi."

We are not a little concerned (wrote Dr. Douthwaite) for our converts on the border, for they are like sheep without a shepherd, and there seems no prospect of our having a suitable man to send them as a teacher. . . . Pray specially, and ask others to pray for them.

Was the Lord unmindful of this little flock and the need of perishing souls around them? Was *He* without resources for Kiangsi? At first there seemed little connection between the weariness through overwork of a young woman in Dr. Douthwaite's station and the evangelization of that waiting field. But this was the first step, when God began to answer the prayers of many in China and at home.

Agnes Gibson must have change and rest. But there was no where to send her. Health resorts and summer vacations were unknown in those days, and she was young to travel to the coast alone. But the need became urgent, and it was arranged for her to go to the outstation of Changshan, a lovely place among the hills halfway to Kiangsi. There was a little chapel there with a room above it, which she could occupy.

Now it happened that all the Christians in Changshan at that time were men. The women of their families were still ardently worshiping idols. There was no one to visit or teach them, and they would not attend the services. Indeed, they persecuted their men-folk so persistently that the latter had been driven to rent a room for themselves, where they could be quiet for prayer and Bible study.

Such was the state of things when the Scotch lassie, who looked younger than her twenty years, went to board with the evangelist and his wife. If only she could sleep for a week, she would be all right! But there was little rest for Agnes Gibson at Changshan. The Christians soon heard of her coming and carried the news home, hoping that curiosity would overcome prejudice. Result: an unceasing flow of visitors from early morning till late at night, and such opportunities for telling the Gospel that the young missionary lost her voice as well as her heart in making friends with the women and children. How they flocked around her and responded to her loving spirit! And with what wonder the men looked on, praising God for such an abundant answer to their prayers. For the women were not only interested; several were led to Christ, and joined their husbands in attending the Sunday services.

It was surely providential that, just at that juncture, Mr. Taylor himself should visit the district on his way to the Kwangsin River. Some years previously he had passed through Changshan and had met the persecuted Christians. He could not but be impressed with the change in the whole situation now, and with the earnestness of their plea for a missionary.

"If the visit of a lady teacher for a single week," they urged, "could bring about such results, what would not be accomplished if we had one with us all the time?"

The argument was a good one and was reinforced in practical fashion. For the group had put together all the money they could spare, and handed Mr. Taylor no less than ten dollars (Mexican) toward fitting up the premises more comfortably for the desired lady.

All this was strong confirmation of Mr. Taylor's growing conviction that the time had come for a new development of women's work along these very lines. He had purposely brought with him on this journey several ladies, older and younger,—including Miss M. Murray, for years the beloved head of the Women's Language School—to test the reaction to their influence of both Christians and outsiders. So he was able to encourage the rising hopes at Changshan, before passing on to the headwaters of the Kwangsin River.

From that point onward for two hundred miles the journey down the river was a revelation. The welcome they received at Yüshan, in Farmer Yü's district, was touching in its eagerness. But the thirty or more Christians were in need of shepherding, and Katie Mackintosh, one of Mr. Taylor's party, seemed as much drawn to them as they to her. They had prayed so long for a missionary, that to have one of their own, and especially one who could share their family life, seemed almost too good to be true. Two other outstations were visited—Hokow, where they found eight women ready to be baptized but waiting a suitable opportunity, and Kweiki, where they witnessed the baptism of the first and almost the only believer. Kiangsi with its vast, unmet needs lay about them. City after city was passed in which there were no witnesses for Christ. In spite of crowding and excitement, wherever the ladies were seen, women came freely to their boats and they had endless opportunities for making known the one and only Saviour.

"It would do your heart good," Mr. Taylor wrote, "to see the response of the women to our young sisters."

The leader of the Mission knew very well what could and would be said about allowing these young workers to take up such a field. But were these multitudes of accessible and on the whole friendly people to be left, still without any knowledge of the Way of Life? That was a responsibility he dared not face. Day after day, in prayer with his fellow-travelers, guidance was sought as to what the Lord would have them do. And before they reached the Poyang Lake, the decision was come to that three of the party should return at once to live and work with the Christians on the river. Another young missionary joined them at Takutang, to go across the border to Changshan, and with quiet confidence in God they set out to put to the test His "exceeding great and precious promises." How gladly would Mr. Taylor have gone with them! As it was, he could only commit them to the supervision of one of the most experienced members of the Mission, the Rev. John McCarthy, and bear them up continually before the Lord in prayer.

So that very summer (1886) a "new thing" was begun on the Kwangsin River, and a gold reef opened up, as far as the evangelization of many a waiting field in China was concerned. For the blessing of God rested in a remarkable way upon this venture of faith, making it manifest that here was an agency after His own heart—"small enough and weak enough for Him to use." The young missionaries were so consciously inadequate to the task that they had to keep very near to the One who had sent them. They were so defenseless that they had to rely, moment by moment, on His protecting care. Without wisdom or experience, they were cast upon Him in all their problems. And the work grew so rapidly that the men among the Chinese Christians had to come forward and take a leading part. All this was to the good.

"The issue of women's work has greatly delighted and somewhat astonished me," Mr. Taylor said a few years later, "and it is a question in my mind whether those provinces and cities in China which seem altogether closed to male evangelists may not prove open to our sisters."

By that time (1890) there were hundreds of Christians and inquirers on the Kwangsin River, and the pioneers would have been overwhelmed with the greatness of their opportunities, but for the coming of reinforcements, including the young workers from North America. For all the women of the party that had come to China with Mr. Hudson Taylor had been appointed to that field. They had been six months at the Language School and gave promise of being resourceful, dependable workers, and it was with joy they looked forward to working with Katie Mackintosh and Agnes Gibson—the first and almost the only missionaries on the River. Great indeed was the need of all the help they could afford!

It must have been a surprise to the seven Canadians and Americans to find that the escort who had come to Takutang to meet them was younger than most of themselves, though she had been several years in China. But Flossie Tapscott was already the missionary-in-charge of a station on the Poyang Lake, and she had with her a bright little Chinese woman, a devoted Christian, who was a host in herself.

With the help of Mr. and Mrs. J. T. Reid, the kindly couple at Takutang, they made all arrangements for the journey of several weeks on a house boat of the most primitive kind. One small cabin had to accommodate all the travelers by day and night. Food was supplied from the boatman's kitchen at the back, chiefly rice and cabbage, though eggs and chicken, pork and fish could be obtained at markets on the way, as well as fruit and a variety of vegetables. Eight rolls of bedding were used as seats and tables during the day and spread out on the floor at night, when the time came for "packing the sardines." But it was a happy party that made light of inconveniences, and enjoyed Chinese dress, eating with chopsticks, and the beauty of river and mountains flooded with spring sunshine. Passing big cities, the travelers had to keep out of sight, as there were so many of them, but in quiet places they could walk in little groups along the towpath or through fields and villages.

Everywhere their hearts were saddened by signs of idolatry—temples, wayside shrines, or haunted trees laden with votive offerings. After traveling for some days they passed the headquarters of Taoism, one of the great religions of China. There the Taoist Pope had his home, in the city of Shangtsing, some miles south of the River, and one of the young women of this party was to be the first missionary to live and preach Christ in that stronghold of demonism. For, whatever may be its philosophical teachings, Taoism means to its followers unspeakable fear of demons in this life and the next.

Moored among other junks at night, crowded together for the sake of protection from thieves, they became used to the bang of crackers and the fumes of incense with which the boat-people were driving away evil spirits or propitiating their gods. Women would come from the neighboring boats to see them and listen by the hour to Mrs. Tu's earnest preaching. And when the boat-people had "eaten rice," they gathered in the cabin and around the door for evening worship. Their thoughtful faces in the lamplight reflected the earnestness with which the Gospel message was given, and one, at any rate, of the hired men seemed truly to believe. He could not hear enough about the Lord Jesus and the Way of Salvation, and his face was lighted with joy as he said, when leaving for his village:

"I am your brother now, by the grace of God!"

All this impressed the newcomers, watching with such keen interest. So did the stories their escort told them of experiences on previous journeys. At one city she had gone ashore, when traveling with only Chinese companions. While the boat-people were laying in provisions, they hoped for some opportunity for telling the Glad Tidings.

Up a side street I found myself invited into a very large home. The courtyard was soon filled with people. Among the crowd was one woman I can never forget. As I was talking, her eyes never left my face. She was a big, tall woman of unusual strength. Strangely earnest, she drew nearer till she was right by my side.

"Did you understand?" I questioned.

"Yes, I understood, and I want to hear more. I want you to come with me."

Alone in that heathen city—for she had become separated from her companions—the young missionary hesitated a moment. Should she go with this stranger? But the woman settled the question.

Taking my hand, she drew me insistently to a side door, and down little streets and byways to a fair sort of house on a back lane. There was nobody there. She led me to the guest hall, and the look on her face was just hungry! She longed to hear more. Forgetting everything but her need, I told her again of the love of God in Christ.

Alone there, she poured out her story, a terrible story of opium and sin—other wives, no son, no peace; nothing in life, nothing beyond, and that awful dread of death! Then I knew that the Lord had taken me there just for her sake—and what a joy it was to tell of One who is a Saviour indeed!

And there are many like that—so many, still waiting for the Gospel! We have the message for them, the Word of Life to everyone who believes.

This woman grasped the thought that there is a Way, a Saviour for her people as well as for us. She had never seen a white woman before or heard the Name of Jesus. Then came a great knocking at the door. Pastor Ho and the cook were seeking me. I wrote a little prayer for her—after we had knelt and prayed together. It was hard to leave her without further help, though I could not but feel that the Lord had met her—and He would never leave her.

Halfway up the River, the first outstation was reached in the important city of Kweiki. There, three of the new workers, Susie Parker, Jeannie Munro, and Edith Lucas went ashore to join Miss Annie Say and her companion. Behind the chapel on a busy street, the little courtyard was taxed to its utmost to accommodate the new arrivals, but the welcome they received was out of all proportion to the premises. Could they have foreseen the blessing that was coming, when that one church would number over a thousand members, past and present, their joy would have been even greater. But there were dark days to go through first—and so soon! For it was only a few weeks later that the first precious life was laid down on the Kwangsin River, when Susie Parker went from that little Chinese courtyard to the very presence of the Lord she loved. There was no shadow yet, however, on the hearts of those who stayed so gladly at Kweiki or those who continued their journey.

A few days later Hokow came in sight, with the Mission House perched high above the River. Steep steps led up to a busy street and the narrow building that only allowed of a chapel below and some little rooms above. Here Agnes Gibson was living alone, with the evangelist and his wife, happy and busy in the growing work. From the boat-people on the river to the officials in the city, she had friends among all classes, and it was with thankfulness she hailed the coming of fellow-workers—Rebe McKenzie and Jessie Gardiner, who proved worthy of even her ardent spirit.

Only two young Canadians were left to go on with their escort to Yüshan. There they found Katie Mackintosh alone among the people she loved with so great a love. Little and gentle as she was, Katie was winning her way into the confidence of town and country-folk alike. She had dispelled early prejudice by the perfectly open life she lived with the Pastor and his family. Dressed like the women of the district, she went about freely, accepting the hospitality of the Christians and losing no opportunity of making known the Gospel. In the mission courtyard there were no closed doors, her rooms being just as open to visitors as those of Mrs. Chang, with whom she boarded at the cost of a dollar a month. All this was known throughout the countryside, and the women flocked to her, sure of sympathy and understanding.

To this ideal missionary, Florence Tapscott committed her remaining charges, Cassie Fitzsimmons and Hattie Turner, who were almost sorry to find that Katie had already a new outstation in a neighboring city waiting for them. In the few weeks before they moved to a bright little home of their own, they had seen enough of Katie's ways to impress them with the same stamp of loving devotion.

Those were wonderful days in Yüshan (Florence Tapscott, who had spent six months as Katie's fellow-worker, recalled). Everything was planned with a view to the people round us, rather than our own convenience, hours of meals and meetings included. Katie was not impulsive, erratic, or unwise. She never allowed liberties. But while standing aloof in her gentle way she was thoroughly one with the Chinese, and full of fun, which they greatly appreciated.

Pastor and Mrs. Chang, with whom we lived, were a great blessing to us. How we loved them and the children! She was a merry little woman, always ready to help people in trouble and to tell the Gospel. Our rooms were above theirs, but when summer came and the thermometer registered 106° by five o'clock in the morning, we simply couldn't exist up there, just under the tiles. We had to find a corner down in the family courtyard. It was only a small white-washed room, but we got so near to the women! They came in and out freely, and would often say, "Truly, this is a little heaven!"

Sunday was the great day of the week, for then the Christians gathered from near and far. Early comers might be expected any time after sunrise, and they were so pleased to find Katie always ready to meet them. Sometimes a bundle of mail arrived, but it was never opened on Sunday, even if we had been five or six weeks without letters. That day was sacred to the Lord and to the Christians. The squeak of the barrows was music to us as they came in from the country, and Katie was just like a mother welcoming home her children. She knew them all by name, and would ask after any who were absent.

There was no time for set meals on Sunday, except the lunch we all took together at noon, usually out in the courtyard. The day never seemed long enough to satisfy the Christians. It was their one opportunity for spiritual fellowship, and we made the most of it. Singing filled up all the intervals between classes and meetings, and precious times of prayer were fitted in with those who were burdened with some special need. The country Christians had to leave before the evening meeting, but they would stay as late as they could, arranging with us when and how we should come to their villages. Last farewells were said right out at the big gate, when they all went off with prayer and singing.

This was the spirit that spread all down the River, as station after station was opened, the spirit that actuated the first missionaries of the Cross, and that still makes effective the preaching of the Gospel.* Writing from Kwangfeng, the outstation mentioned above, Hattie Turner and her companion were soon able to tell of real conversions and the faithfulness of young believers under cruel persecution. And from Iyang, below Hankow, came similar tidings. Successful in obtaining a footing in this busy city, Rebe McKenzie and Jessie Gardiner found the people turbulent at first. Crowds came about them so constantly that they were thankful for an occasional day of rain that gave them a breathing spell. But they were making friends all the time and laying the foundation of a strong, self-governing church. They were growing too in faith, and winning a fellowship with Christ so precious that it far outweighed the cost.

Faith for temporal supplies was very real in the experience of all these young workers. There was constant need for prayer, not only that funds might be sent in at home, but that remittances might reach them safely, so far from the coast.

Since coming to Kwangfeng (Hattie Turner wrote) we have had many tokens of the Lord's protecting care, especially in providing for our daily needs. Four times in this city we have come to the last of our money, yet, before nightfall, fresh supplies arrived. Once, we had to live very carefully for several days on a single dollar. Our

---

* See Acts 20:18; 1 Thess. 1:5, 7-12; 1 Cor. 9: 19-23.

rice came to an end. At midday we finished our bread and the remains of a chicken. We had plenty, but not another scrap of food was left in the house.

"Did you have any supper that night?"

Yes, the Lord knew our need! Three o'clock, four o'clock, five o'clock came—and still no help. But, praise the Lord, we were not afraid. And at half-past five a messenger arrived with mail and money. . . . We have never once been in want. Hallelujah!

And as to the loneliness they often felt, that too was made a blessing, as Jessie Gardiner found one memorable evening, not far from Iyang.

I was spending a few days with our Bible-woman in her own home, hidden away among the hills. Village after village had been visited, crowds had heard the Gospel, and we were wending our way homeward at dusk when a deep feeling of loneliness came over me. I remembered how far I was, many thousands of miles away from my home and loved ones. And then the Lord just filled my soul with His peace—unspeakable peace, the gift of God's love. Though tired in body and weary in heart, I could not but praise the Lord for the blessed privilege of walking even *one* step of the long, weary way my blessed Master trod for me. I would not give that hour in China for all the years spent at home.

Words are poor to tell what such experiences mean in the enrichment of life, now, and still more hereafter.

CHAPTER

XXII

INNS AND LONELINESS ON THE KAN

SIX months after the women of the North American party had entered upon their work in Kiangsi, most of the men who had come out with Mr. Taylor were on their way to the same field. They had been longer at the Language School than usual, as there were no senior workers on the Kan River and no occupied centers to receive them. Pioneering work of the stiffest kind lay before them, and they were happy in having as their escort from Anking, Mr. F. A. Steven with his bride (née Florence Tapscott), shortly to be connected with the North American branch, as we have seen. Both were pioneers. They knew well the kind of experience that lay before their companions, and very helpful were the times of prayer and fellowship they had together.

Ten days in junks on the flooded Yangtze—a perilous journey—brought them to Takutang, beautifully situated near the northern boundary of Kiangsi. From the Mission House high on the hill, they looked out over the Poyang

Lake toward the valleys and distant highlands of the Kan
River—a territory comprising three great prefectures that
were to form their parish. Seven to eight million people
occupied that southern part of the province, enclosed by
mountain ranges on the east and west and south. Seven to
eight millions—spiritually in darkness and "the shadow of
death," a prey to sin, superstition, and endless fears, with
no witness to the saving-faith that is in Christ alone!

In face of needs so great, so overwhelming, that missionary band was indeed as nothing. Five loaves to feed five
thousand! Only a year in China, they had little of the
language and still less experience to guide them. This, in
one way, was an asset, for they did not know enough to hold
them back. Their hearts were warm with faith and love.
The Master's command was clear. They were there in
simple obedience, sure that He could not fail.

Sixty miles up the Kan River, the party divided, James
Lawson and J. S. Rough going ashore at the busy city of
Changshu, to herald the Glad Tidings throughout the prefecture of Linkiang. There Mr. Steven and the rest changed
into long, flat-bottomed boats, able to negotiate the shallows
and formidable rapids that lay ahead.

Eighty miles farther south (several days' journey), William Horne and John Meikle were left at Kian, governing
city of the important prefecture of the same name. There
the River, half a mile wide, still offered an open highway,
south, and ever southward.

For nearly a hundred and forty miles, George Duff and
Mr. Steven traveled on, preaching and leaving tracts by the
way, till they came to Kancheo, the prefecture that reaches

to the extreme south of the province. Almost two million people traded in its markets, lived in its cities, and cultivated its beautiful valleys: a strong and turbulent people they proved, but among them, from the first, were those whose hearts the Lord opened.

Happily for themselves, the young evangelists had come unannounced. No one was expecting them; so they were not troubled by official attention, and were able to carry out their plan of action unhindered. This was to travel widely, visiting as many cities and markets as possible, simply to scatter the good seed in the form of Scripture portions and tracts and make known the chief elements of the Gospel. After a couple of months of such work, they were to return to Takutang, where Mrs. Steven was waiting, for further conference and prayer and for a period of language study.

Needless to say, this program was not carried out without plenty to test courage and endurance. Far apart in their appointed fields, the young men had a great variety of experiences; but one thing they all had to meet was the intense, overpowering curiosity of the crowds that assembled wherever they were seen. In spite of Chinese dress and *queue,* they were immediately recognized as foreigners, and so far in the interior this caused no little excitement. Another experience in common was the discomfort of life in ordinary inns. Too often dark, damp, and dirty, they were always alive with small but voracious foes, and afforded little if any privacy. If a room had a door, in place of a scanty curtain, that was encouraging. If the door could be fastened, it was still more so. But even a barred door may not deter the very curious—as George Duff discovered when a man came tumbling in, through a space over the top of the door, so determined was he to see the "foreign devil." His perplexity was amusing on that occasion when, after looking under the bed and in every corner, he could not find the object of his search. In vain the missionary assured him that the room had no other occupant. That dark-eyed, dark-haired young man was too like themselves to be a real "foreign devil"! But if he was disappointed in one way, he found more than he had expected in another. For he carried away some knowledge of the Glad Tidings.

Unfortunately, as it proved, another of the young evangelists did *not* have dark hair and eyes, and his sandy type of coloring brought him much undesired attention. At one place, where he and his companion were spending Sunday, he had actually to sit outside the inn from nine in the morning till five o'clock at night, just to be stared at, listening to shouts of "Red-haired Foreign Devil" from the changing crowd, not to speak of other uncomplimentary remarks. The people were so noisy that he could not make himself heard; but they bought books freely, and he comforted himself with the thought that his fellow-worker was having a quieter time inside.

On the whole, the crowds were friendly, however, and many interesting conversations were held in the inns at night. The eagerness with which books were purchased was an encouraging feature of those first journeys, though it gave rise to some trying situations. In the busy market of Tongning, Horne and Meikle were so rushed that they had to back up against a wall to save themselves from being trampled under foot by the crowd.

We could not hand out books quickly enough to suit them (wrote the latter). And what a scene the market presented when the rush was over! One old man was in a sad plight, gathering up the rice cakes he had been boiling in oil—his stove upset and his oil scattered—while others who had been able to save their wares were spreading them out again on various stalls. Our stock of books was completely sold out.

But at the near-by city of Tongsin, a young barber was met who seemed really to accept the truth. An old man also listened with the deepest interest, and said, with tears in his eyes, "When will you, Teachers, come again to tell us more of this good Message of Salvation?"

Thankful and encouraged, though weary after six weeks and more of tramping and preaching, the young men reassembled at Takutang to compare notes and give themselves to prayer and study. Winter over, they set out in good heart to return to the south of the province, little expecting the changed conditions which awaited them. For, by that time, the authorities were alive to their movements, and had determined to hinder and thwart them in every way possible. Their passports entitled the young missionaries to travel freely, but did not provide for residence or the purchase of property. Not that they wished to settle down. Their prayer at that time was not for opened cities but for open hearts. And that prayer was graciously answered, in spite of all opposing forces.

In February we set out again for the south (wrote Mr. Rough), expecting to go ahead with our work in peace and quietness. False hopes, alas!

Lawson and I landed one evening at Changshu in a great welcome of mud and rain. With difficulty we got to the inn. Half an hour after entering its fetid atmosphere a commotion arose. A messenger had arrived with an urgent invitation for us to visit the Mandarin at once. A second hurry-up messenger soon followed. So forth we went, encouraging each other with the promise to those brought before magistrates for Christ's sake. . . .

From then on, for a long time, officials troubled us incessantly. Our passports were constantly demanded. A *Wenshu* was attached to us.* A soldier (save the mark!) accompanied us wherever we went. Innkeepers who harbored us were arrested and beaten, and every device was employed to keep us moving on.

"Riots and beatings were not unknown in those days," Lawson added, from painful experience, but it was all for the Lord's sake.

At Kanchow, on their arrival, Horne and Meikle almost despaired of finding accommodation. Every inn, it appeared, was full. The boatman who had brought them was pressing to be set free. And, after hours of searching, there seemed no place on shore that would receive them. They could only look up for help, in earnest, united prayer. And then, as night was closing in, their servant returned, saying he had found a place. It was the meanest kind of an inn, on a back street, but they were made welcome.

The innkeeper and his wife gave us their own room (Meikle wrote), the best they had, poor things! Just beside it was the hogpen, with six big, fat pigs. The noise and smell can be imagined! Still, we were thankful for shelter under the circumstances.

"When do you leave and where are you going?" was the question that met them next morning from aggressive *yamen* runners. And while they were out, preaching and book-selling, these underlings cruelly beat the landlord who had dared to shelter them, right on the public street.

---

* A *Wenshu*, or Government despatch, may prove a troublesome document, though it is nominally a request for protection, passed on from one official to another.

"Move on! Move on!" was now the urge that followed the missionaries in all three prefectures. "But this moving on," as they thankfully proved, "gave us the opportunity of witnessing in hundreds of small towns and villages, in which, otherwise, the story of Jesus and His great redeeming love might never have been heard." Hard as their life became on those long tramps and in easily excited cities, they were not without evidence of a growing interest in their message. In Kanchow, Horne and Meikle made many friends. They were even able to rent small premises to which inquirers came night after night for meetings.

This was too much for the enemy, who stirred up the *literati* against us, so that we were obliged to leave the city. Several of the inquirers escorted us to the boat with real sorrow, and supplied us with provisions. We left, commending them to God and to the Word of His grace, thankful for the testimony we had been able to bear in the city.

Three months later (Mr. Horne continued), I went back to Kanchow, putting up in an inn outside the East Gate. There the inquirers gathered round me again, bringing others with them. They themselves rented two rooms in a private house, which they pressed me to occupy. I had no sooner done so than the landlord who had sheltered me was severely beaten, and I only saved the owner of the house by offering to be beaten for her. The official, fortunately, "would not presume," and I got him to promise not to touch her after I had left.

For they had to go away—making another long itineration—but this time one of the inquirers carried on the work in a little store they had rented, doing business as a doctor or herbalist. There the Christians gathered for meetings, and a quiet witness was maintained that attracted other inquirers. Brightest of these was the incense-maker, old Mr. Tseng, who always seemed to have some new experience of the Lord's goodness. His business had brought him in a profit of two hundred dollars annually, for he was the sole maker of a spiral coil of incense much used in the city, which would keep on burning for forty-eight hours. Of his own accord, he gave it all up, when he came to know the Saviour. He would not even sell the utensils he had made, of which there were no duplicates, but smashed them up for firewood. His idolatrous books, a well-thumbed pile, he brought to the Christian drug store to be burned. His missionary friends, when they heard of it, felt some concern as to how the old man would make a living. But he was full of joy. His faith was unquestioning, and the Lord honored it. Many were the stories he had to tell of answered prayer in his new undertaking—buying and selling pigs—in which he was remarkably prospered.

Alone at Kian, for Mr. Steven had been called down to the coast, George Duff had like encouragement. He was able to stay on in the inn on the high bank of the river, and with a few simple remedies did a good deal of doctoring. This of course made friends, and gave opportunity for many a conversation on spiritual things. On several journeys, also, he found interested inquirers, before he had to leave on account of serious illness.

It was throughout the Linkiang prefecture that opposition proved most persistent. Again and again, James Lawson and his companion came back from long itinerations to find the old antagonism at Changshu, on the part of the authorities. Places they rented once or twice had to be given up, and there was nothing for it but to go on scattering the Good Seed far and wide, leaving it to the Lord to give the increase.

On one lonely journey Lawson found interested listeners at the city of Yüanchow, with its seventy-thousand inhabitants, far up a tributary river, toward Hunan. He even entered that most antiforeign of all the provinces, and found an attentive hearing in several cities, bringing back, however, scars due to severe handling, "as a memento of my visit to Hunan."

All this meant a fight against discouragement, as time went on, for it was six years before Lawson's brave and patient itinerations resulted in the establishment of settled work. Two thousand Christians in that Yüanchow district and more than twenty congregations meeting for regular worship were yet to rejoice his heart, but in those first few years there were times when he was almost giving up. Indeed, but for the dear Scottish couple at Takutang, as Mrs. Lawson tells us, the story could never have been what it is today.

Mrs. Reid's loving mother-touch did for the young men of that pioneer band what nothing else could have done, while Mr. Reid's comprehensive, staunch grasp of the Word of God made him a rock of strength to his younger brethren.

On one occasion, several years before we were married, my husband had been having repeated attacks of malarial fever, accompanied by repeated attacks of temptation. Physically down, the lonely life of wandering from inn to inn made him an easy prey to depression. He felt that his work was useless and he had better go home.

Accordingly, he left Changshu and started for the coast. But he could not go without first seeing his friends at Takutang. Arrived there, Mr. and Mrs. Reid saw the situation and tactfully met his need. Mrs. Reid "mothered" him in real Scotch fashion—mended his socks, called him by his Christian name, and treated him as a son. Mr. Reid soon took him to his study for a talk, and listened to his plans about going home, and the reasons that impelled him.

"But what does the Word say, Brother?" was, as my husband often told me, his way of meeting difficulties.

Needless to say now, a few days in that atmosphere brought the young missionary's heart and mind back to their true position; and with soul and body strengthened, he went back again to the inns and the loneliness.

Those were days when Mr. Lawson carried most of his belongings in a small bundle with him. In summer he pawned his bedding—not needed in the heat—which, wrapped in waterproof cloth or paper, was well taken care of by the pawnbroker, to be redeemed when cold weather came again.

"Back to the inns and the loneliness"—but there was One who knew just what it all meant: One who will yet say, "Ye did it *unto me*."

CHAPTER

XXIII

"WE WOULD SEE JESUS"

NEEDLESS to say, the experiences just outlined meant much to the leaders of the Mission. There was a heart in Shanghai, watching it all, and planning as well as praying for such help as could be given. So it came about that Mr. Frost had hardly time to realize that he was in China before a delightful suggestion was made to him. He could not expect to visit, in person, all his American and Canadian children, but why should not they come together at the coast to meet him? Mr. Hudson Taylor was there himself to facilitate arrangements, thankful for the occasion which offered just the rest and refreshment he knew the young workers must need. So letters went out, calling the pioneers from Kiangsi and the students from the Language Schools down to Shanghai for a week's conference in April (1891).

Mr. Frost, meanwhile, was gathering impressions that made him thankful that he had come to China.

The special discovery I made (he wrote) was of our missionaries. . . . It was a wonderful event in my life when, in 1887, I had my first contact with the Mission in London and became acquainted there with its leaders, returned missionaries, and candidates. But it was a more wonderful one when I came in contact with it in China and saw there its larger missionary personnel. China, after all, is the true home of the Mission, and I soon perceived that it was in its environment that the missionary leaders and followers found it most easy to adapt themselves to a life of separation from the world and unto God. For, somehow, as they were contributing to heathenism, heathenism was contributing to them. Heathenism either makes or breaks the foreigner; in their case it was making and not breaking them. I soon discovered, therefore, that the Mission's officials and missionaries were, spiritually speaking, a unique body of men and women. There at Shanghai were the Rev. J. Hudson Taylor, the Rev. John W. Stevenson, the Rev. W. J. Cooper, Mr. C. T. Fishe, Mr. J. F. Broumton, and Mr. J. N. Hayward—all of whom are now with the Lord. These were leaders in the work, each in his own position and sphere; and the combination produced as sanctified and able an administrative body of men as I had ever hoped to see.

It was a time of remarkable growth and development in the Mission. There was scarcely a gray head among its more than four hundred workers on the field, and young life was pouring in to the Shanghai center from new and old sources of supply. Well was it that this growth had been foreseen and providentially provided for. Only a year previously, new and adequate premises had been given in answer to prayer, without any expense to the Mission, in which the enlarging work could be cared for for a long while to come.

When our small party arrived at the Mission Home (Mr. Frost continued), we were impressed by the fact that our "poor faith Mission" had received some pretty generous treatment on the part of our Father in heaven; for first, there was an extensive compound which was beautifully bedecked with grass, palms, and flowers, and then there were large and splendidly equipped buildings reaching around three sides of the compound, one side being left open for sunlight and ventilation. The buildings had been built with money furnished by Mr. Orr-Ewing, and they had been planned on a large scale because recently united prayer had been offered for many additional missionaries and Mr. Taylor felt it wise to get ready for the influx. Mr. Taylor's faith was not altogether appreciated by some foreigners in Shanghai, for a number of these dubbed the buildings, on account of their size, "Taylor's folly"! However, we were glad just then that they were as large as they were, for parties from the home lands began to pour into Shanghai like a flood. There had preceded us a party of thirty-five Swedes from the western States; then came our party of five; there followed us three men from Australia; and finally there appeared another company of Swedes from the States, numbering fifteen. It was no longer a question as to whether the buildings were too large, but rather, as to whether they were large enough.

The much-debated question of "Church union" was quickly solved at that time and place. We gathered in the dining room, meal by meal, numbering from sixty to eighty missionaries, differing in nationality, speech, temperament, and denominational affiliation, and yet conscious of the fact that we were all one in Christ Jesus. The noon prayers were confusion so far as language is concerned, for besides the different accents of the Englishmen, Australians, and Americans, there were the Swedes, and while these began their intercessions in English they seemed possessed with the thought that the Lord did not quite understand that uncouth tongue and so broke forth into the pure and melodious speech of Scandinavia. Happily, the word "Amen" is about the same in all languages, and, whether or not we had understood the prayer, we united in saying this word of approval at the end. And as for music, the Swedish brethren and sisters, with their sonorous voices and accompanying guitars, filled at times the big dining room and at other times the bigger prayer-meeting room with such melodious praise as we had never before heard. What days they were! I learned more about Christian fellowship at that time than I had ever dreamed was possible.

And there were further surprises, in connection with Mr. Frost's own contingent from North America. For as the young workers began to arrive from their distant fields, he simply did not know them. It was not only their Chinese dress and, in the case of the men, partly shaven heads and bronzed faces that so changed them. Nor was it the Chinese manners and Celestial speech with which some of them approached him, to prolong his uncertainty. There was something more intangible by far that made them different. As he recognized them, one by one, at length, he was not only impressed with their improved appearance, "tremendously proud of them" as he put it, but he became conscious also of a change below the surface that moved his heart. For these were men and women whose willingness to suffer with and for Christ had become reality, and who knew Him —and still more longed to know Him—in a new and deeper way. *"We would see Jesus"* became the conference hymn from the very first meeting, and seemed to gain in meaning as the days of fellowship went on.

Mr. Frost was not the only speaker at the conference. Mr. Hudson Taylor and other experienced missionaries took part, and the sessions covered practical as well as directly spiritual topics. There were hours in which the young missionaries told of lessons they had learned since coming to China—revealing hours, that went far to explain both the joy and hunger of their spirits. There were times of prayer in which the Lord drew very near. And in the Bible Readings, day by day, Mr. Frost was so helped that the conference hymn had to be modified, and before the close of the week they were singing with radiant faces, "We *have* seen Jesus, and our souls are strengthened."

> "We *have* seen Jesus—the great Rock-foundation,
>   Whereon our feet *are* set with sov'reign grace;
> Not life, nor death, with all their agitation,
>   Can thence remove us, *for* we see His face."

Reality was the undertone of it all, for there were gaps already in the North American contingent that spoke loudly to those that remained. Not only was Susie Parker's place empty—Hamilton Racey, William Souter, and Robert Randall had also finished their earthly course. Four specially promising young lives, so soon cut off, amid needs so great, had a message as urgent as it was sorrow-laden and yet glorious! For, had they not been promoted to higher service? Of the thirty-one still in China, twenty-nine were at the conference, but Alexander Saunders of Toronto—the first North American worker to join the Mission—and E. M. McBrier of New York were so far away as to make the journey impracticable.* They were with the conference group in spirit, however, and their letters were effectual in calling forth prayer for the great needs around them.

The conference ended with a memorable Communion Service conducted by Mr. Taylor, and on the following day (April 22) there was a beautiful though simple wedding, when Jeannie Munro and John S. Rough, both of Kiangsi, were married in the Shanghai Cathedral. They had been engaged before coming to China and had waited the two years the Mission required of all new workers, so that their happiness was well deserved. And it was generously shared with others, as Mr. Frost discovered when he set out in their company on his first inland journey.

Of all his new experiences, this was the strangest! For it began with a barber, a shaven head, a borrowed *queue*,

---

* Mr. Saunders, who had come out from England in The Hundred (1887) was already active in evangelistic work around Taiyüen, capital of Shansi, while Mr. McBrier was learning much beside the language in his happy association with Mr. D. E. Hoste and Pastor Hsi, farther south in the same province.

and a complete set of Chinese garments, in which Mr. Frost hardly recognized himself. He had a new name too, a regular Chinese name, to which he learned in time to answer. And he was reduced to dependence on others such as he had never known, not having a word of the language. But, to make up for it all, he had a delightful interpreter and traveling companion in Mr. Stanley P. Smith, one of The Cambridge Seven, whose picture on the cover of a book picked up at Niagara-on-the-Lake had been his first introduction to the China Inland Mission. All through that spring and early summer they traveled together, ministering both to the missionaries and Chinese Christians in the stations visited.

By the time Kiangsi was reached, Mr. Frost was ready in a new way to appreciate both the work and the workers. The burden of heathenism lay heavily on his heart. So many great walled cities, towns, and busy markets; so many homes of the living and graves of the countless dead; so few who had ever heard of Him who, alone, is mighty to save—and on all hands evidences of idol-worship and demon-power! He had more understanding also of the cost of making known the Gospel, especially among the women of inland China.

Quite a party set out with him from Shanghai, destined for distant stations, including two young Canadians, Maggie and Tina Scott. With six governing cities and four hundred villages in the district to which they were returning, there were only two other missionaries (a married couple) and five professing Christians. Yes, there was no question about the need for those loving, Christlike young workers at Hweichow. But how it tested Mr. Frost's faith in God, as well as his missionary convictions, to let them leave the protection of the party at the crowded junction of two rivers to continue their journey alone!

But the sisters were not in the least perturbed. There they stood at the prow of their boat—fair-haired Maggie and dark-eyed Tina—bravely waving their hands in farewell and sending us cheering smiles across the widening water. They evidently knew the God in whom they trusted, and were persuaded that He is able to keep.

Coming a few days later to the Kwangsin River, it was no little comfort to see the outcome of just such sacrificial service. Barely five years had elapsed since the first women missionaries had gone to these undeveloped outstations, and already scores of new believers were gathered into well-established, all-alive churches, in four centers. Immediately upon entering the city of Yüshan, Mr. Frost became aware of a new element in the life around him. Passing in a sedan chair along the crowded street, he noticed several men whose faces were bright with an unusual light. They proved to be Christians, and were only a sample of the larger number met with during the ten days of his stay. And happy, tell-tale faces were not confined to the converts. Mr. Frost's impression of the "angel" of the church in that beautiful region is interesting:

It was at Yüshan I became acquainted with one of the most remarkable women it has ever been my happy lot to know. . . . I refer to Miss Katie Mackintosh, afterwards Mrs. H. N. Lachlan. In physical make-up, she was small and somewhat frail, though wiry. In disposition, she was gentle and very quiet. In character, she was as strong as a rock, and devoted to God and man. In accomplishment, she had broken down almost unbreakable walls of prejudice and opposition, and was esteemed by Chinese officials and people, followed by Christian leaders, and adored by the Christians at large. In daily influence, she held the church and its adherents in the

hollow of her hand; and the strangely beautiful thing about the
situation was that she did not realize it and her people were only half
aware of it.   As to her face, it was the face of an angel, with light
radiating from it, whether in animation or repose.   It was worth
having come to China just to see this one woman, living in the
midst of heathenism with the Christians about her—her joy and
crown.

What heathenism actually meant to those under its dark
and terrible influences, he was beginning to realize.

For this same Miss Mackintosh, in spite of her great love for the
Chinese, told me some sad facts about them.   She took me walking
into the country and pointed out, as we passed along, brick towers
some ten feet high, with a hole toward the top, where not-wanted
babies were dropped and left to die, hundreds being killed by their
parents, thus and otherwise, every month of the year.   She showed
me a foundling-home (Chinese) where undesired babies were passed
through a hole in the wall, and where those in charge fed them with
rice water till they pined away and died.   She took me to the city
temple and pointed out the city idol in its gaudy dress and scowling
face, before whom throngs of worshipers were making offerings and
mothers were teaching little children to bow and knock their fore-
heads on the ground. . . . She told me tales of woe, such as I had
never before heard, of opium-sots and suicides, of gambling fiends,
tyrannical and murderous women, and of wives and children sold
into slavery.   In short, she revealed heathenism to me till I could
stand no more, and wondered how she could live, year in and year
out, in such surroundings and be the happy, triumphant Christian
that she evidently was.

And that wonder only increased as Mr. Frost traveled
from station to station.

Wherever you chance to be (he wrote), the larger cities in China
are much the same—with walls, battlements, gates, towers, many
high temples, countless slate-roofed houses, and throngs of laboring,
bartering, yelling, and chattering people.   A modest mission home
in such surroundings does not make a striking impression, and yet,

to turn off a narrow, busy, noisy, and noisome street into an abode of quietness and love is not altogether different from what it must be to pass from earth to heaven.

This was apropos of a visit to Hokow, where Agnes Gibson's gentle but heroic spirit was telling upon the opposing forces around her:

The next morning after our arrival, I heard from my room the loud, harsh, angry voices from street and courtyard below, and felt deeply the pitable condition of those poor, loveless lives. But suddenly a child's voice sounded out, sweet and clear, singing, "Jesus loves me, this I know." I could hardly believe that the voice and song were real, so unexpected were they and so strange did they seem among the strident sounds of heathenism. Miss Gibson told us also of a rich man's son, about five-years of age, who had been at some of the children's meetings. Forbidden by his parents to come again, he would watch his opportunity and just run in to Miss Gibson from the neighboring house, and say,

"Listen, Teacher! Jesus died; Jesus rose; Jesus is coming again: is that right?"

Then he would run back to his dark, idolatrous home.

At Iyang, only opened a little more than twelve months, it was encouraging to see the progress that had been made. Several men as well as women had been led to Christ through the prayers and devoted labors of the North American sisters. Grace Irvin had joined Rebe McKenzie and Jessie Gardiner, and to Mr. Frost's surprise they were already helping quite a group of new arrivals. Five Swedish and two German visitors were with them, studying the language, and Miss McKenzie had her hands full, as the senior worker. To be entertained in their own station by young missionaries he had himself sent out was a new and joyful experience to Mr. Frost.

Fifteen of us sat down to dinner in quietness and peace (he wrote) where, only the year before, the first missionaries had realized that at any moment the house might be pulled down over their heads.

The cook at Iyang was among the converts we met. Not long after he believed, he was taken sick and was at the point of death. His relatives were preparing to give him a heathen funeral. He protested, got up and tore down the house idols, went back to his bed, and recovered! Now he is an evangelist as well as cook. The barrowman is also a convert. He is a stalwart, both in size and character, preaching wherever he goes. His face is a veritable beacon light for Christ, as he trundles his wheelbarrow along the city streets or country roads.

How thankful the missionaries must have been for such an ally in their itinerations!

June days brought hallowed memories as the travelers reached Kweiki, for it was there that, just two years previously, a beautiful young life had been laid down. "Precious in the sight of the Lord is the death of His saints," and precious it was to Mr. Frost to hear from those who had been with her of the Home-going of Susie Parker, only a few weeks after she reached Kweiki. Already, while still at the Language School, she had been the means of winning her teacher and his wife and mother to Christ.

"Jesus is now King in that home," wrote her companion, Jeannie Munro (Mrs. Rough). "Is not that worth coming to China for?"

And no sooner had they reached Kweiki than the two began to visit in the homes around them. They found the women very friendly. How could they but be?

"Susie loved them and would hold their hands while our woman (a Kweiki Christian) explained the Gospel."

The heat that summer was intense in the little rooms up under the tiles, and Susie was brought down to the guest hall when she began to suffer from that terrible fever. There the air came in more freely, through the big door that opened on the courtyard, and there the Chinese friends who loved her did all that was possible for her comfort.

A few days before she left us (Mrs. Rough continues), I said to her, "Susie, are you sorry you came to China?"

"When I think what Jesus suffered," she answered, "I praise Him that He has privileged me to suffer *with Him*."

On the evening of her death (Monday, July 8), I was alone with her for a little while.

"Sing some hymn," she whispered, "with the name of Jesus in it *often*."

"All the way long it is Jesus," was in her mind.

I quoted softly, "When thou passest through the waters, I will be with thee."

"Yes," she answered, "He is faithful that promised."

One of her favorite passages came to my mind, and I began, "Watchman, what of the night?"

"The morning cometh," she went on, "and *this* time a morning without clouds."

Then Edith Lucas came in. She had a lovely voice, and we sang together for the last time, "Jesus, Saviour, pilot me." After that, our dear one prayed—and they were the last words she said:

"Father, I am Thine. I give Thee all I've got— Nothing, nothing too precious for my Lord Jesus."

But though she could no longer speak intelligibly, she responded to the name of Jesus, and at the very end her face was lighted with a wonderful smile.

A rich harvest was to be reaped at Kweiki where this precious seed had fallen into the ground. Mr. Frost met there on this visit, the young Scotch missionary who was herself to see more than a thousand men and women baptized in that city on profession of their faith in Christ. Already Chang, the converted Buddhist priest, was pastor of the little church, and his friend Li, who had been with him in the monastery, had found Christ through his faithful witness.

Up in the hills was another Buddhist temple that had yielded two of the early converts. For more than thirty years it had been cared for by a nun who in her old age had taken a nephew to help her. He cultivated the small plot of land, and with the gifts of worshipers they made a comfortable living.

This nephew, in his visits to the city, heard of the "Jesus Hall" and the converted Buddhist preacher. There he too found the Saviour—"Jesus, our precious Friend," of whom Chang loved to tell. He carried back the Good News to the little temple. But his aunt was indignant and accused him of slighting the idols.

"Who but our gods," she said, "could have made the river and the trees? You say that the foreigners' God made heaven and earth! If they have books, bring them here to me. I will get someone to read them."

Out on the hillside the old nun listened and listened, while the Gospels were read aloud by a neighbor who knew characters. Light began to dawn, and the stern old woman felt her heart strangely moved. But she was far from satisfied. Could it be that all her service to the gods was in vain? She determined to test their power.

Picture the scene, and what her feelings must have been, when she took her long staff and went alone into the temple. Standing before her favorite idol, she said,

"For years I have set food and incense before you, and moved you from place to place. You have never helped me. Now, see if you can help yourself!"

With one blow, the idol fell in fragments at her feet.

Her heart was still sore with loneliness and disappointment when she came to Kweiki, not long after Susie Parker's death, and told all this to Jeannie Munro, sitting on a low seat in her little upstairs bedroom. Gradually she was comforted, as she learned more of the living Saviour. Again she came from her temple-home, asking to be baptized. It was explained to her that she could not be received into the church as a Christian while she still served idols.

"It is too much!" she exclaimed. "I cannot give up the temple. It is my living." And back she went to the hills.

But her heart was hungry. The Christians in the city were praying for her, knowing how dark and empty her life must be. At last she could bear it no longer. Turning her back on the old life, she sought her friends in the city.

"I have left all for Jesus," she said simply. And they knew how much it meant.

When she was baptized, Jeannie Munro took her hand as she came up out of the water. Her face was radiant.

"I heard a voice," she explained, a little later, "and it said, 'I am pleased with you!'"

At the time of Mr. Frost's visit, still dressed in her nun's garb, and with her bowl and chopsticks, this little woman was out among her relatives and friends and the many who had known her in the temple, telling of the wonderful Saviour she had found.

As they neared the great Poyang Lake, the travelers came to another district in which trophies were being won for Christ. The three young English women they found in Anjen had faced a riotous mob of hundreds when they first settled in the city. Yet, even there, a new day was dawning.

We were told while at Anjen that ten miles away there was a village of three hundred inhabitants, where all the idols had been pulled down and not a single person smoked opium; also that if you asked anybody there whether he had heard the Gospel,

"Oh, yes!" he would reply, "Old Chang has told us."

This Old Chang was a farmer who had been saved and become a preacher, and all the village had turned to Christ.

I saw this redoubtable soldier of the Lord. He hardly looked the part, for he was small of stature, homely of face, dark-skinned, and bald. His *queue* was thin and short, his legs bare, his feet shoeless, and his whole aspect that of lowly life and poverty. But he was great in the sight of the Lord; one of those whom the Spirit uses to overthrow dominions and powers.

But how few of this sort there were! The great multitude was still undelivered. After a day at Anjen, we went back to our boat as night was falling. Passing in the darkness through a narrow street, we met an elderly woman who was holding lighted incense in her outstretched hand and uttering loud cries as she walked along.

"I burn incense for merit. I burn incense for merit," she kept saying.

This was the best she knew in order to obtain her soul's salvation.

We left our moorings at four in the morning. As we floated out silently into the stream, past the long, dark wall of the city, it looked like a place of the dead. Nevertheless, stars were shining overhead, and we accepted their assurance that there is a God of light and love, even in dark China.

CHAPTER

XXIV

HOLDING THE ROPES

AN UNUSUALLY close and helpful relationship had grown up between Mr. Hudson Taylor and the young American Secretary. Wherever he went in China, Mr. Frost's ministry proved to be just what was needed for the comfort and quickening of fellow-workers. He could not only listen; he understood. People opened their hearts to him and found far more than sympathy; for, somehow, they were left aware of God—His Word, His ways, Himself, in all their situation. Greatly desiring to extend such influence, Mr. Taylor was arranging for several long journeys which would take the visitor to many of the stations of the Mission, when these plans were swept aside by letters and a cable bringing sad news from America. Mr. Frost's family was in distress. Several of his children were ill, his mother still more seriously so, and his father urged his immediate return.

Leaving China was harder than Mr. Frost could have expected, and the apprehensions of the journey were sadly realized when he learned, upon landing in Vancouver, of the death of his beloved mother. In painful suspense he traveled on, not knowing what awaited him in Toronto. Owing to a misunderstanding about the time of his arrival, there was no one at the station to meet him; and, to add to the strangeness of it all, he had to search for his family in unfamiliar surroundings. Much had taken place during his absence, and the Shuter Street home had been exchanged for premises more suited to the growing work. The new address led to a residential neighborhood, and it was with amazement he stood before the large Church Street house in its garden that now formed the headquarters of the Mission. Could this be the C. I. M.? And if it had been difficult to meet the rent at Shuter Street, what would it be here?

Strangest of all was to ring the bell and have to ask to be shown the way to Mrs. Frost's rooms. But there was no doubt about its being *home* when wife and children welcomed him! To his great comfort, a glance assured him that they were all there, though it was easy to see how serious had been their illnesses and the strain upon the brave but tired mother.

And now began a period in the work at home that reminded Mr. Frost of the early days at Shuter Street. There is a "need be" for all affliction that is allowed to come to the children of God,* and, later on, it was not difficult to see why faith had to be strengthened and spiritual life deepened by trial permitted at this time. It was still a "day of small things" in the North American work. The missionaries on the field, thirty-one in number, were well cared for

---

* 1 Peter 1:6, 7.

ABBIE ELLINWOOD FROST
This portrait of Mrs. Frost was taken after the move to Philadelphia

through the Toronto office, even when there may have been serious shortage for those holding the ropes at home. It was, perhaps, undue sensitiveness on the part of the young Secretary that led him still to keep the home and China accounts entirely separate, only using in Toronto money specially designated for their own and local expenses. Later on, experience led to a more normal arrangement, as in the old country, and meanwhile the Lord wonderfully met the needs of His trusting and sometimes much-tried children. The comfort of answers to prayer under such conditions will not be lessened for us by the fact that we too find ourselves, at times, in emergencies due to human failure or misapprehension of God's purpose. He knows the hearts of His servants and is very patient with the limitations of those who are truly seeking to do His will.

It was a July day when Mr. Frost arrived from China (1891), and writing to Mr. Taylor a few weeks later he told of some recent experiences:

Two days after my return, our funds were wholly exhausted, nothing being left but a day's supply of food. The Lord, however, did not forget us. That evening Mr. George Duff's mother came over from Hamilton and brought a gift of two hundred dollars, specifying it as for the General Fund. Once since that time we have been reduced to our last dollar, and upon that day a gift of eighty dollars was sent to us from a far-away city in Nova Scotia. This gift also was for our General Fund. At the present time our finances are again very low. But we are assured that the same loving Father who has supplied our needs hitherto will continue to care for us. Having loved His own who are in the world, He loved them unto the end.

In September, with six or eight candidates in the house, there came a day when there was not enough left for another meal. A little bread, a modicum of rice, and half a canister of tea was all that could be found when Mrs. Frost went to the kitchen to consult the maid—who was, happily, much in sympathy—and there was no money for fresh supplies. Nothing daunted, for she knew how much prayer there had been, Mrs. Frost had the table set for dinner and a kettle of water put on the stove to boil. She was sure that, in some way or other, the Lord would undertake.

Just then the doorbell rang. Gertrude answered it, and what was the thrill with which she returned a few moments later, holding five fat partridges in her outstretched hand!

"They are from Mr. Gartshore," she explained, "and he says they must be used at once, as they will spoil if kept!"

So dinner that day was quite a feast—and long to be remembered, for such experiences go deep.

It had come to be a recognized thing, even at Shuter Street, that whenever fresh candidates were received there was sure to be fresh trial as to funds, as though it were a necessary part of their training. This experience was even more marked in the new and larger Home. A number of earnest young people were under consideration for the work in China, and they had more to learn than Mr. Frost could teach them, fresh though he was from the field.

For us, as well as our candidates, those were kindergarten days (he wrote of this period) when our Father was giving His little children object-lessons of a simple and striking kind as to what life with Him really means. . . . To be forewarned is to be forearmed, and happy the man who discovers the way of the Lord and is not surprised when apparent calamities come. They are meant for good and not ill, and they will make for blessing, if only the soul will first submit and then learn.

At one period of prolonged scarcity that fall, a remarkable answer to prayer impressed these lessons.

We had come to a place of almost greater extremity than we had ever before been allowed to reach. Our money was entirely gone, and the food in the house almost so, while our family was a large and hungry one. We did not understand why our gracious Father should allow us to be so close to want . . . but we were enabled to trust and confidently rest in the perfect love that works no ill. Believing that the promises of God would be fulfilled, we made known our needs to no one outside of our Home, but individually and as a family continued to wait in prayer upon the living God.

A devoted friend of the Mission, who had given a son to China, was sitting up just then with a patient, and one night had some quiet hours for thought and prayer. It was natural that her heart should turn to China, but she was surprised to find herself wondering what she could do to help the work financially, for she was not a person of means. Then a small sum of money came to mind which she had laid aside, and the Lord seemed to say:

"Go and give the China Inland Mission ten dollars."

"But Lord, I am saving that money for a cloak," was her first response, "and I need it."

Again the impression came: "Go and give the China Inland Mission ten dollars."

Again she answered, "Lord, I need the cloak."

But still He seemed to say: "Go, give the China Inland Mission ten dollars."

Not without a struggle, the dear mother at length replied: "Yes, I will do so."

Next morning early, she hastened home for the money, and was at the Mission House soon after breakfast. Mr.

Frost was surprised to receive so early a visit, and still more so when the gift was put into his hand—for almost the last particle of food in the house had been used up. Greatly interested in her story, he asked in what way she would like the money to be used.

"It is for your home expenses," came the definite answer.

If I was surprised before, I was almost startled now. For it was plain that the Lord had indeed spoken to His servant and sent her to us in answer to our prayers. But still I hesitated. Remembering about the cloak, I had no heart to take the proffered gift. I urged our friend to reconsider the matter, reminding her that she undoubtedly needed the cloak.

"Oh, no!" she said, decidedly. "I shall have no peace until I give you the money."

I could hesitate no longer, and accepted with grateful thanks that which the Lord had so evidently sent. . . . I may add that the friend who was thus used of God to minister to us found that she obtained, through her gift, one of the largest blessings of her life.

"Living from hand to mouth," do we call it? Yes, but listen:

We found before we were through that it was not our hand but God's hand, and that is a distinction that makes all the difference—from God's hand to our mouth. We gradually gathered, therefore, that times of scarcity were intended to be new revealings of God's love and power, if only we could be attentive to the inner meaning of things and see below the surface. We thus came to a place where our chief anxiety, when some new experience of want confronted us, was not to have our physical needs supplied, but to discover the spiritual blessing hidden within the happening. And frequently it was not difficult to do this. God's purposes of grace are generally very patent, for He desires us to be blessed, and hence makes manifest the blessing.

It became delightful, in this way, to walk with Him, even in narrow places, since all we had to do was to keep our eyes open at the various turns of the way; for we always found that at such places there would suddenly arise before our wondering sight some new manifestation of infinite good. Fear, therefore, largely vanished away and joy as largely took its place. This sense of comradeship and security finds expression in Oxenham's lines:

> "Not for a single day
> Can I discern the way;
> But this I know,
> Who gives the day
> Will show the way;
> So I securely go."

Life reduced to fellowship with Christ makes the complicated very simple. We follow and He guides; we follow and He gives; we follow and He acts. In other words, we do not do anything but keep with Him, and then He does all necessary things. Who would not walk with a Master who works like this?

Not all gifts were as opportune as those recorded above; indeed, there was one at this time that had quite a humorous side, of which the kind donor knew nothing. For while funds were still exceptionally low, a letter was received containing five dollars, with the surprising request that it be used to provide ice cream for the Mission family!

It was always our rule, in accepting donations, to carry out the expressed wishes of the giver, and we kept to it in this case. So for some days we fed upon bread without butter and tea without sugar, but with elegant ice cream to finish up the repast!

To the end of the year (Mr. Frost continued), we experienced our ups and downs, financially. But, by God's overruling, a wonderful thing took place—our ups were always ups and even our downs were always ups! For every experience, whether seemingly good or bad, proved good, since all led us to God and God is always good.

Many other instances of providential care might be given, did space permit, for they kept pace with daily needs. Helpers too were provided as the work developed—notably Mr.

John McCarthy, who came from China early in 1892, and gave six years to the home department in Canada and the States. His experience as one of the early pioneers of the Mission made him invaluable, whether as deputation speaker or in connection with candidates. The following remarkable answer to prayer, recalled by his name, belongs to this period.

Coming into the Secretary's office one day, Mr. McCarthy could not but see that Mr. Frost was burdened. The reason was soon apparent for, taking up a bill that had been delivered, Mr. Frost explained that a sum of one hundred and fifty-six dollars was due for rent on the Mission House, and that he had nothing like that on hand. It was not that the matter had been neglected. All through the quarter he had tried to reserve money for the rent, according to his usual procedure, but funds had not allowed of it. And now, strange to say, the bill had come in several days before it was due. Scarcely glancing at it, Mr. Frost had laid it aside with the thought, "If the agents are thus early, God will not be behind time. In some way or other, He will provide." But prayer had seemed unavailing.

Readily Mr. McCarthy responded to the suggestion that they might, together, lay the matter before the Lord. They were about to pray when, looking again at the none-too-welcome paper, he suddenly exclaimed:

"Why, this is not a bill at all! It is a receipt!"

I could hardly believe what he said (Mr. Frost might well write), but taking the supposed bill in my hand, to look at it more closely, I saw under the amount charged to us the magic words, "Received payment in full," duly signed by the agents. Now we understood why the money had not been sent to us in answer to prayer. God had otherwise provided, and it was He, not the agents, who had been ahead of time! We never learned who paid the bill; it remains a mystery to this day. Happily, God had His eye upon the saint, whoever he was, and has abundantly rewarded, according to His promise.

Another way in which prayer was being answered was in the maintenance of unity and harmony throughout the work. And this was the more remarkable as not a few different denominations and even nationalities were represented in the Council and membership of the Mission. So true was the oneness of heart between the workers on the field and the staff in Toronto that the North American missionaries, hearing of financial trial at home, made up a gift of over fifteen hundred dollars, out of their personal remittances, and sent it to Mr. Frost as an expression of loving sympathy. And as to the Council, it was with thankfulness he was able to write of those early years:

We learned, as we had never imagined that we should learn, what is the spiritual unity of the body of Christ, and what are its implications. This unity had been manifest from the first in the persons whom the Spirit had joined together. Mr. Taylor, I believe, was a Baptist; Mr. Sandham was, I know not what; I was a Presbyterian; the members of the Council were connected with Anglican, Presbyterian, Congregational, Baptist, and Methodist churches, and with the Society of Friends. The missionaries who had gone to the field were as varied in their denominational views as were the Council members, and the candidates offering to us were connected with all the leading evangelical churches. We were thus a somewhat mixed multitude, and from a natural standpoint there was reason to suppose that we should become dismembered and fall apart. But nothing of the sort took place, nor was there any apprehension of its happening. There were divergent convictions among us. But also, there was the Holy Spirit in our midst, and He was our love and peace. The outcome was that we were all drawn close and ever closer together, and I can truly say that there was never a jar nor mar in our fellowship. . . .

When the China Inland Mission, in the year 1888, became international, a friend remarked to Mr. Taylor:

"The project is impossible. You don't expect that Americans will work happily with Englishmen, Scotchmen, and Irishmen, do you?"

And Mr. Taylor replied in his gentle, uanswerable way:

"Well, I don't know; but it seems to me that the Holy Spirit is equal even to that!"

And this He was proving to be, interdenominationally and internationally. How wonderful the Holy Ghost is, and how wonderfully He works!

But it was only as the control of the Spirit was real and unhindered that such unity could be maintained. Far away from Toronto, a crisis had arisen that threatened this vital fellowship among leaders of the Mission; and, remarkably enough, it was the young Secretary and two members of the North American Council whom the Lord used to harmonize differences of a serious nature in London. But first He had to prepare them for this important service. Knowing nothing of the situation, Mr. Frost was increasingly pressed in spirit to go to London to see Mr. Hudson Taylor. There were matters about which he needed to consult him, and the guidance seemed confirmed when, at their own expense, two members of the Toronto Council offered to accompany him. Together they set out just after Christmas (1892), glad rather than otherwise of a slow steamer that took ten days for the crossing. They wanted time for quiet thought and prayer for, as Mr. Frost recorded, they were strangely heart-hungry.

The divine Spirit had been dealing with each of us for a good while past, searching our hearts and giving us vehement desires for Himself, and thus for higher and more ample spiritual experiences. We did not know of one another's state of mind until we came together for prayer in my cabin. But once on our knees, we found that this hungering after righteousness was common to us all.

Mr. Frost's companions then asked him to take the lead in daily Bible study, and the theme chosen was "The Filling of the Holy Spirit." Deep and reverent were the conclusions to which they were led, which Mr. Frost summarized as follows:

That the Holy Spirit is a Person;

That He abidingly indwells the believer;

That He is the source of holy living and fruitful service;

That there was one initial "baptism" of the Spirit, at Pentecost,* but that there may be many fillings;

That a filling is to be sought for and obtained, according to the need of life and service;

That a filling is not necessarily dramatic or emotional, but often silent and without sensation;

That a filling is to be secured by a simple act of faith, as based on the Word of God;

That the result of a filling is not that we should have more of God but that He should have more of us;

That the process of such filling is a fourfold one: to acknowledge; to ask; to accept; to act.

"Act as if I were, and you shall find that I am."

When we had been brought thus far (Mr. Frost continued), the question remained whether or not we were prepared to accept the Holy Spirit as the absolute Lord of our lives and thus put ourselves at His disposal for anything and everything. I confess that there was with us all something of a struggle just here. But the day before we reached Liverpool we abandoned ourselves entirely to God the Holy Ghost, leaving results with Him.

This experience is dwelt upon because, just at this time, the Lord was dealing with many others in the Mission in

---

* Repeated in the case of the first Gentile believers. Cp. Acts 1:5 and 2:1-4 with ch. 11:15,16.

the same way. Known to Himself only, a baptism of sorrow and suffering awaited those engaged in the work, both at home and in China. Fruitfulness lay beyond the cross and grave—such fruitfulness as the Mission had never known before. And it was on these quiet, unemotional, Scriptural lines that members of the Mission, as well as leaders at home, were being prepared. For spiritual life must be deepened at home as well as on the field, if advance is to be sustained and adequate.

All unconscious of the near or more distant emergencies, Mr. J. D. Nasmith and Mr. J. S. Helmer traveled on with Mr. Frost to London. They only knew that their lives were under the control of the Holy Spirit as never before. It was not all at once they discovered the situation which the London Council was facing. The penetrating cold of the English winter was their first consciousness, though the warmth of their welcome at the Mission headquarters more than made up for unheated houses. It was some satisfaction to Mr. Frost to discover that one chamber he occupied had not seen a fire for over a hundred years—"which I knew to be a fact, for the building was that age and there was no fireplace in my room." And it was January weather!

Perpetual shivering, however, gave place to genial warmth in Mr. Taylor's study, for having been in America he had special fires made up for his guests. He moved them into warmer bedrooms too, when he found how they were suffering, and had abundance of coal provided for their use. The difficulties in the Council at the time did not hinder his giving ample attention to the questions Mr. Frost brought before him. These were talked and prayed over until conclusions were reached which the developments of after years clearly proved to have been God-given.

Meanwhile, Mr. Helmer and Mr. Nasmith had been introduced to the London Council and had shared Mr. Frost's unmistakable welcome. The new element thus introduced, somehow lessened the tension and broadened the outlook upon matters of serious moment in which their judgment was asked. At first the points of view with regard to necessary organization in the growing work seemed irreconcilable, and the only resort was prayer—more prayer, much prayer. Then there came a spirit of yieldingness on both sides. Suggestions were made with which all could agree. A workable plan was arrived at and, better still, full harmony was restored through a deepening of spiritual blessing. Mr. Frost was requested to draft a statement expressing his views upon the questions under consideration, which was unanimously accepted as a working basis for the future.

In addition to this (he wrote with thankfulness), we had all learned the valuable lesson that there is always a way out of difficulty, however great it may be, if men will face their differences in the love and patience of Christ and the humility and meekness of the Holy Spirit. As a proof of this, I may add that from that day to this (some forty years later) the principles then adopted have prevailed, with habitual concord following. It is true that difficulties have since arisen, but they have not been those that were at that time considered and settled. As a result of all that we had passed through, I got new light upon the filling of the Holy Spirit. It was this. Evidently, a filling did not mean that difficulties would not arise, but rather that when they *did* arise there would be deliverance, to the glory of God. . . .

Thus our gatherings were brought to a close with thanksgiving and praise. . . . I was specially grateful to God for the blessing which Mr. Helmer and Mr. Nasmith had been, from first to last, to all concerned. Mr. Benjamin Broomhall made the remark that if all the members of the Toronto Council were like these two, he should never have any fear concerning the future of the work in North America: a statement which greatly pleased me, for I knew they were.

All this opened the way for advance, in view of new opportunities for evangelization that were cheering many a pioneer in inland China. The prayers of long, lonely years were being answered, and soon Mr. Taylor was leading a Forward Movement to carry the glorious message of salvation throughout that wide field. Mr. Frost had by this time been appointed Director in North America, with Mr. F. A. Steven as Secretary-Treasurer. Whole-heartedly they threw themselves into the advance movement, greatly helped by a visit from Mr. Hudson Taylor in 1894, when he came to speak at the Student Volunteer Convention held in Detroit. Streams of blessing were started at that time, through a marked outpouring of the Spirit of God, which have been flowing ever since in many parts of the world. Thirty new missionaries went to China in the following year from the Toronto center, and wonderful answers to prayer continued to cheer the Council and home workers.

But in the midst of all this, Mr. Frost was carried beyond his strength. A long absence from his office became necessary, and at the same time a devoted friend in Montreal offered to meet all the expense of a visit to China. For the second time Mrs. Frost was willing to spare him, and Mr. Steven undertook to fill his place as far as possible. A year and a half were to elapse, little as they realized it, before the beloved traveler's return; for on the way, and in China, his life was once and again almost despaired of, and it was only after long convalescence that he was able for some interesting journeys with Mr. Taylor.

The voyage home, via Suez, helped to restore his health, and it was with joy he noted the substantial progress made during his absence. The prayer circles started by Mr. John McCarthy were growing in number, enlisting praying friends in little groups in many parts of the country.*

Nothing gave Mr. Frost more encouragement than this, unless it was the prayer spirit in the Toronto Home itself.

When I got in touch with Mission affairs, I found that the income of the Mission had considerably increased. This was encouraging. But times of testing had not ceased, and I would express the hope that they never will. For if life were all made up of receiving, where would the occasion be for believing? It is when good gifts are withheld that faith rises up and lays hold upon the good Giver. We rejoiced, I need not say, in the increase of supplies, in view of our increasing needs. Also, we rejoiced in the trial of our faith, deeming it more precious than the gold that perishes.

One of the most uplifting experiences I have ever had, and I have had many, has been to kneel in the living room of that Toronto Home with certain harassed saints, gathered for prayer when funds were entirely exhausted, who did not know where the next meal was coming from, and to discover that they were more filled with praise than care. Such an experience is a conquest of faith, only to be obtained in face of great conflict. This was the state of things I found when I was once more in contact with Mission affairs; and at the same time applications for service in China steadily continued.

---

* The China Inland Mission Prayer Union, organized by Mr. Frost a few months later, was an outcome of this work. It took immediately, and by the summer of 1894 numbered over 600 members. So marked was the blessing resulting from it that a similar Union was started in England, by the express wish of Mr. Hudson Taylor (1898). Later on, Australia and New Zealand added the Prayer Union to their organizations. Mr. Frost's original thought has thus in large measure been realized: "I felt that if we could obtain enlarged and united prayer, we should secure enlarged and united blessing."

One morning at family worship, they were praying in that living room for a fresh supply of coal. It was wintry weather, and one who knew that both range and furnace bins were empty repeated the request, asking definitely for two tons, one of each kind. At that moment, Mr. Elias Rogers, a leading coal merchant in the city, was driving down town to business. Impelled, he knew not why, to call at Church Street to inquire for the Mission family (he was a member of the Council), he resisted the impression and drove rapidly onwards. But the constraint was not to be set aside and, anxious though he was to reach his office, he turned back, drove several blocks out of his way, and stopped at the Mission House. The family had just risen from their knees and were coming into the hall as he entered. After a brief but pleasant visit he was about to leave, when he suddenly stopped and said:

"By the way, there will be two tons of coal for you at my office, whenever you wish to order it."

Wondering at the surprised and happy smiles this occasioned, Mr. Rogers inquired the reason, and Mr. Steven could not but tell him of those empty bins and the prayer of a few moments before. The coal merchant strode to the near-by telephone, called up his agents, and told them to hurry two tons of coal to the Mission House, for range and furnace. When he left, it was under a deep sense of the nearness of Him whom we are privileged to call our heavenly Father. This was the first of many consignments of coal from the same generous friend, who seemed to find his gifts to the Mission a good investment.

At another time, a little old lady in a near-by city was the messenger when help was urgently required. A remittance to China was almost due, and the money in hand was two hundred dollars short of the normal sum. Needless to say, much prayer was made about it at the Mission House, considering the need of fellow-workers far away. Just then there came from Scotland a legacy that made this dear old lady feel quite rich. Moved by an earnest desire to help forward the work of God in China, she promptly set out for Toronto, taking with her a roll of bills to put into the hand of Mr. Steven. And when he came to count them, to make out the necessary receipt, he found that they amounted to just two hundred dollars.

We could never tell (Mr. Frost commented upon these experiences) where the answer to our prayers would come from—whether from the north, south, east, or west. The result was that we learned to look, not around, but up.

But the praying that most of all impressed him at this time was on another line. It was the outpouring of a heart burdened with a great need and, being "effectual, fervent prayer," in the name of the Lord Jesus, it accomplished much for His glory in China. Mr. Frost goes on to tell how, through Mr. F. A. Steven, the needs of the aboriginal tribes, numbering millions of warm-hearted mountaineers, inhabiting chiefly the regions bordering on Burma and Tibet, were kept before the Mission circle in Toronto.

Mr. Steven had seen the pitiable condition of these interesting and promising people, and the divine Spirit had put into his heart a great compassion for them. When he came to Toronto and associated himself with us, he was possessed of a strong desire to see something practical done for them. From thenceforth we heard of the tribes on almost every occasion. If with most of mankind all roads led to Rome, with Mr. Steven they led to the aboriginal tribes. This was particularly true at the time of prayer, for wherever our friend started he was sure to end up in the hills of West China. Wednesday, in our cycle of prayer, was the day appointed for intercession in behalf of the aborigines; but to Mr. Steven every day was Wednesday, for he prayed for them all the week through. I have to confess that the rest of us became weary at times, with the oft-repeated names of the Miao, Lolo, Lisu, and others. But to judge by the result, God never became weary. For as Mr. Steven prayed, He listened and worked. . . .

It must not be inferred that Mr. Steven originated the great work among the tribes of western China, for that honor belongs to others. But he undoubtedly had much to do, through his compassion and unwearied prayers, with the developments that took place. Thus our living room in Toronto had become a temple of the most high God, and our brother a chosen priest of the Almighty.

It is interesting to note, in connection with the marvelous awakening among the tribes which has since brought thousands into the Kingdom of God, that the very first missionaries to give themselves to this work and to make their home among tribal people were Mr. and Mrs. F. B. Webb, who in 1896 went to live in a Black Miao Village in Kweichow. And the link with North America was a close one, for Mrs. Webb (as Miss Van Lear) was from the southern States, and had been accepted and sent out by the Toronto Council.

And so, passing reluctantly over much of interest, we come to the close of the first decade of the Mission's history in North America. It was wonderful to look back on the eventful years and see the hand of God in it all. No fewer than a hundred and twenty-three young men and women had been added to the ranks of the Mission in China. Funds to send them out and sustain them had been adequately supplied, and the home work carried on without debt or deficit. While the income had varied with the years, a total of over two hundred and fourteen thousand dollars had been received, to the amazement of the leaders who had begun with nothing but the two hundred and fifty Mr. Taylor had been able to leave with them in Attica. That it had come from the Lord Himself and told of His presence with them there could be no doubt, for as Mr. Frost wrote:

No collections had been taken in any meetings held, no appeals made either by voice or pen or by authorized agents of the Mission, and no special needs made known in public or private. In other words—prayer, and prayer only, had been our method of access to God and our means of obtaining supplies.

We proceeded on the assumption that God was our Father, that Christ was the "Lord of the harvest," and that the Holy Spirit would move upon the hearts of those who were His stewards, whether rich or poor. And judged by the record given, our assumption was happily and blessedly true. We had had our testings. Also we had received full and rich supplies. In these circumstances we were encouraged to hold to the financial principles adopted and to continue in the life of prayer and faith to which we had been led.

CHAPTER

XXV

THE FORWARD MOVEMENT

THE Forward Movement—how it was needed! Access had been gained to the far inland provinces. The long closed door was opening. Here and there, in hitherto Christless regions, little groups of believers had been gathered, and multitudes were accessible as never before to the tidings of Redeeming Love. But how great the work that remained to be done! With its representatives already scattered in nine provinces, the North American section of the Mission was well to the fore among the pioneers. Already, toward the close of its first decade, tidings were coming to Toronto that called forth prayer not only for Kiangsi with its far-reaching river systems, but for the crowded plains of northern China, the turbulent cities of Hunan, and the waiting millions of the West.

Seven walled cities and no fewer than four thousand market towns and villages formed the district, for example, in which Mr. and Mrs. Alexander Saunders were the only missionaries (1894). Mr. E. M. McBrier, also from North

America, had preceded them in the same field, the Pingyao plain of central Shansi, and when they took it over there were some scores of Christians to shepherd, as well as the great multitude for whose souls no man cared.* When Mr. Saunders was out in the district—a hundred and twenty miles across, with its teeming population—Mrs. Saunders was alone in the central station. The only white woman in that large city, she was busy and happy with the friendly visitors attracted by the little foreign baby, and had no small share in building up the work which, until then, had been one-sided. Soon there were women in the church as well as men, and the missionaries longed for fellow-laborers.

There is a field here for several men (Mr. Saunders wrote, eager to give Bible teaching to the Christians and their children). Pray not only that we may be much used in proclaiming the Truth throughout this immense district, but that coworkers may be raised up, both foreign and Chinese.

Even larger and more populous was the plain in the adjacent province to the west (Shensi) which claimed another North American worker. Lagerquist, Marshall, and Thor had been the very first foreign missionaries to go out from the Moody Church in Chicago and from the Moody Bible Institute, first of many hundreds. When the time came for their designations in China, Mr. Hudson Taylor appointed the two latter to the Kan River district, in Kiangsi, and Lagerquist to the Sian plain, on which there was as yet no settled station. Millions thronged its cities and rich farming country, but the spiritual harvest to be reaped was still

---

* Though Mr. E. M. McBrier of Lockport, New York, was not able to remain long in China, through pressure of home claims, his interest in the work continues to this day—as the fine buildings of the Christian High School at Hungtung, his gift to his first station, and the provision made for Bible School equipment, there and elsewhere, abundantly attest.

a matter of faith. As an instance of the quiet, steady seed-sowing that was going on there and in many other parts of inland China, apt to be overlooked in the ingatherings of today, the experiences of the group Lagerquist had the privilege of joining in 1891 may be touched upon.

Six weeks by boat and riding over mountainous country brought the young American to the city of Fengsiang, toward the west end of the plain, where he found his senior missionaries. An inn of the poorer sort was their only home, and they were living under conditions that in these days seem almost incredible, save to those who still carry the torch far afield into the darkness.

They had a preaching place at the front of the inn, which opened on a busy street. At night the Bothams slept there on the *k'ang* (brick bed). When the front of movable doors was taken down, we always had a crowd to hear the Gospel.

Back of this hall, or shop, was the living room, measuring some eight feet by ten. Here the rest of us slept when not out itinerating. Bland had the table against the wall, being the shortest. Lagerquist slept under the table, and Redfern on a bamboo couch at one side. Mrs. Botham had to live in that little place most of the day. The way she managed to make home out of it all was simply marvelous. And she was always so brave and bright! A hole of a kitchen opened out of the inner room, and the charcoal fumes were none too pleasant.

We had a cook, a kettle, and a saucepan. Mrs. Botham had also a tin of milk, kept in case of sickness. When someone did get ill and the tin was opened, it was bad! We could not get stores from the coast in those days, and there were none to be had locally. Mail reached us only once in three or four months, and we never knew when to expect it. For butter we had sheep's tail, melted down, and our Chinese food was of the simplest. But we were all young and well and felt it only a privilege to be there for Christ's sake. Mr. and Mrs. Botham were people of prayer. They were sure that there would be great results on the Sian plain.

And so there were; though for years, both before and after Lagerquist joined them, they had to move from city to city, never permitted to stay long in one place. They literally carried out the Lord's injunction, "When they persecute you in one city, flee ye to another," being careful, however, to flee in a circle, so that they kept coming back again and again to the same places. In this way, the cities and many of the towns and villages became more or less familiar with the Good Tidings. Ten thousand baptized believers in the province today, connected with the China Inland Mission alone, are cheering evidence of the blessing of God, both then and in later years.

Even in Fengsiang, in those early years, the missionaries could not stay too long at a time. Experience had taught them when it would be wise to leave for another itineration. Traveling with one or another of the party, the young American soon came to know many of the cities on the plain, to one of which he was specially drawn, the city of Chowchih, in which he was to see many souls won for Christ. Sometimes they would meet the rest by appointment, in a quiet country place where they could have united prayer—precious hours of soul-strengthening. Eagerly they would compare notes as to any signs of interest in their message. Sometimes there were none, but even then, faith triumphed.

"What were you able to do in that last city?" Botham questioned on one occasion.

And how he appreciated the brave answer: "I was able to praise God!"

Strong and resourceful, Lagerquist became a valued addition to the pioneer party. At one time their domicile in the

Fengsiang inn was threatened by the persistent annoyance of beggars, hired to make trouble. A couple of these poor creatures camped on the busy street, under the eaves of the preaching hall, and kept up a continuous howling for money, which Botham dared not give them, as to do so would only have attracted others. Lagerquist, coming "home" just at that time, considered the situation; and when night fell and the beggars were lying up against the wooden partition, smoking opium, he quietly took the field. With a large medical syringe well filled with water, he came behind them, and through a hole in the woodwork put the instrument well out, so that no water should be seen on the door. Presently there was a shout, as a chilly stream poured down the neck of one of the slumbering intruders.

"Raining, raining! Just see how wet I am!"

But there was no sign of rain. After much strong language, they settled down again, until the same thing happened to the other. More excitement! More outcry!

"Truly, there must be demons here!"

Thoroughly alarmed, the beggars cleared off, and the trouble was over.

When the first house was actually rented on the plain, the problem was how to keep it. It was tenanted by people who did not wish to move, and they kept the entrance so carefully closed that there was no chance of getting in at all. The purchase money had been paid over and the missionaries held the deeds, but all they could do, since they wished to maintain friendly relations, was to pray about it. And prayer was not in vain.

"Quick! Quick!" called the cook, running into the inn one evening, "the door is open!"

Catching up a couple of folding chairs, Botham hastened to the spot. Mrs. Botham followed with a teapot and a stool. Lagerquist took some bedding.

"Oh, do not come in, in all this filth!" protested the surprised occupants. "We will clean up and invite you tomorrow."

But the Bothams were too wise to leave, and though trouble ensued that almost threatened a riot, prayer and patience won the day. That house near the West Gate of Fengsiang—the first settled station on the plain—was to become the birthplace of many souls and is still the center of a growing work.

When Lagerquist opened a station of his own, in Chowchih (1893), like difficulties were encountered. Indeed, it seemed as if the house he had been able to rent would be pulled down over his head. Darkness brought some relief, but the rabble went away vowing to come next morning and burn the place to the ground. About midnight there was such a thundering at the door that Lagerquist thought they must have returned. Peering out anxiously, what was his surprise to see that the impatient group consisted of *yamen* runners with lanterns, from the chief official of the city.

"Come at once, Foreign Doctor," they called; "the Mandarin's lady is dying!"

Wonderingly, he opened the big door and was hurried to the *yamen*. In vain he explained that he had no medicines and was not a physician.

"Her Ladyship has taken mercury," the great man said. "Save her life! I will give you anything you require."

The young wife, little over twenty years of age, was manifestly dying.

She was already blue in color, and her teeth were so loose that I could have taken them out with my fingers. Crying to God in my heart, suddenly a thought came—

"Bring me eggs, not a few!"

They came by basketfulls. At first the patient would not touch them. I had to open her mouth and make her swallow the whites of what I hoped would prove a sufficient number. To my immense relief, she took a turn for the better. I left at daylight, as she continued to improve, the official escorting me to the door and sending me home with all courtesy, in a sedan chair.

But the riot was not over. A noisy crowd gathered that morning, according to arrangement, and were about to break in the door, when events took an unexpected turn. To everyone's surprise, the chief Mandarin appeared, riding a big black mule. This animal had been trained to kick violently, whenever his rider gave a certain tug on the reins. Round and round the mule went, in front of the door, kicking in all directions.

"What's the matter?" cried the official, as the crowd began to scatter. "What is all the row about?"

Explanations were hurriedly given. The Foreign Devils took out people's eyes to make medicine, and so on.

Then the great man harangued the crowd, telling them what had happened in his own household a few hours previously.

"I called all the doctors in the city. This foreigner alone was able to help. I am very fond of my wife. She is a fine woman. And look at the money I have saved! To replace her would have cost two thousand *taels.*"

That touched the spot!

"Yes," said an old man in the crowd. "My daughter-in-law killed herself a short time ago, and my son's present wife cost us two hundred ounces of silver, besides a feast and many presents."

Another spoke up: "My daughter-in-law also committed suicide. I had to pay out a hundred *taels* for my son's new wife. If the foreigner had been at hand, it would have saved all that!"

"Well, there you are!" the Mandarin said impressively. "If you leave the foreigners in peace they will be able to do good deeds, and think of the money you will save in domestic troubles!"

"Yes, yes. Quite true!"

The people began to scatter and Lagerquist remained in possession.

That official was a very good friend to us (he continued). He sent me a lot of presents. We gave him a New Testament and tracts. He must have read them, for he came to know a great deal about the Gospel. The lady fully recovered.

By that time reinforcements had come to the plain, in the bright, courageous workers of the Scandinavian Alliance Mission. The echo of their favorite song long lingered in the Shanghai compound, where Mr. Frost had loved to hear it:

"It's best to go singing, singing all the way."

Faith and prayer and music, but above all the love of Christ won their way, as these new colleagues entered into the labors of those who had sown precious seed all over the plain and watered it with their tears. As many as four settled stations were opened in 1893, and when the pioneers married, including Lagerquist, and missionary ladies came to these cities, many a despairing life was transformed by the touch of Christ, and "domestic problems" began to find their real solution.

Oh, the anguished heart of heathendom without Christ! That glimpse into the homes of Chowchih is enough to show the cruel suffering that sin brings, especially into the lives of women. And the searching question still remains:

"If thou forbear to deliver them that are drawn unto death, and those that are ready to be slain; if thou sayest, Behold, we knew it not; doth not he that pondereth the heart consider it? and he that keepeth thy soul, doth he not know it? and shall not he render to every man according to his works?"

This was the burden on Hudson Taylor's heart as he prayed over and planned the Forward Movement, and on the hearts of all his fellow-workers, many of whom he was able to see and to encourage on his visit to China in 1894. He had come via North America, as he always did when possible, and had been impressed afresh with the resources of the Church, both in men and means, for the supreme task of world-evangelization. Facing the great audience in the Student Volunteer Convention at Detroit, one of the other speakers had whispered to Mr. Taylor on the platform, "This is the epiphany of youth!" And the power of the Holy Spirit in that great gathering was enough to prove how easily He could equip and provide for those whose lives were handed over unreservedly to Him. Mr. Taylor's addresses there and in the Annual Meetings of the Mission did much to call forth prayer for China and for the Forward Movement, in which Mr. Frost and the Toronto Council were taking so earnest a part.

Only a few weeks later, Mr. Taylor himself undertook a difficult journey through the heart of China to strengthen and advise several groups of Forward Movement workers in the northern provinces. Though it meant traveling through the heat of summer by wheelbarrow, cart, and mule litter, and all the discomforts of inns specially infested at that season by insect-plagues and fever-breeding smells, he did not hesitate to embrace the opportunity for giving needed help. From May to September he traveled on—for there were no railways or airplanes then to annihilate distance—and though the heat in the loess gullies of south Shansi nearly cost his life, he was richly rewarded by the gratitude of those he was able to help and by the joy of seeing for himself the new thing that God was bringing to pass. For the same developments met him everywhere—open doors that before had been barred; signs of the passing of age-long prejudice; a new willingness to give heed to the claims of Christ as Lord and Saviour; and the urgent need for more laborers to "buy up the opportunity." Yes, the Forward Movement was not only called for: it was begun. God was indeed doing "a new thing" in China. There was "a sound of going in the tops of the mulberry trees." And, surely, it meant as long ago, "thou shalt bestir thyself, for the Lord is gone out before thee."

Mr. Taylor was specially thankful to be able to reach Sian on this journey—the great city, once capital of China—and there to meet young men from the five centers already occupied on the plain. Lagerquist came up from Chowchih with tidings of the beloved leaders detained at Fengsiang by serious illness. For Mrs. Botham was lying at the point of death from typhoid fever. As soon as the news was received, Mr. Taylor and those with him at Sian gave themselves to prayer for the life that could so ill be spared, while the doctor son, Howard, who was of the party, set out to travel by forced stages to Fengsiang. The five-days' journey was done in three, and when he reached his destination it was to find that prayer had been answered in a wonderful way. For the patient was up and able to welcome him! At the very hour of that united calling upon God in Sian, the fever had abated. Long-continued delirium had given place to natural, refreshing sleep, from which she had awakened, as she declared, "almost well." To the doctor's thankfulness, the healing was complete, and he was able to rejoin the party of which his bride was one, as they entered Shansi.

There Mr. Taylor's impressions were further deepened by conference with Pastor Hsi (founder and leader of the Opium Refuge work), Mr. D. E. Hoste, and other missionaries who came together to meet him. Personal talks with Mr. and Mrs. Saunders, from Pingyao, emphasized the evident need for reinforcements, and especially for Bible teaching to equip the Chinese Christians for more effective evangelization. The great opportunity for winning women and children, through newly established missionary homes in many districts, and the appalling need for medical help in the almost total absence of qualified doctors in Shansi, were everywhere apparent; and the leader of the Mission returned to Shanghai only to find the same story repeated in letters from many other parts of the interior.

"God always blesses us when we undertake Forward Movements" had been the experience of the Mission from the beginning, and was the conviction with which Mr. Taylor faced the sacrifices and problems that such obedience must involve. His heart had been specially gladdened by the advance of women's work in the far west, in which several young missionaries from Toronto were being used of God. Miss M. Bee, as Mrs. Ben. Ririe, was strengthening the hands of her husband at Kiating, an important city in which little had been done among the women; while Florence Haynes and Annie Hastings, after two years of work in the capital of Kweichow, had gone to the help of pioneers in their own province. Mr. Thomas Windsor, shortly before his marriage to Miss Hastings, had in answer to much prayer obtained a footing in the busy city of Tuhshan, near the Kwangsi border, and Mr. James Adam had taken his bride to Anshun, where wonderful opportunities were opening up around him. For the movement among the Miao, rightly called "God's great prairie fire," owed its origin to his devoted labors at this time.

And now, within ten months of their marriage, came the heavy tidings that the young wife whose presence seemed so needed at Anshun had been called to higher service. How Mr. Taylor's heart went out to the lonely mourner who, from the grave where he had laid their little one beside the mother, set out again for the mountains she had loved to visit with him, staying with the Miao people in their simple homes. From the Tating district, in which he was to have the joy of seeing hundreds turn to Christ, Mr. Adam wrote that September*: "The country and markets are all open and the people friendly," and after returning to Anshun he was cheered by the coming of a clan of heathen Miao to ask him to pray for rain.

Drought had been long continued, and word had reached their remote valley of a God who loves people, even the Miao. So they took counsel together and the whole village came—men, women, and children—all the way to the city, sleeping on the mountainsides at night and living on the parched grain they carried in little bundles, mixed with cold water from the streams. It was a precious opportunity, and after teaching them more of the truth, James Adam joined them in earnest prayer for rain. After that it must have been with difficulty that they got home again, for "a great rain came pouring down that night and continued for several days."

With much to encourage in these and other ways, there were also serious developments of an opposite nature at this time. The troubled reign of the young Emperor, Kwang Hsu, was rapidly running its course. Reforms he was seeking to make were broken in upon by the disastrous war with Japan, which commenced while Mr. Taylor was still on that northern journey. Before Christmas the issue was virtually settled, though the treaty of Shimonoseki was not signed until April of the following year (1895), which gave the Island Power her first foothold in China. Rudely shaken from the exclusive policy of ages, that great Empire was faced with a situation with which its rulers were ill-fitted to cope. The reform

---

* Mrs. Adam (née Florence Haynes) had passed away only one month previously, on the 17th of August, 1894.

movement gained a new impetus from China's humiliation. The need for modern equipment and education stood out with startling clearness. Edict after edict, put forth by the Emperor, sought to sweep away the old order and bring in the new. But there was strong opposition in Government circles as well as among the conservative *literati*, who saw their age-long privileges threatened. At the same time, Japan's hold upon China unfortunately aroused the cupidity of European powers, and a period of unwarrantable aggression began which threatened nothing less than the partition of the Middle Kingdom. All this started strong opposing currents. On the one hand there was growing resentment throughout China against the attitude of foreigners, and on the other an eagerness for knowledge that opened wide the door for whatever help they could give. To the missionary, it was the opportunity for which he had long waited. While there was a resentful spirit abroad that led to rioting and even loss of life in some places, there was also a willingness to hear and a response to the Christian message such as had never been known before. It was the hour for advance in the most important of all ways, and missionary evangelists as well as teachers responded to it gladly.

On the Kan River, the changed attitude of the people at large came as an answer to many prayers. It was there that the Mission planned a special development of the Forward Movement, with the object of bringing the Gospel not only to every city, town, and village, but to every home. Nothing could be clearer than Mr. Taylor's conviction that this was the Master's will and our duty. In a series of articles entitled *To Every Creature*, he pointed out that simple obedience was not impossible, and showed how the task, great as it was in China, might be accomplished within a very few years.

Let us just obey and cease to reason (he pleaded). . . . If as an act of obedience we were to determine that every district, every town, every hamlet in this land should hear the Gospel and that speedily, and were to set about doing it, I believe that the Holy Spirit would come down in such power that we should find supplies springing up, we know not how. We should find the fire spreading from missionary to flock, and our Chinese fellow-workers and the whole Church would be blessed. God gives His Holy Spirit to them that obey Him. Let us see to it that we really apprehend what His command to us is, now in this day of our opportunity, this day of the remarkable openness of the country. . . . This work will not be done without crucifixion, without consecration that is prepared *at any cost* to carry out the Master's command. But, given that, I believe in my inmost soul that it will be done.

Lawson, Horne, and others who had laid broad foundations through the steadfast endurance of those early years on the Kan, were fitted now to lead the new effort, and to them the men of the Forward Movement were sent for preparatory training. And the field was ready for the advance they planned. Fifty governing cities in Kiangsi alone, capitals of counties, were still without witnesses for Christ; and on a test journey in 1898, Horne found much to encourage.

We visited thirty-eight large villages and five walled cities (he wrote), preaching many times every day, distributing Christian literature, and claiming every foot in the Name of the Lord as we passed along. The people received us kindly everywhere—such a change from the time when Meikle and I first itinerated in this district, ten years ago!

On the second day we stopped to take breakfast at a wayside inn, where we found unexpected encouragement. For the old proprietor, almost eighty years of age, proved to be a firm believer in the Lord Jesus. He had given up his idols upon hearing the Truth from us years ago. His daily "grace" before and after meals and his continual prayer has been: "Lord Jesus, I thank Thee for Thy great grace; forgive my sins and save my soul—Amen." . . .

The first Sunday a literary graduate listened to the Gospel all day long, reading our books when we were not preaching. . . . In one of the cities our innkeeper became much interested. We left the Word of Life in his hands. . . . In another city a Taoist priest and also a barber came regularly to the evening meetings, and on Sunday to the services. Pray for them. They will help each other.

We found an open space in another place, one Sunday, and soon had a large crowd. I had not been speaking long when an old man edged up in front of me, listening attentively. He soon began to ask intelligent questions. Inviting him to our inn, we learned that he belonged to a strange sect that denied the real existence of things, much as so-called Christian Scientists do. But he found no comfort in it. It was a joy to preach to him Jesus and see him drink in the truth. His son-in-law also seemed to be an earnest seeker. They bought Scriptures and tracts, and urged me to come again soon. We commended them to the Lord and to the Word of His grace, believing that He would perfect their salvation.

Kanchow city itself was also opening, the place in which it had been impossible, hitherto, to obtain a settlement. The only home the missionaries had was in a town some fifteen miles away, but on returning from this journey they made another effort.

Plenty of middlemen came forward and proffered their assistance . . . and no one seemed to thwart us in the least.

A large and very suitable property was found in an elevated part of the city.

When the negotiations were complete, the official stamped the deed without any questioning . . . and the neighbors came to a feast and congratulated us. We could not but contrast all this with our former experiences, when we were chased from inn to inn in this same city and never allowed to stay long in one place. Any attempt to get a home was nipped in the bud by the gentry. The owner of one place we did succeed in mortgaging was thrown into prison; his relatives fled the city; some of the middlemen took refuge with us; our teacher, who had made out the deed, was put in jail and his home pillaged; and we had to give up the house to save his literary degree. Now, all is peace, and the gentry come to make calls! You will praise the Lord with us for this great change. . . . Please pray that the new home may be the birthplace of many souls.

All this was typical of the change that was coming in many parts of the interior. Hunan itself, the last province in China to tolerate the advent of foreigners, was opening its gates to messengers of the Gospel. A permanent station had been opened at Changteh, in the north, by British representatives of the Mission, and near the Kiangsi border, Dr. Frank A. Keller from the United States was in the midst of happy and fruitful work at Chaling.*

Meanwhile, strange to say, there had been a check upon the coming out of reinforcements for the Forward Movement by unusual shortness of funds at home. All through 1897 the income of the Mission had fallen off in England, so that by September a decrease of no less than ten thousand pounds, as compared with the previous year, was giving cause for concern. A remarkable answer to prayer turned this crisis into a glorious victory for faith. We are indebted to a Chicago editor for the details, as Mr. Taylor himself gave them a few weeks later, when again in America on his way to China.

---

* A riot stirred up by the students, some months later, was quickly settled, and the gentry themselves found a house which was much better than the former premises had been, and from which Dr. Keller wrote in November, 1899, "The people on the streets are most cordial; everyone seems happy. They congratulate us on having a house and treat us better than ever in the past."

"Have you experienced definite and striking answers to prayer in the course of your career?" questioned the interviewer.

"Many of them," was the reply; and among other instances, Mr. Taylor went on to tell the facts in which he was specially rejoicing.

"Last August and September, I was sick in Switzerland. This has been our 'Jubilee Year' in England, and some societies that make no solicitation for funds have suffered in consequence.* The lessening in contributions to our own Mission amounted to no less than ten thousand pounds, as compared with the previous year. And we had at the same time over fifty new workers, accepted and ready to go out to China, which called for a large additional sum for passages and outfits. This looked very much like a crisis, and it was one. But God was equal to the emergency. We made no appeal to any man and, as you know, we never go into debt. We just kept the whole matter before God in believing prayer. And then, before the month closed, we received from a comparatively new friend in London a donation of no less than ten thousand pounds. It was the largest single gift since the commencement of the work. Ah, yes! 'This God is our God for ever and ever: He will be our guide even unto death.'"

And there was more, that did not come out in this interview. For a wonderful thing had happened that filled Mr. Taylor's soul with a new deep sense of responsibility. Within a few weeks of that gift of fifty thousand dollars, the gener-

* Sixty years from the accession of Queen Victoria (1837). "Jubilee funds" were the order of the day, and appeals were being made on all hands for beneficent purposes.

ous donor had passed to be with the Lord, and when his
will was made public it was found that he had left a fourth
part of his residuary estate to the China Inland Mission,
amounting to more than ten times his previous gift. This
large sum was to be used in China, in annual installments
covering ten years, and mainly for evangelistic purposes.
Could there be any doubt but that God was behind the Forward Movement and had a purpose in it all?

Not fifty, but seventy new missionaries went out that year,
soon to be absorbed in the growing work. And, best of all,
Chinese fellow-laborers were being raised up, men of true
missionary spirit. Such were the Kan River converts who
accompanied Dr. Keller into Hunan, one of whom became
his life-long colleague; and such was the evangelist in the
northern part of the province, himself Hunanese, of whom
the Rev. George Hunter said at this time:

What a joy it has been to work with him and to see his faith and
love and zeal! That man keeps praying every day that the Lord
will open up Hunan. He can hardly ask a blessing at meals without
bringing in Hunan. I have heard him say, as we sat down at the
table:
"God bless this food and nourish our bodies with it, and open up
Hunan, and deliver its people from the snares of Satan."
I wanted him to go with me the first time I was planning a
journey into the province. He said, "I will think about it." Next day
he handed me a little document, the essence of which was as
follows:
"If you are just going down to Hunan to look round and come
back again, I had rather be excused. But if you mean business, if
you are going to preach there and are ready to endure hardness, I
will go with you. It is the very thing I desire."
He told me also that if I did not go, he had a plan of his own.
He was looking and praying for some whole-hearted man to whom
he might say: "If you come with me to Hunan, the people will

curse you and very likely beat you, and perhaps kill you.   But shall we not go and trust the Lord, so as to make known His glorious Gospel?" He was planning a Forward Movement on his own account.

"We will go to a village," he continued, "and stay three days to let everybody hear the Glad Tidings.   If they want to hear more, we will remain a day or two longer; if not, we will go on to the next place."

Happily, he and I were able to pull together.   He is there now carrying on the work, and when I had to leave for furlough, his parting words were:

"Do get the folks at home to send out more missionaries and to pray more earnestly for Hunan."

CHAPTER

XXVI

A GOD OF DELIVERANCES

THE century closed stormily in China. The reform movement had been "strangled at birth" by the *coup d'état*
of the Empress Dowager (1898) and by her fierce suppres-
sion not only of the reformers, many of whom she sum-
marily beheaded, but of the young Emperor himself. Forced
into seclusion, he was practically a prisoner for the next ten
years, while Tze Hsi resumed the reins of Government. Her
antiforeign attitude and encouragement of the rising "Boxer"
element were rapidly leading to the devastating crisis of
1900. Yet the early months of the year were encouraging
to all forms of Christian effort. Signs of promise, as we
have seen, were bright on the spiritual horizon, although the
ship of state was heading for tempestuous seas.

Meanwhile, in quietly effective ways, the home base of
the Mission in North America was being strengthened. The
loss of Mr. and Mrs. F. A. Steven had been seriously felt
when, after six years of devoted service in Toronto, family
circumstances called them to England. Happily Mr. John

McCarthy was at hand to care for *China's Millions*, which under Mr. Steven's editorship had grown into a magazine full of interest and spiritual uplift. As Treasurer, he was succeeded by one of the charter members of the Council, Mr. J. S. Helmer, who, though living at a distance, gave much time to the Toronto office. But the Missionary Home and most of the Secretary's work had still to be provided for.

Gladly would Mr. and Mrs. Frost themselves have resumed a service for which they were so well fitted; but his serious illness in China and slow convalescence compelled them to live apart from the many claims at headquarters. And where could foster parents be found to assume such responsibilities?

It has been my experience (Mr. Frost wrote in this connection) that it is comparatively easy to find those who can serve acceptably in such matters as the care of home and office—bookkeeping, correspondence, and the like—but decidedly difficult to secure those who, while doing these things, can maintain a life of praise and prayer, come to decisions under the guidance of the Holy Spirit, and convey blessing in all contacts, whether with high or low.

Such a man was Mr. Helmer, and it had long been Mr. Frost's hope and prayer that the Lord would bring him and his equally devoted wife into full-time service in the Mission. The desire had seemed impossible of realization, for the Helmers had no small sphere of usefulness in their beautiful home at Lockport. But prayer changes things—though, like buried seed, it may be long in coming to fruition.

Nothing could have been more unexpected than the series of events which stirred up the nest of these beloved friends and set them free to accept Mr. Frost's repeated invitations. Nine months after the Stevens had left, Mr. and Mrs.

Helmer took charge in Toronto to the blessing of all concerned. To the last moment of her life, sixteen years later, this gracious lady mothered the family at Church Street as if it had been her own, while of her husband's co-operation Mr. Frost could write:

For twenty-seven years Mr. Helmer and I were associated in the official work of the Mission. In all that time, though our united service was often exacting as well as full of perplexity, not a shade of misunderstanding ever crossed our fellowship. In and through all, he was to me a true and tried friend . . . a pillar of strength.

Another valuable addition to the staff at this time was the young stenographer and bookkeeper who began work under Mr. Helmer in 1899. Who could have thought that the candidate from Colorado who failed to pass the medical test, and was declined as not strong enough for China, would through the blessing of God prove a stand-by to the work at home in almost every department, for more than thirty years? Yet such was the gift given to the Mission when Mary E. Brayton joined the staff in Toronto. And it all grew out of a seemingly trivial happening. Miss Brayton had never even heard of the China Inland Mission until one gusty day, in Pueblo, when the wind blew to her feet a torn copy of a magazine which proved to be *China's Millions*. This made the contact. Correspondence with Mr. Helmer followed, and led to a full course at the Moody Bible Institute, so that—in addition to college and business training—Miss Brayton brought to her service in the Mission a well-established faith. Does anything happen by chance in the life of a child of God?

One more gracious answer to prayer must be noted as the summer of 1899 drew on. The Church Street house had long been too small for the growing work, and the landlord, while refusing to make needed repairs, insisted on raising the rent to an unreasonable sum. It became necessary to move the Mission headquarters and Mr. Frost greatly desired to purchase rather than rent, with a view to lessening expense and avoiding such difficulties for the future. But no suitable place was to be found at a price the Mission could consider; and, moreover, there were no funds in hand for such a purpose. So the situation was a trying one, and prayer was the only resource.

It did not make it any easier that every time Mr. Frost went down town he had to pass a residence on the opposite side of Church Street that seemed to be in every way what the Mission needed. It was a large, plain, well-built house, standing on a corner lot which secured air and sunshine. That the owner had no intention of moving was evident, for he was adding a billiard room on the ground floor, reaching out into the garden. As this building went up, Mr. Frost's hopes faded, if he had had any in that direction. In another direction, however, they were brightening, for he was in receipt of a most surprising letter.

One of Mr. Hudson Taylor's oldest friends, it appeared, had passed away, leaving him a legacy of a thousand pounds. This was for himself, personally, but the money came to hand just as he was praying for funds for the needed Home in Toronto. With his accustomed attitude that all he had was at the disposal of the work, Mr. Taylor could not but see God's purpose in this coincidence, and it was a joy to send the whole amount—almost five thousand dollars—to Mr. Frost without delay. The draft came to hand on the 23rd of July, Mr. Frost being specially touched to receive from Mr. Taylor in this way the largest single sum so far contributed to the North American branch of the Mission.

Where to look for premises was now the question—and, strange to say, Mr. Frost and Mr. Helmer had not far to seek. The very next morning, the former had occasion to go to town, and passed again the corner house which had seemed so desirable.

I turned to give it, as it were, a last look—and what was my surprise to see in front of the parlor windows a huge sign advertising the property as for sale! I hastened home to Mr. Helmer, but before I could tell him my good news he asked if I had seen that Number 507 was for sale. We prayed together then that the place might come into our possession, unlikely as it seemed.

The next step was to call on the owner, who proved to be pleasant and interested. As he showed them all over the house and connecting stables, both visitors almost felt as if it had been planned for the purposes of the Mission.

The living room I dubbed "Solomon's Temple" (wrote Mr. Frost), for it was finished on the walls and ceiling in gold. The large dining room would make a fine gathering place for our staff, missionaries, and candidates. The new room opening out of it would be ideal for prayer meetings, and the stables at the rear could easily be fashioned into offices. By the time we had finished our inspection we were ready to buy, provided Mr. Somerville would sell at any figure within our reach.

Out in the garden the matter was talked over, and Mr. Somerville heard for the first time of the China Inland Mission. Though so near a neighbor, he had known nothing of its existence, and the facts he learned must have impressed him favorably, for he forthwith made a reduction of two thousand dollars on the price he was asking for the property.

This was encouraging, but even so we lacked eight thousand of the required sum.   Mr. Somerville then inquired as to how much we could pay down, and remarked, when I said five thousand dollars, that he supposed we would secure the balance by a mortgage. Our friend seemed much surprised when I told him that we could not put our signatures to a mortgage, as the Mission never obligated itself beyond the cash in hand.   He confessed, at this, that he did not see how we could proceed.   We did not see either, until suddenly it came into my mind to propose that several of our well-known Council members should act as trustees for the property, receive and pass on to the owner such payments as we were able to make, and arrange to have the house and grounds deeded to us when the purchase was completed.   Mr. Somerville smiled at this and said it certainly was a unique proposition.   He consented to it, however, and told us to have our lawyer draw up a contract along the lines suggested.

And the sequel?   Mr. Sampson, the lawyer, objected, saying that no such agreement had ever been heard of in Toronto.   But he drew it up, and to his surprise Mr. Somerville signed it.   Four of the Council members, Messrs. Rogers, Nasmith, Kilgour, and Gartshore, put their names to it, and the property was at the disposal of the Mission.   More than this, within ten days of obtaining possession, Mr. Frost was able to make a further payment of two thousand dollars, besides meeting all the expenses of moving and necessary adaptations.   And within twelve months the final payment was made, with much thanksgiving to God.   Great indeed is His faithfulness!

In thankful acknowledgment of the Lord's goodness, a motto text was hung in the front hall of the new Home as the year was closing, bearing the words: "This is the law of the house . . . the whole limit thereof round about shall be most holy.   Behold, this is the law of the house."

We fervently desire (wrote Mr. Frost) that our whole equipment, and we ourselves, may be only and ever for the glory of
God.

Shortly after this Mr. Hudson Taylor came again to
America—one of the invited speakers at the Ecumenical Mis-
sionary Conference. This great gathering, held in New
York in the early spring of 1900, impressed many besides
Mr. Frost as "one of the major events in the history of the
Christian Church."

It sprang out of the consciousness of a great need (he wrote); it
was convened by spiritually minded men; it was addressed by
speakers whom the Lord had signally used; and its influence was
profound and far-reaching.

A special interest attaches to Mr. Taylor's share in these
gatherings, as it was the last of the long series of conferences
to which he richly contributed over a period of five and thirty
years.* It is tempting to linger, with Mr. Frost, over these
impressive scenes, but one must suffice:

The test of influence is the good it brings to pass and its quality
of continuance; and according to this standard, the impressions produced by Mr. Taylor were nothing less than phenomenal. I can see
him now—there in Carnegie Hall—as he comes forward to speak.
Dr. Judson Smith of Boston is in the chair; Dr. A. H. Strong of
Rochester has just given a masterly address upon *The Authority and
Purpose of Foreign Missions*. Presently Mr. Robert E. Speer of
New York and Dr. William Ashmore of China are to follow. The
platform is filled with the most learned, eloquent, and distinguished
men in the missionary world. The great auditorium, with its two
tiers of boxes and its three encircling galleries, is packed with a
mass of humanity whose interest is intense. And there, at the front
of the platform, Mr. Taylor stands a moment in silent prayer. As

---

* From the Perth Conference of 1865, in which God so wonderfully used
the young and unknown speaker, Hudson Taylor, that it led to the birth of
the China Inland Mission.

he raises his head, a bright smile overruns his face, and as he begins
to speak, his voice takes on a kindly, companionate quality. A hush
which can be felt falls on the vast audience. Old and experienced
leaders in missionary service, seated on the platform, lean forward
to catch the quiet words. The people in the body of the house are
deeply moved. And all through the audience, hearts are opened to
the Lord, spirits become eager to be and to do what God desires,
and resolutions are formed to give and go.

When Mr. Taylor finished, there was almost an audible sigh of
spiritual relief, so many of his hearers realizing that they understood as never before the will and way of God. His topic was *The
Source of Power,* and not a few who listened felt that the speaker
was himself a demonstration of the truths of which he spoke. Thirty-
two years have passed since then, and I am still meeting men and
women who declare that Hudson Taylor's address that morning
radically changed their lives.

And it was almost the last address Mr. Taylor ever gave.
The voice that so long had pleaded the cause of Christless
millions, the cause of Christ Himself, faltered a few days
later in a meeting in Boston—and was silent. Recovering
from the threatened stroke, Mr. Taylor continued his journey
to England, but it was evident that he must be sheltered from
the heart-breaking tidings coming by frequent cables from
China. For the storm of Boxer madness was sweeping over
many stations, and precious lives were falling before it. In
a remote valley in Switzerland, news only reached him gradually; but even so, the heart that so long had cherished these
beloved fellow-workers, as a father does his children, almost
ceased to beat.

"I cannot read," he said when things were at their worst,
"I cannot think, I cannot even pray; but I can *trust*."

Of the martyrs of that summer—fifty-eight of whom were
members of the China Inland Mission—seven were from

North America.   Two of these fell in the massacres in
Shansi, two succumbed on the long journey to the coast, and
three were put to death in an uprising in Chekiang.   And
there were others who lived through indescribable sufferings.
Of these, Mr. and Mrs. F. C. H. Dreyer were from Allentown,
Pennsylvania, while Mr. Alex. Saunders and Mrs. John Falls
(then Miss M. Watson) were Canadian.*   Not only were
they preserved by marvelous deliverances, they were spared
to lives of exceptional and prolonged usefulness.   Mr.
Saunders died in harness only a few years ago (1934), and
the rest are still engaged in literary and evangelistic work in
China.*   Was it the dying daily of that terrible time that,
by the blessing of God, made these and other spared lives so
fruitful?

A stormy sea of danger lay before Mr. and Mrs. Dreyer
when, with a party of British fellow-workers, they set out
from Shansi for the only accessible treaty port (Hankow)
seven hundred miles away.   They knew that, already, scores
of missionaries had perished in their much-loved province,
and that the only hope of life lay in flight.   The only official
protection they could obtain was a document to pass them
on as prisoners, common criminals, from city to city.   This
secured them an escort, though the soldiers too often proved
rough and cruel, and more friendly with the Boxers than
with their charges.

Mr. and Mrs. Saunders, in a city four-days' journey away,
had not been able to obtain even such a poor pretense of
protection.   The blackest of all the edicts put out by the

---

* Mrs. Alex. Saunders was from England.

* Since the above was written, Mrs. Saunders has had to retire from
Yangchow on account of the Japanese invasion.

Empress Dowager had come, saying, *"Iang-ren pih shah; iang-ren t'ui-huei ki shah"*—"Foreigners must be killed; even if they retire, foreigners are to be killed." With their four children and six fellow-missionaries, they left Lucheng with very little hope of reaching the coast. Attacked, robbed, destitute, they struggled on, mostly barefooted, and with no protection from the blinding heat of August. Food and even water were refused them, day after day, and night brought little respite—for, wounded and weary as they were, they often had no shelter from the stones of villagers or the annoyance of dogs.

Yet there were daily deliverances. Death was turned aside again and again. Strength was given to endure and comfort to sustain. Food was provided when they were half-starved, and clothing, such as it was, when their own had nearly all been taken. Friends appeared among cruel foes, and a way of escape was made in desperate situations, though for some it was escape into the very arms of Jesus.

Little seven-year-old Jessie Saunders was one of these. How her simple faith had cheered her suffering fellow-travelers! She was so sure that Jesus was with them, and so quick to see His loving care.

"Mother, pray again," she pleaded, when a crowd of Boxers cruelly attacked them in an inn. After that prayer, their tormentors suddenly went off with one accord; and how the dear child's eyes glistened as she said, "Jesus sent them away!"

Many times she reminded us that Jesus too was hungry and had no place to lay His head. One day, lodged in a sort of stable, we put the children in a stone trough where animals were fed. It was the cleanest place. I was fanning little Jessie, who was at that time very weak, when she looked up and said so sweetly:

"Jesus was born in a place like this."

And the thought was full of comfort.

After we had been a month on the journey, our sweet baby, Isabel, was taken by the Good Shepherd. . . . A week later, Jessie joined her little sister. She was tired and worn out, and the last few days said more than once,

"Mother, I do want a comfortable place."

Jesus heard her cry and took her to the place He had prepared. What a change from our distressful surroundings to His own home and presence!

The other party, traveling much the same road, was spared some of these experiences, though their first escort proved to be in league with the Boxers. Attacked and robbed, with swords brandished over their heads, they fully expected to be killed. But even in that extremity the Lord delivered them, and sent a friend in the darkness of the night to supply money for the further journey.*

Crowded into heavy, springless carts, they were often twelve to sixteen hours without being able to move. Large carts were exchanged for small ones, as they went on, and these again for farm carts drawn by oxen, and even for wheelbarrows that left them exposed to the turbulence of excited mobs. Through all this, Mr. Albert Lutley, an English member of the party, was very ill, often delirious with fever. Mrs. Lutley was far from well, and in Honan they

---

* Of this brave man, Mr. Marshall Broomhall wrote at the time:

"During the reign of terror in Shansi, no one has done more devoted service than Elder Chang Chih-heng. . . . At the risk of his own life, he has labored to assist those who were in distress, both Chinese and foreigners. . . . When the Swedish missionaries were obliged to evacuate, they left in his care a considerable sum of money to succor any who might be in need. With this he was able to organize a secret service and give help to not a few." In doing so, he faced, himself, every kind of danger.

were bereaved of both their children. At Chengchow, little Jessie died, crying for the drink of water they could not give, and farther on the baby breathed her last on one of the jolting wheelbarrows. The grief of leaving them both in nameless graves by the roadside cannot be told.

Soldiers were passing through the province, and to hide us from them we were kept in prison for five days. The mud floor of the room into which we were all crowded was lower than the ground outside. Water oozed in from the filthy courtyard and the stench was awful as we lay there, right on the ground. For forty-five days, in the worst heat of summer, we had no change of clothing, and what we suffered from mosquitoes and loathsome insects may be imagined.

Four Shansi Christians who would not leave them were an unspeakable comfort, and after getting well into Honan their sufferings were mitigated by the humanity of high officials who, disregarding instructions from Peking, supplied them with food and medicine, as well as better escorts and conveyances. But before Hankow could be reached, three of the ladies had fallen by the way, as well as the four precious children.

Written in blood, the records of that summer cannot be read without anguish of heart; yet victory is the note that rises above all, by the power and grace of God.

The sufferings are almost forgotten (said one who reached a place of safety, but whose life was even then ebbing away). All is deep praise to God for the experience has been so blessed—the experience of His power to cover and keep in perfect peace, only seeing glory when face to face with death; the experience of His tender care and enabling love. . . . *All* has been a blessed experience of Him.*

---

* Mrs. A. E. Glover, the story of whose journey to the coast, with her husband and children, is told in that memorable book, *A Thousand Miles of Miracle in China.*

"Precious in the sight of the Lord is the death of His saints"—precious too the lives brought through the furnace seven times heated. Among these was the group of Honan missionaries with whom Miss Watson was working. Unable to escape before the riot came, they were hidden by Chinese friends for thirteen long, anxious days, before they could even attempt the journey to the coast. Again and again they were almost discovered, and had the baby (Nora Conway) made any sound, all would have been over. It was a daily miracle that an infant of a month old was kept so well and happy—in spite of noises, excessive heat, and lack of everything a baby needs except her mother—that she actually did not cry in all those days of suspense and danger. She began to once, when they had hurriedly to climb a wall behind which they were crouching in the blazing sun, but even then she was soon quieted. The wonderful story of their long series of deliverances is told in the biography of one of the party, Dr. Whitfield Guinness, who lived to devote thirty years to medical work in Honan.† Nora Conway returned as a member of the Mission, with nurse's training, to the city of her birth. Her parents had the joy of reaping a rich harvest in the district which had been the scene of their prolonged sufferings. And Miss Watson (Mrs. John Falls) has long been with her husband a spiritual power among the churches of Shansi. To this little group alone has been given the privilege of more than a hundred years of active service in and for China since that terrible summer of 1900.

---

† *Guinness of Honan,* by his sister, Mrs. Howard Taylor.

With seven hundred members of the Mission scattered in fifteen provinces, the only wonder was that the losses were not greater, when the ruling power was bent on the extermination of all foreigners. But for the heroism of the Southern Viceroys who dared to disregard certain mandates from Peking, the tragedy of Shansi would have been repeated in many other parts of China. The relief of the Legations in Peking by the international forces changed the situation, shortly before the Dreyers and their party reached Hankow. The Court had fled, the Empress Dowager was in hiding, and the worst was over, but it was long before tranquility was restored.

The seven beloved workers from North America had by this time sealed their testimony with their blood. Two were of Mr. Saunders' party—Miss Hattie Rice and Miss M. E. Huston, who had proved singularly devoted in their work among the villages around Luan. Unavoidably separated from the others, Miss Rice had received injuries from which she died early on that fateful journey, and though Miss Huston was enabled to rejoin the rest of the party, her sufferings too were ended before they could reach the coast.

Far north in Shansi, Mrs. John Young (with her husband) and Miss M. E. Smith fell in the cruel massacre at Tatung; and three other workers, Miss Josephine Desmond, Miss Etta Manchester, and Mrs. George F. Ward (with Mr. Ward) were killed in a local uprising in the province of Chekiang. All these young missionaries had won the love and esteem of their fellow-workers. A future of much usefulness seemed opening before them, but it was to be where His servants serve Him seeing His face.*

Meanwhile, the leadership of the Mission had been invested in Mr. D. E. Hoste, whom Mr. Taylor had long recognized as raised up of God to be his successor. At headquarters in Shanghai, Mr. Hoste was in close touch with party after party, as they arrived from the interior. It might be some time before they could return to their stations, and the problem of resuming work in the stricken areas was not more pressing than that of restoring the stricken workers. It was comparatively easy to provide relief for worn-out bodies, but more than this was needed. The shock had been great in the spiritual realm as well. Faith needed reassurance and hope quickening.

One of Mr. Hoste's first measures was directed to this end. The earliest refugees had hardly reached Shanghai before he was in communication with Mr. Frost in America and Mr. W. B. Sloan, the Secretary in London, asking them to come to China for special meetings of a devotional character. Both responded favorably, and both were well-fitted to meet the situation. They found broken hearts in need of healing, much-tried faith in need of reassurance, and a situation among the Chinese Christians as well, that only the Word of God could touch.

It was a sacred privilege to go from center to center where members of the Mission were gathered, to learn of their

---

* The Chekiang martyrs numbered eight in all, including five British workers, and were the only missionaries whose lives were sacrificed outside Shansi and the adjacent province of Hopeh, or on the journey to the coast. Too much honor can hardly be paid to Chang Chih-tung and like-minded Viceroys whose strong, far-sighted measures limited the trouble. Even so, a hundred and thirty-five missionaries, of all societies, lost their lives that summer, of whom fifty-eight were members of the China Inland Mission.

experiences, and to seek to strengthen their hands in God. After memorable meetings in Shanghai and Chefoo, Mr. Sloan went on to Peking and Mr. Frost returned to the Yangtze Valley. He was much impressed with the wisdom and prayerfulness of the Acting General Director of the Mission and with the steadfast spirit of the China Council, gathered for its quarterly meeting in Shanghai.

Searching indeed were the hours spent together, in the presence of the Lord (he wrote). Much lay behind us and much before, and we all felt the need of humbling ourselves before God and seeking the guidance of the Holy Spirit. For the first two days we did nothing but pray. After that we conferred together as touching the future. It is not necessary to go into detail as to our decisions. But I would record that there was no thought of turning back. On the contrary, there was full determination to go forward, whatever the cost.

One other memorable occasion stands out above the rest. It was at Kiukiang, in the home of Mr. Orr-Ewing, who was then Superintendent of the work both on the Kan and Kwangsin Rivers. At great risk to himself, he had gone inland to all the ladies' stations and brought the young workers in safety to the treaty port. Many of these, as of the young men from the south of the province, were Mr. Frost's own "children" from Toronto. Little had they expected to meet again under such circumstances.

Our meetings were held in the large drawing room of Mr. Orr-Ewing's home (Mr. Frost recalls), and never had I felt so intensely the divine Presence as in those gatherings. The Consuls had just given permission for the missionaries to return to their stations, and those present were preparing to leave on Monday for the places where they had been so ruthlessly treated and from which they had been obliged precipitately to flee. Mrs. Steven had come up river with me, and she spoke with great sympathy and helpfulness to the lady missionaries present. I made my addresses as searching and yet as comforting as possible.

The climax was reached on Sunday evening, when it was my privilege to lead in the celebration of the Lord's Supper. As I did so, my heart was deeply moved. There before me sat some twenty young women, as well as a number of men, whose faces were resolutely set toward distant parts of the province where persecution might arise at any time. Yet there was no faltering. For love of Christ and also for love of the Chinese people they were ready and eager to go forward, though pain and death might be their portion. What a sight for God, angels, and men! Happily, by the good hand of the Lord upon them, they went forth *not to die but to live*.

CHAPTER

XXVII

THE ISSUES FROM DEATH

VERY deep was the impression made in Shansi when the attitude of the Mission regarding the losses it had sustained in that province became known. It would have been possible to claim large indemnity. The foreign powers had taken up the situation vigorously, and China, humiliated and in extremity, was ready to accede to any demands. It was partly the regrettable action of some of the foreign troops at this crisis that determined the line taken by Mr. D. E. Hoste and those associated with him, who gave much prayerful consideration to the subject. With regard to the losses of the Shansi Christians, "it was felt that this was a matter between the Chinese authorities and their own subjects," but so far as the missionaries were concerned—the living and the dead—it was decided to waive all claim for compensation. What money could compensate such sacrifice? And what better opportunity could there be of manifesting the spirit of the Gospel, of making real the love and the teachings of Christ?

A careful estimate was made of the Mission's losses, and this was presented to the Foreign Office in Peking, with the statement that no compensation was asked or would be accepted. At the same time, Mr. Hoste went in person to Shansi, accompanied by Mr. Orr-Ewing and others who had also labored there as missionaries, to attend the impressive Memorial Services arranged by the highest Chinese authorities. They were received in Taiyüan, the capital, with every possible honor—arriving on the anniversary, as it happened, of the very day when more than fifty missionaries and their children had met death in that city at the hands of Governor Yü-hsien. Hardly could the facts be credited when it became known that there were to be no reprisals on the part of the Mission which had suffered most. The effect produced may be judged from the proclamation put out by the new Governor. After enumerating fifteen cities in which the Mission had suffered serious loss of property, he continued:

In rebuilding these churches with its own funds, the Mission aims to fulfil the command of the SAVIOUR OF THE WORLD, that all men should love their neighbors as themselves. . . . Contrasting the way in which we are treated by the missionaries with our treatment of them, how can anyone who has the least regard for right and reason not feel ashamed of this behaviour? . . . JESUS, in His instructions, inculcates forbearance and forgiveness, and all desire for revenge is discouraged. Mr. Hoste is able to carry out these principles to the full. . . . From this time forward, I charge you all, gentry, scholars, army, and people, those of you who are fathers to exhort your sons, and those who are elder sons exhort your younger brothers, to bear in mind the example of Pastor Hoste, who is able to forbear and to forgive, as taught by JESUS.

All through the document, the characters for the sacred Name were "exalted," that is, raised above the perpendicular lines in which Chinese is written, as a token of the highest honor. "Posted up throughout the province," Marshall Broomhall wrote, "this proclamation was an object lesson to all, and was calculated to do more to make known the spirit of Jesus Christ than many years of preaching, and from this standpoint alone was worth far more than any amount of compensation."

Thankful for the reëstablishment of the work upon so favorable a basis, Mr. Hoste and his companions continued their journey to the south of the province, everywhere receiving the warmest welcome, but unutterably saddened by what they learned of the suffering of the Christians. Tortured and put to death by the hundreds, they had witnessed a good confession, comparatively few accepting deliverance at the cost of denying the Lord they loved. But the cruelties perpetrated had been beyond telling, and the prevailing famine added to the distress of those left homeless and destitute.*

In the Pingyang district there had been many martyrs. Passing through, a few years previously, the writers had visited the home of Pastor Hsi, meeting his aged mother. She had long been a Christian, and when the Boxers came they could not make her burn incense to the village idols. Enraged, they threatened to cut off both her hands—and actually did so—but through it all the dear old lady was kept true to her Lord and Saviour.

In the city, we went at the same time to see one of the church members who, little as we thought it, was to win a martyr's crown. The old man was nearing eighty years of

---

* Relief funds were being wisely distributed, and during the succeeding winter not a single Christian died of exposure or starvation.

age, but the Boxers had no pity. Dragged to a neighboring temple with a number of others, he was required to worship the idols. To refuse meant death. But he was steadfast, and was cut to pieces—they all were—in that temple outside the walls of Pingyang.*

It was the venerable Pastor in that same city who said to his missionary friends—the Dreyers and their company, as they were being driven out to face the Boxers on the long road to Hankow—*"Kueh neng mieh; Kiao mieh-puh-liao"*: "Kingdoms may perish; but the Church of Christ cannot be destroyed!" And so it proved. For within a year or two of the Boxer outbreak, work was resumed in nearly all the vacated centers, and the following decade witnessed unprecedented advance.

Very cheering was the reception met with as the missionaries were able to return to their stations, and many were the accounts they heard of answers to prayer and protection in times of danger. For Proverbs 14:26 still holds good: "The fear of the Lord is strong confidence and his children shall have a place of refuge."

I shall never forget my return to Yangkow (wrote Miss Grace Irving, one of the American workers on the Kwangsin River). How the men and boys ran—and women too, on their tiny feet—until our lane was filled with the dear folk, laughing and shouting and throwing up their hands with delight at seeing us once more. Joy and tears were mingled in the welcome of not a few. One dear woman exclaimed, "Now you will not leave us for a hundred years!"

---

* Had Pastor Hsi been there in 1900, he too would doubtless have been sacrificed for Christ's sake. His death in 1896 cut short one of the most apostolic careers China has ever known. See, *Pastor Hsi*, in two volumes, by Mrs. Howard Taylor.

But best of all it was to hear of the steadfastness of the Christians. Inquirers had increased in number and leaders had been raised up to care for the country stations. One woman, not long baptized, had proved most faithful and fearless.

People had persecuted her and tried in every way to turn her back. They said that foreigners had all been killed and that the missionaries would never return again. Even the Christian chapel-keeper fled. But Mrs. Ching stayed on and strengthened many—saying, "God has not gone away!"

At Iyang, Miss Mackenzie and Miss Standen were rejoicing in the baptism of nineteen men and nineteen women, all of whom had stood firm through the perils of 1900.

It is wonderful to see with what favor the Gospel is now received (Miss Standen wrote in 1901). We have fresh people coming from all directions to the Sunday services. Some have mixed motives, no doubt, but there do seem to be a number who are truly seeking the light.

First to return to the Kan River was Mr. William Taylor, accompanied by a younger worker from North America, Mr. E. G. Bevis. In station after station their hearts were gladdened by much that they saw and heard.

All the Christians (Mr. Taylor wrote from Kian), though persecuted, have remained faithful. We had good meetings with them the two Sundays we were there.

A Mrs. Chang came to see him whose beaming face was a benediction. Her house had been broken into by a band of men bent on plunder. There were more than fifty of them, but passing through their midst she stood in the field opposite her door, praying to God for protection. The men heard her, and after a few minutes of amazed silence they began to scatter, taking nothing with them. Little wonder her testimony was, *"God helps!"*

Others had had like deliverances, for example a Mr. Liu, the one Christian in the village of Blue Bridge. He was a farmer, and his only fellowship amid the troubles of 1900 was with a neighbor who had become an inquirer. Much opposed at home, they met every evening in a quiet corner of the village Ancestral Hall, for reading and prayer. But they were marked men, their chief enemy being an underling employed in the city *yamen*. This dreaded "small official" had come to Mr. Liu's place with a rabble of followers to frighten him into a return to idolatry. They tore down his Christian scrolls and vowed that unless he replaced the gods and worshiped them, they would come back, beat him, and raze his house to the ground.

All this was very alarming, and Mr. Liu's family besought him to give up his new-found faith. In the end, he yielded so far as to take down the ten commandments from a prominent place in the living room, but idols and incense he would not have. That evening, not a little troubled, he went to the usual rendezvous, but his inquirer friend did not appear. Had he turned back in fear? It was lonely, waiting. Had God too forsaken him? Then he fell asleep. Raised on a slight eminence, he seemed to see company after company coming against him, all armed with swords and staves. But as each group drew near, strange to say, they disappeared into the ground! This he could not understand, until a voice seemed to say to him, "Look behind you." This he did, and there, sitting in a sedan chair he saw a beautiful

Form, radiating light. He knew that it was the Lord Jesus, and awoke fully assured of His protection.

Hastening home, he told his wife and mother that it was all right; the Lord would deliver! They still feared, but his heart was manifestly at peace. And the dreaded underling did not return. A day or two later, he got into a fight in a near-by village and was killed. His threats to Mr. Liu had been generally known, and it was said throughout the countryside, "Beware! The foreigners may be away, but the God of the foreigners is present."

This was the feeling that led, in many places, to mass movements in favor of Christianity. The people had seen evidences not only of the power of foreign armies, but of the fact that there is a living God, who watches over those who trust in Him. The demand for Christian literature increased surprisingly, and Mr. Hoste, in touch by correspondence with all parts of China, was constrained to write:

My letters from the interior all tell the same story of wonderful readiness to hear among the people, and of a real spirit of interest on the part of many. China presents an opportunity for consecrated, humble-minded servants of the Lord that has never been surpassed, if indeed equaled, in the history of the Christian Church.

* * * * *

Meanwhile, at home in North America there was also much to encourage. Mr. Frost had long felt that the time was coming when a center would be needed in the United States as well as in Canada. Even before leaving for China on his mission of comfort, in 1901, he had received the first intimation that his prayers to this end were being answered. A friend from Philadelphia had broached the subject, urging

that Mr. Frost should visit the eastern States to see where
such a center should be located.   There had not been time
just then to take up the matter, and on his homeward journey,
Mr. Frost was delayed by a serious shipwreck and by subsequent visits in Europe.   But the late summer saw him back
again in Toronto and ready for new developments.

One remarkable happening in connection with that shipwreck should be recorded.   On her maiden voyage, the fine
vessel had crashed on a foggy night into rocks off the China
coast, and her passengers had to spend some days on an
uninhabited island before they could be rescued.   Among his
losses, Mr. Frost sorrowed most for the disappearance of a
box containing all his Bible notes and outlines of addresses.
The fruit of years of prayer and study, these papers were
invaluable, and he felt stranded like a workman robbed of
his tools.   All he and his companion, Mr. Nasmith, could do
was to pray about it, but it must be confessed that Mr. Frost
continued his journey to England with very little hope as
to his lost belongings.

Weeks later, in London, the Mission received a notice
from the ship's Company that some of the passengers' effects
had been recovered and would be available for inspection on
a certain day.   With little expectation of finding anything
worth while, Mr. Nasmith went down to the docks alone, as
Mr. Frost had a previous engagement.

When my friend reached there (wrote the latter) he found a mass
of goods piled high together, in a condition which would have
justified Carlyle's exclamation in *Sartor Resartus*, "Old clothes and
nasty!"   Mr. Nasmith found none of his garments and none of mine.
But as he was turning over with his foot part of the pile, he saw a
large manila envelope which had a familiar look.   Picking it up, he
found that it belonged to me and had some of my Bible notes in it.

At this, he put his foot into action again, coming across more such envelopes, until at last he had twelve of them. Then he found an old suitcase with my initials on one end, containing nothing but a soiled collar and a chicken feather. He put all the packages into this case and brought it home to me.

When I examined the envelopes, with an eagerness which may be imagined, I found that the flaps of some of them had been torn off and that a good many of the loose leaves inside must have fallen out, for they were stained with mud and water. But *all the envelopes were there*, and *not one Bible Reading was missing*. Besides the old suitcase, collar, and feather, these packages were all I recovered from the wreck. But the notes were everything! And they were the things for which I had prayed.

How slow we are to believe that God hears and answers! And yet we have so many evidences of His faithfulness in this way. Another wonderful experience of this sort came to Mr. Frost when he went down to Philadelphia that fall, and was taken by Mr. Horace C. Coleman to see the house he had in mind for the Mission. It was one of the most attractive on old De Kalb Street, Norristown, not far from the city. After showing him first one house he had thought of, then another, Mr. Coleman drew his attention to a property they were passing, farther up the hill, and asked him to observe it without seeming to do so.

I looked then without looking, and what I saw was simply fascinating. There before me was a place of an acre or more, beautified by broad lawns and stately trees, and in the center a large, roomy home of Colonial type. My feelings by this time were deeply moved, but I was almost silent. I was too grateful to say much, and besides I had about exhausted my adjectives lower down the street. However, I gave Mr. Coleman to understand that I should fervently thank God for the gift of such a place. My friend was not a man of many words, but he knew how to act expeditiously. Within a day (on Tuesday, October 8) he had bought the property, paying for it over twelve thousand dollars. It was immediately deeded to me as a trustee—we were not then incorporated—and over night, as it were, the prayers of ten years were answered and the China Inland Mission had a center in the United States.

That was in 1901, and until his Home-going, thirty-five years later, Mr. Coleman was a friend whose sympathy and helpfulness knew no limit. As a member of the Philadelphia Council, his services were invaluable, and his generous giving never outran his prayers.

And in those days of enlargement and blessing, both at home and in China, prayer was sorely needed; for if 1900 had witnessed a devastating, external crisis, the years that followed brought internal perils of an even more serious kind. There had been problems before, connected with the inner working of the Mission, but now a situation arose that threatened to destroy its unity and spiritual usefulness.

One big, loving heart in China had been carried away with the teaching of "the larger hope," and circular letters began to appear in which a change of doctrinal position was urged upon others. The matter had to be dealt with at last by Mr. Hoste, Mr. Taylor himself, and the Councils. It took Mr. Frost to Switzerland for personal conference with Mr. Taylor, and took him again to China. For Mr. Hoste saw plainly the danger that arises from protracted correspondence in such a situation. He believed that united waiting upon God would harmonize differing points of view and make continued fellowship possible, when letters were apt to result in misunderstandings. After much prayer, he therefore called a special Council meeting in Shanghai, to which Mr. Frost as Director in North America and Mr. Sloan as Assistant Director in England were invited. Both were deeply taught in the Word of God, clear thinkers, and uncompromising in their convictions. And both were wholly true to the doctrinal position of the Mission, that of the evangelical faith.

From Europe and North America the leaders came—Mr. Frost accompanied by Dr. Howard Taylor—their hearts subdued by a deep sense of dependence upon God. It was not creeds or dogmas that occupied them, but a fresh study of the Word of God itself, in every part, and they were deeply imbued not with its teachings only but with its spirit.

Those Council meetings, by the grace of God, resulted in a great deliverance. Had the leaders of the Mission failed or even faltered then in loyalty to the Word of God or love to one another, the blessing of succeeding years could never have been. But instead of being torn asunder, the bonds of mutual confidence were strengthened by love and patience, and all proved to be of the same mind regarding the principles at stake. Mr. Frost's final statement as to the way in which he would deal with any member of the Mission whose doctrinal views had undergone serious change was received with thankfulness, and paved the way for the following Minute:*

After prolonged deliberation, it was agreed that we record our continued conviction that the Doctrinal Basis of the Mission, as hitherto existing, should be maintained; and it is understood that, while the discretionary action of the Directors in dealing with individual cases affecting doctrine among members of the Mission is to be exercised, such action shall be in view of and in harmony with the said Doctrinal Basis.

To make matters still clearer, Mr. Taylor, as his last official service to the Mission, put forth a restatement of the Doc-

---

* Dated February 11, 1904.

trinal Basis upon which it had operated from the first. It was an unspeakable sorrow to him that the beloved fellow-worker whose change of views had brought about the situation, had finally to withdraw from the membership of the Mission. But fundamental principles had been clearly re-stated and the whole work safeguarded, at home and on the field, from the subtle changes that cut at the root of spiritual power and fruitfulness.

It was no little comfort that the years that followed brought such rich return in the ingathering of precious souls. Up to 1900, the Mission had received by baptism a total of thirteen thousand converts, within a period of thirty-five years. But after 1900, more than seventeen thousand were received within the first eight years, and the increase continued.

In the midst of this tide of blessing (spring, 1905) Hudson Taylor returned to China. Mrs. Taylor had passed away some months previously, and in his great bereavement it was a comfort to go back to the land he loved. On the way from Switzerland, he had the joy of visiting the new Philadelphia headquarters, and it was in one of the North American stations in China that, a few weeks later, Mr. Taylor also received the Home-call.

Dr. Frank Keller, after the Boxer troubles, had been enabled to gain an entrance into Changsha, capital of Hunan, the province that so long had resisted the coming of missionaries. There he was rejoicing in a remarkable work of God. After visiting a number of inland stations, accompanied by the writers, Mr. Taylor was strengthened physically to accept Dr. and Mrs. Keller's invitation to visit them. Never had the Founder of the Mission received more loving welcome than from these fellow-workers and from the believers who formed the first church in that great city—the church in Dr. Keller's home. And it was from the midst of these Hunan Christians that dear Father passed, in one painless moment, to his eternal service and reward.

"It was not death," we wrote at the time, "but the swift, glad entry upon life immortal."

And in that quiet room, "full of unutterable peace," we opened Father's Bible—the last he had in use—and found there a little sketch-map on thin paper, sent to him by James Adam of Kweichow, to show the district in which he was working among the mountain people whom he loved. In Father's hands it had been much prayed over. The closing days of his life had been rich in fruition, as he saw for himself the last of China's inland provinces opened to the Gospel, and heard of the wonderful developments, there and elsewhere, since 1900. And how his heart thrilled to the promise of that little map! For the great ingathering among the long-waiting tribes of the Southwest had indeed begun.

PART III

FAITH'S CROWN

"Behold, I come quickly: hold that fast which thou hast, that no man take thy crown."   REVELATION 3:11.

"What is our hope, or joy, or crown of rejoicing? Are not even ye, in the presence of our Lord Jesus Christ at His coming? For ye are our glory and joy."

I THESSALONIANS 2:19-20.

"Be thou faithful unto death, and I will give thee the crown of life."   REVELATION 2:10.

"Blessed is the man that endureth temptation: for when he is tried, he shall receive the crown of life, which the Lord hath promised to them that love Him."   JAMES 1:12.

CHAPTER

XXVIII

REVOLUTION AND
THE GREAT WAR

TIMES of special trial in the experience of the Mission have always led to times of special blessing. We have seen this in connection with financial trial in the early days of the North American work; we have seen it in the overwhelming crisis of 1900; and now we are to see it on the scale of national and international developments, up to the present hour. For, more even than in the past, we are proving in these latter days the faithfulness of God amid unprecedented emergencies, and are seeing His hand overruling evil for good.

China was entering upon troublous times as the rule of the Manchus drew to a close. Only one day after the death of the deposed Emperor (Nov. 14, 1908), the Empress Dowager also passed away, leaving as heir to the throne a child of two years, the unfortunate P'u Yi, now nominal ruler of Manchukuo. Three years later, the dynasty in power since 1644 tottered to its fall. Revolutionary forces headed up to the swift developments of 1911, when China's four hundred millions were swept out upon a new and perilous way. On the first of January, 1912, Dr. Sun Yat-sen was declared President in Canton. And six weeks later, in the hope of cementing union between the North and the South, he resigned in favor of the former Viceroy, Yüan Shï-k'ai, in Peking.

Widespread suffering accompanied the Revolution, "when some of the finest cities in China were given over to looting by the soldiery." But, thanks to the stable, peace-loving character of the people, the reign of terror was limited and comparatively brief. It introduced, however, a period of lawlessness, due to the breakdown of constituted authority in many places, when the worst elements of the populace came into power. Thus the amazing career of "White Wolf" was made possible, who in the two following years devastated province after province. Supported by armies of brigands, this powerful outlaw attacked and burned cities with unspeakable barbarity, torturing and killing thousands, and moving with such rapidity that he overran a large part of the North and West. Terror spread before him, and where missionaries held on, it was at the gravest risk. Early in the Revolution, two associate members of the Mission, with six European children under their care, were massacred in the city of Sian. This, though, was due to a local uprising.

As is so often the case in the providence of God, this period of national calamity had been preceded by a period of marked spiritual blessing. During the years immediately prior to the Revolution, there had been a wonderful quickening in the experience of Christians in China. Conferences for the deepening of spiritual life had taken on new meaning and power. There had always been such gatherings in local districts, but now they began to assume almost national importance. Both in Korea and in Manchuria there had been truly marvelous outpourings of the Spirit of God. Dr. Jonathan Goforth, who had witnessed these revivals, came back to his station in Honan moved to the depths, and longing for similar blessing in China. First in Shansi, then in other provinces, he was used of God to kindle fires that spread far and wide. Before long, he was set free from station work to respond to calls from all over the country, and others who had caught the inspiration, both Chinese and foreigners, were also giving themselves to nation-wide evangelism. It was a great advance in Christian testimony, and was accompanied by mighty manifestations of divine power. Nothing less could account for the deep conviction of sin, the repentance, restitution, and changed lives that resulted. Just as in the days of the Apostles, whole communities were moved by the joy and victory of men and women saved from bondage to sin, through faith in Christ, healed of sickness, delivered from demon-possession, and filled with the Holy Spirit.

Among those specially used of God at this time were several members of the China Inland Mission whose lives had been spared in 1900 for wide and fruitful service—Mr. A. E. Lutley, Miss Jessie Gregg, and Miss Margaret King, whose work in soul-winning and building up the churches took them to every province in China; Mr. F. C. H. Dreyer, becoming known as a Bible teacher, and Mr. Alexander Saunders, pioneer evangelist among soldiers as well as civil-

ians.   Mr. Percy Knight also, who had been helping Mr.
Frost in America during the Boxer troubles, was successfully
developing short-term Bible schools.   The Church in China
had caught a new vision of what the Christian life should
mean, and he was deeply impressed with the importance of
building up awakened souls in the truth of God.   Station
Bible classes in Shansi led before long to the establishment of
a full-time Bible School, in charge of Mr. and Mrs. Dreyer,
which eventuated in the production of his invaluable Com-
mentaries now in use all over China.

Another providential development, before the days of suffering that were drawing on, was the appearance of a new
type of leadership among Chinese Christians.   There had
always been leaders used of God to the upbuilding of the
church in their own localities.   The influence of some of these
had reached adjacent provinces.   But now, filled in a wonderful way with the Holy Spirit, evangelists and Bible teachers
who had the great advantage of being Chinese nationals began
to take a wider field.   Prominent among these was Pastor Ting
Li-mei of the Presbyterian Church in Shantung, to whose
ministry "all the schools, colleges, and universities throughout the country" were opening at this time, and who later
became known as "the Apostle of China."

Scarcely less remarkable has been the record of Hsieh
Meng-tseh of Anhwei, connected with our own Mission, who
was brought into fullness of blessing at one of Dr. Goforth's
conferences.   Traveling on foot, in the plainest of cotton
clothing, taking no salary, enduring hardness, and living a
life of true faith and prayer, this man of God has done a
unique work in many parts of China.   To all who will re-

ceive him in town or country, be they few or many, rich or poor, Christians or outsiders, he rejoices to unfold the treasures of the Word, maintaining also a regular correspondence with hundreds who have been blessed through his labors, to whom his circular letters form almost a Bible course.

Such men are among God's best gifts to the Church of any land. It was not that there was anything specially new about their message; but coming from Chinese lips and in purely Chinese garb, it had a new appeal. A new standard of Christian holiness had been raised, and new apostles were living as well as preaching it in the power of the Spirit. And with it went a new emphasis on Bible study, calling to mind Mr. Hudson Taylor's words:

The best evidence of Christianity is a Christlike life, and the best evidence of the inspiration of the Word of God is found in that Word itself. When studied, loved, obeyed, and trusted, it never disappoints, never misleads, never fails.

When the Revolution came, followed by years of suffering through cruel brigandage, all this was put to the test. And it was heartening to see how the Church stood and grew. In the China Inland Mission alone, the troubled decade, 1909 to 1918, witnessed no fewer than *forty-thousand baptisms*— more than in all the previous forty-three years of its history. It was a day of glorious opportunity, in spite of almost overwhelming difficulties. Mr. H. S. Conway, for example, was rejoicing in a wonderful work of God in the district in which he and his colleagues had suffered in 1900, but of 1913 he wrote:

This has been a most tragic year for us. Seven times have our outstations been plundered; four times have robbers been quartered on our premises; nineteen times have workers (Chinese) been held up and more or less robbed by highwaymen; twice have workers been condemned to be shot, but the Lord delivered them; one worker, sad to say, was shot and still lies in a precarious condition; two of the church members have been killed; three times have Christians been seized and held for ransom; seven times have their homes been wholly or partially destroyed; five times has the Lord interposed to deliver them from fire, when on each occasion nearly the whole village was burned; eleven times have their homes been wholly or partially plundered. . . .*

On the other hand, never have we known a larger opportunity than the crowded towns have afforded us. To speak of this place only (Shekichen), over seven thousand families have been registered at the gates as refugees, and our chapels present one long scene of interested people coming to see and hear. The number of voluntary preachers, helping in the hall and on the streets, has been a real encouragement.

To be able to minister to the suffering was no little comfort, under such conditions, and happily the prestige of foreigners at this period was unusually high.

Never in my experience of thirty years have missionaries had so much influence with the officials, people, and even brigand chiefs (wrote Bishop Cassels from West China). Again and again they have been called in to act as peacemakers or go-betweens. They have secured protection for ousted officials and for defenseless women and children; they have obtained from brigands more moderate terms for the cities captured; and have even secured safe passage for Government troops through districts held by powerful brigand bands.

Among many who had the privilege of being useful in these ways was Dr. Lagerquist, one of the early pioneers on the Sian plain. After a brief medical course in the United

---

* But God's protecting care was very evident, for when "White Wolf" attacked the town, putting up scaling ladders in the darkness of a Christmas night, his bold strategy was discovered and he was repulsed by a well-directed fusillade of stones from the city wall. So the community was spared, though individuals suffered.

States, he had returned to China, taking up work at Laoho-kow, an important commercial center on the Han River. Attacked by "White Wolf," the place was given over to plunder. No fewer than fifteen hundred people were killed during that awful night and the day that followed. The city was set on fire in forty-seven places; and when the brigands retired—taking with them some five hundred young women and girls as well as the loot they had gathered—thousands of wounded were left without succor. The missionaries had been in gravest danger, but the opportunity of helping in such a crisis more than made up for all they endured. In recognition of his services, the highest authorities in the province presented Dr. Lagerquist with a memorial tablet bearing the inscription in great gold characters, *"Laboring for all, in order to save and relieve."* Civil and military officials, as well as the gentry of the city, took part in the presentation, and attention was widely called to the mission-ary's spiritual message.

Remarkable answers to prayer confirmed the testimony of Chinese Christians also, amid these distresses. When "White Wolf" devastated a large part of the distant province of Kansu, Mr. and Mrs. Lloyd Rist from Canada, were in Tsin-chow, and wrote of such experiences.

Praise the Lord! He kept us in perfect peace all through that awful day and night (when the city was looted), and *not one of our Christians was harmed*. . . . Some, whose neighbors on all sides were robbed and many of them killed, did not even have their compounds entered. Others whose courtyards were entered lost nothing, neither they nor their possessions being touched.

One poor woman was alone in her home when a band of brigands came in, demanding silver and opium. She told them, quite truthfully, that she had neither. They then ordered her to make them some food, but her supplies were all used up.

"Make us tea!" they shouted angrily.

She dared not say that she had no tea leaves, nor could she slip out to borrow any. All she had in the house was a pound of charcoal she had just managed to buy. Lighting a fire with this precious bit of fuel, she put on water to boil, praying in her heart all the while that the Lord would make some way of escape. Just as the water was ready to make tea, there was a sudden commotion on the street.

"Never mind, we can't wait!" shouted the intruders as they rushed out to see what it was.

And she was left to praise God for a great deliverance.

Such instances might be multiplied, for everywhere God was watching over His own, and many were the ways in which He was overruling evil for good.

The coming of the Republic did not bring the millennium in China (wrote one well qualified to judge), but it was undoubtedly accompanied by a most extraordinary opportunity for preaching the Gospel. There was awakened on all hands an almost passionate desire for better things than the past had afforded, and many sought to find their ideal in Christianity.

Comparatively peaceful conditions over a large part of the country enabled a majority of the missionaries of all societies to go on with their work as usual, and to take advantage of new openings as they pressed upon them. This was the case with Mr. Alexander Saunders, to whom came a great opportunity among soldiers. He was Superintendent of the work of the Mission in central Kiangsu and was living in Yang-chow when some fifteen thousand revolutionary troops under General Hsü Pao-san were quartered in and around that city. Mr. Saunders had received a considerable grant of Gospels and tracts, and longed to get them into the hands of these men, but knowing how peremptorily such efforts had been forbidden in the past, he saw no way of approach. After much prayer, however, he decided to send his card to a subordinate military official, with unexpected results.

I felt I would rather risk a refusal from him than from a higher authority, but my card and request reached the General, and he asked for an interview. The result was that we were not only granted permission to distribute Scriptures and tracts to the troops. "Preach to them!" he said. And his own brother, who was then Military Governor of the city, was appointed to accompany us as we visited all the camps.

This work took seven half-days. We were received with military honors at each camp, and had opportunity for conversation with the regimental officers. The troops were then drawn up in hollow square . . . and for half an hour we explained to them the Gospel. The books were then distributed, but not by us. We simply handed them out in packets, and the officers distributed them to their own men.

More than this, the General gave us a badge to admit us to any camp, without question. . . . It bore his own seal, with the words on the reverse side, "A deputy of JESUS, to preach the Gospel."

A month later Mr. Saunders was again in Yangchow, after a visit to the northern part of his district, where there were many inquirers.* Accosted on the street by a Secretary, he was told that the General wished to see him. After conversation on various topics, the missionary ventured to say:

"General, how do you occupy the troops on Sunday, seeing they do not drill?"

"I would like you to preach to them," was the unexpected reply.

And that was how it began. For the General was as good as his word. He appointed a place, gave the necessary

---

* On his return, after furlough, he had the joy of baptizing two hundred and two of these new Antung believers, at one time.

orders, and requested that the first three meetings might be for officers only. They were wonderful gatherings, followed by a long series for the rank and file of the army. So great was the impression made that when Mr. and Mrs. Saunders had to go home on furlough, leaving the work to others, the General took the lead in expressing good will. All the members of his staff, with a Guard of Honor five thousand strong, accompanied the missionaries to the launch on the Grand Canal, when they set out for Shanghai and home. What a contrast to their experience in 1900! China was changing, and in many places a reaping time had come.

It was so, very markedly, in Kiangsi, where the pioneers on the Kan River were rejoicing in signs of a new day. The district in which James Lawson had been homeless for eight years, living in inns, sowing the precious seed often with tears, now had three settled stations and groups of Christians in many other places. Leaving the older work in the care of Mr. R. B. Whittlesey and other colleagues, Lawson had gone on westward to the Yüanchow prefecture, with its population of a million, living, dying without Christ. In the governing city of that beautiful region, he was prospered in effecting a settlement (1903) and in spite of the notorious wickedness of the place, a work of God had begun which compensated for all the toil and suffering of earlier years. In 1913 he was able to write:

At present, over two thousand people are in touch with us, all of them receiving instruction in spiritual truth. Ten outstations have been opened (from Yüanchow), in each of which there are now church members, and an attendance at worship of from four hundred down. . . .

This beautiful spot is a modern Sodom! Here the Gospel has been preached for ten years and, thank God, where sin abounded grace has much more abounded, and the power of God is being revealed in the changed lives of men, women, and girls. A chapel to seat four hundred has been built (in the city) and is filled each Lord's Day. A boarding school for girls and two day schools for boys are doing good work. . . . At least five new workers are needed. . . . God has given the open door; it is for us to enter in.

Urgency in the great task certainly characterized both the Lawsons and their beloved fellow-workers, Mr. and Mrs. Robert Porteous. When driven to take furlough a little later, Mrs. Lawson, who had been the first to bring the Gospel to the women of that Yüanchow district, quoted memorable words which were much upon her heart—though, indeed, they applied to the home churches more than to themselves:

We have been acting as though we had an eternity in which to do our work, and the people we seek to reach had an eternity on earth in which to be reached; whereas the fact is, that our term of service and their term of life must both very soon expire.

The same spirit was to be found in all the stations up the Kan River. In the far south of the province, W. S. Horne was no longer at his beloved Kanchow. His place was filled by British colleagues, both of whom had married North American workers—W. E. Tyler and C. A. Bunting.* John Meikle had gone on to Sinfeng, carrying the light always farther into the darkness, and so changed was the situation from early days that Mr. and Mrs. Horne had been called to the provincial capital (1909) to open a Bible School for

---

* In the year that followed the Revolution (i.e. 1912) Mr. Bunting spent 143 days itinerating in the Kanchow district, accompanied on some of his journeys by a fellow-worker from Canada, the Rev. L. C. Whitelaw. "Throughout the entire district," wrote the latter, "there seems a ready response to the Gospel message, and a demand for books hitherto unknown. . . . The need certainly is appalling, and the response such as no one, a few years ago, would have deemed possible."

Kiangsi Christians. There, in the busy city of Nanchang, they were prayerfully and patiently laying the foundations of the richly fruitful Bible training and evangelistic center of today.

At Kian, the prayers of years were being answered, and the William Taylors were happy in reinforcements, including the Rev. E. A. Brownlee and Mrs. Brownlee, and their little son, from Toronto. Not only had the church grown from nine members in 1900 to over a hundred and thirty, the growth was genuine spiritual increase. Great care had been taken to avoid the dangers of the mass movement common at that period, and to baptize only true believers. This was the case also in other Kiangsi stations, and the character of many of the Christians was a rich reward for long prayer and patience. When the William Taylors came home on furlough in the year of the Revolution, he could truly speak of some of them as "among the brighest and most devoted Christians I have ever known." A Confucian scholar was one of these, converted, strangely enough, through the recurring word in Ecclesiastes, "All is vanity." Another was a Mrs. An, whose story has a special interest as she is still living, respected and beloved by the Kian Church, after nearly forty years of faithful and fruitful witness.

Left a widow early, with one little girl, this woman was in the unprotected position of having no son. She was well-to-do in her village community, and moreover was decidedly attractive, always well dressed, good-looking, with steady eyes, and rosy cheeks, and well able to manage her little patrimony. But she was open to special danger.

For in that remote part of the country (as Mr. Taylor discovered)
likely young widows belonging to small clans are often carried off
by larger clans to be forcibly remarried. A few dollars, prudently
distributed where they would "do most good" to opium-smoking
clansmen, probably simplified matters. So it happened to this "vir-
tuous widow." She was forcibly seized one evening, a sack was
thrown over her head and tied round her arms, and she was roped
on a wheelbarrow and trundled off. A resourceful young person,
she kept her wits about her, and when released in the guest hall of
the home to which she was taken—where a feast was ready for the
expected wedding—she seized a stout carrying pole and laid about
her vigorously, attacking her abductors, smashing the dishes on the
table, and then, back to the wall, faced them, her eyes blazing with
indignation.

"Enough, enough!" cried the prospective bridegroom. "I don't
want that kind of woman. Take her away!"

So she was released; sent off with firecrackers, to "save her face,"
and escorted home in a sedan chair.

But the experience left her anxious. It was more than
likely to happen again. Not knowing how to protect herself, she had almost decided to enter a Buddhist nunnery,
but before doing so went to consult a nephew of her late husband. This young man had been given a Gospel when up in
the city for one of his examinations.

"Why don't you go to Kian," he suggested, "and join the
foreign religion? I am sure they could protect you."

The result was that one Wednesday afternoon as the
Christian women were gathering for their weekly meeting,
two strangers appeared who had walked more than thirty
miles from their village homes. They had brought food-
money with them, and asked if they could stay a few days
to learn the doctrine. Gladly Mrs. William Taylor received
and taught them, explaining, when she learned of Mrs. An's

trouble, that though the missionaries could not protect her, the living God assuredly could.

When they left us, their faces showed that they had found what they sought—true peace and gladness. Though it was not possible for any of us to visit them during the next few months, the Holy Spirit was their teacher, and we found when they came again that both of them had grown in grace and in the knowledge of the Lord Jesus Christ. Mrs. An could read most of the New Testament by that time, having engaged an old teacher for a daily lesson. She and Mrs. Tsien (her cousin) had also been meeting regularly on Sunday for worship in the latter's home. They were baptized the following spring, and in spite of not a little opposition continued to witness joyfully to the Saviour's love and power.

In their isolation, two-days' journey from the nearest gathering of Christians, these young believers were much encouraged by definite answers to prayers. At a time of prevailing sickness, for example, a messenger came to Mrs. An in haste, saying that her cousin had been "caught by the epidemic demon." Setting out at once for the village, a walk of two or three miles, she arrived there toward evening. To her distress, she found Mrs. Tsien delirious, in high fever, and the heathen relatives busy preparing for idolatrous ceremonies. It was difficult to persuade them to desist, but at length they consented to wait twenty-four hours.

Mrs. An's position was a serious one, with no medical help or older Christian to advise her. After caring for her cousin as well as she could, she went up early in the morning to the dusty loft where farm implements were kept, and gave herself to prayer and fasting. The sick woman was unconscious then and apparently dying. But Mrs. An prayed on, hour after hour, audibly much of the time, until about four in the afternoon. Then suddenly she heard a call:

"Cousin, aren't you hungry? Come down and cook rice."

It was the patient, conscious but weak, and with joy Mrs. An clambered down the ladder to do as she had said. When the rice was ready, Mrs. Tsien was able to take some of the gruel, and before nightfall was manifestly recovering. This was the more wonderful, as two others in the same compound, who were ill at the same time, died of the fever, in spite of all the idolatry and propitiating of demons.

Mr. Taylor, having heard of this experience, went out to the village a few weeks later, wondering why Mrs. An had turned in her extremity to prayer with fasting. He certainly had never spoken in her hearing of this Scriptural procedure.

"Why did you fast as well as pray?" I questioned.

Mrs. Ann seemed a little disturbed. "Perhaps I was mistaken," she replied, "but I thought I remembered reading somewhere in the Bible that this kind of demon 'goeth not out but by prayer and fasting.' Was I wrong? I cannot find the place now."

It was a joy to turn up the passage she had in mind and show it to her. And how she feasted her eyes upon it!

I learned that day as never before the littleness of my faith, and the power of the Spirit to use the simple reading of the Word of God to teach those whose trust is in Him.

In the ladies' stations also, on the Kwangsin River, reliable Christians were growing in usefulness. This was notably the case at Iyang, where Miss McKenzie had for some years the help of Miss Maybeth Standen, another Canadian worker.* In the early days, Evangelist Kiang had saved Miss McKenzie's life at the risk of his own, and now the church, grown to over three hundred members, was "a sturdy, work-

---

* Miss C. C. Macdonald, who joined them in 1898, remained on to share Miss McKenzie's labors, when Miss Standen had to go north to Honan, to seek a more bracing climate. All three are still engaged in their loved work in China.

ing church," largely composed of men who—perhaps because
the missionaries were ladies—undertook a full share of responsibility.

Teacher Hong was one of these, converted through reading *Pilgrim's Progress*, before the Revolution, when he was
an able ultra-Confucianist. Though highly esteemed as a
scholar, he was fearless in his confession of Christ. Miss
McKenzie recalls him as "a bold, clear, earnest preacher of
the Gospel."

Once, on the main street of Iyang, he had the attention of a crowd
of two hundred or more, when a local Taoist (a leader in spiritism
and demon-worship) attacked him in bitter argument. Other
Christians who were there were fearful, but Hong was unperturbed.
Kindly and ably he met every argument, until the crowd was won to
sympathy with the followers of Jesus. The Taoist was angry and
threatening, so much so that the Christians, on considering the matter, felt that the weekly street-preaching had better be discontinued
for a time. Hong was for going right on, and a special prayer
meeting was held to seek the Lord's help and guidance. The
Taoist, meanwhile, had to go to the country on business. There he
was taken ill, and before the next week's meeting was due, he was
in his coffin! All the city knew of it and was moved.

When Hong was too old for street-preaching (Miss McKenzie
continued), he used to go to a Christian's inn, just opposite his
home, and sit there for hours, speaking to all who gathered round
him of the Gospel. Till nearly eighty years of age, it was said of
him that he could talk for two hours in his loud, clear voice, "without
even a drink of tea!"

That inn he frequented was the place where the innkeeper's wife had a secret for maintaining peace of heart amid
all the claims and distractions about her. She was a true
Christian (though at one time her life and that of her husband had been flagrantly evil) and when tried beyond

bearing would retire to a hidden corner in the stable, with her precious New Testament. "They looked unto him, and were lightened."

"I wear out many Bibles,"* she said to the present writers, and this explained the strength she found to go on with shining face.

Many were the men and women, born again and brought into spiritual blessing, whose stories might be told in connection with even the restricted sphere of our present survey —the North American section of the Mission. For when Canada and the United States became involved in the terrible war in Europe, there were no fewer than fifty-four stations, scattered throughout thirteen provinces, in which North American members of the Mission were at work. Many of these were already experienced leaders among the tribespeople of the mountains or the Chinese of the plain. It is difficult to refrain from going into further detail as to their labors, sufferings and successes, and the overwhelming needs with which they were surrounded. Opportunity everywhere, and so few to enter the open doors! But from the records of those days, brimful as they are of interest, we must of necessity turn away. For something remains to be said as to the repercussions of the World War and the serious situation in which it involved all missionaries in China.

It was not only that discredit was thrown upon the Gospel message by the sight of "Christian" nations engaged in such a conflict. Nor was it the financial crisis, grave as it was, that threatened disaster. In the case of the China Inland Mission especially, it was its international character. Of the

---

* The thin Chinese paper then used for printing would not stand long handling.

four hundred German missionaries in China at the time, more than one hundred were connected with the China Inland Mission, and when China joined the Allies the situation, tense before, became, humanly speaking, untenable. What could hold together such a fellowship, united only in the bonds of Christian love? It will easily be seen that the Mission was threatened with disruption from within, as well as the breakdown of its faith standards, through the failure of temporal supplies. And yet, in the faithfulness of God, the very reverse was what actually came to pass.

From the first, the Mission has been interdenominational (we quote Mr. Marshall Broomhall, then Editorial Secretary), and in the Lammermuir Party* there had been representatives from England, Scotland, Ireland, and Switzerland. With the passage of years, members or associates from many countries joined the work. All associates from the continent of Europe were supported by funds contributed in their own countries, but on the field the work was one. When the war broke out, there were workers from the following lands: England, Scotland, Ireland, Wales, Canada, Australia, New Zealand, South Africa, the United States of America, Finland, Russia, Belgium, Holland, Germany, Austria, Sweden, Norway, Denmark, Switzerland, Italy, Sicily, and India. In a remarkable manner the Mission was demonstrating the possibility of co-operation, and even union both interdenominational and international. The bond of love in Christ was a real thing. Could it survive the clash and cataclysm of war? It was a stern and vital test. Was love stronger than hate? Were the claims of Christ greater than those of country? As the months ran on into years, and the bitterness and the strain intensified, it seemed as though it was more than flesh and blood could bear. But grace and love conquered. Without any sacrifice of patriotism, the supernatural nature of Christian fellowship triumphed. The Mission came through the war without break or division. The strain on both sides was intense, and not least on the part of those whose countries were defeated. It was a conclusive

---

* The first party of the new Mission, including Mr. and Mrs. Hudson Taylor, who sailed for China on the *Lammermuir*, in 1866.

answer to the Apostle Paul's great question: "Who shall separate us from the love of Christ?" If the bond with Him remained, then the fellowship of His children would survive anguish and peril and sword. And it did. Love was tested, and it did not fail. . . .

The other great problem was financial. Here is one testimony from the Superintendent of the Liebenzeller Associate Mission. "Though we were cut off from our homeland for months through the war, yet we were not cut off from our heavenly Father. More than ever before, the children of God learned to pray for their daily bread, and amply God has answered. He opened new springs, even from among the Chinese, and especially at Christmas time. One gift from a Chinese gentleman, a Christian, amounted to a hundred dollars."

The courage and tenacity of the German Associates of the Mission were beyond praise, for, as is well known, their financial difficulties did not diminish with the cessation of the war, but rather increased. Yet financial stringency has never driven them from their posts.*

Financially, the experience of the Mission as a whole was no less remarkable. Foundations were sorely tested, for the purchasing power of gold remitted to China fell steadily during the war. At its commencement, five gold dollars would purchase as much as eight *taels*, or Chinese ounces of silver (the currency in general use); after its close the same sum would barely purchase three. This meant that the money sent from home was reduced by more than half before it could reach the workers on the field. It was a crisis as serious as it was unforeseen and, as far as human resources were concerned, unprovided for. And what happened? Why, just the very thing that met the situation! The income of the Mission at home rose as the exchange in China fell. Without appeal for funds, but solely in answer to prayer, more and more came in from faithful and beloved donors,

---

* From *By Love Compelled*, by Mr. Marshall Broomhall, pp. 63-66. The diagram on the following page is from *Our Seal*, by the same author.

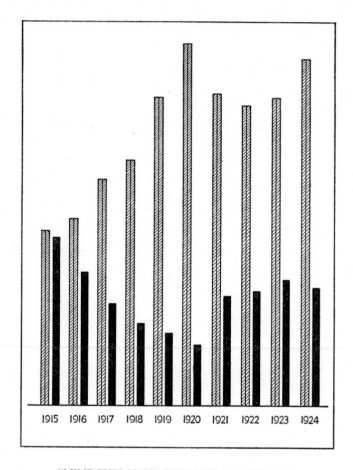

"MINE EYES HAVE SEEN THY SALVATION."

The black column represents the number of *taels* or Chinese ounces of silver
for which about $5000 exchanged during the ten years 1915-1924 inclusive.
The shaded column represents the Mission's approximate income in U. S.
dollars during the same period. It will be seen that as the black column
fell the shaded column rose, so that in 1920 when the exchange was most
adverse the income was at its highest.

"*Whoso is wise, and will observe these things, even they shall understand
the lovingkindness of the Lord.*"

most of whom knew nothing of the special need, so that sufficient silver could be obtained in China to carry on all through those war years, without debt or too serious difficulty.

The accompanying diagram will make plain the wonder that God wrought. The black column falling year by year was natural enough, but that rising column—who can account for it, in the general financial crisis? It was God's doing. With Him there are no emergencies. He knew what was needed. And He is ever faithful to His promises. To Him be the glory!

CHAPTER

XXIX

"LACKED YE ANYTHING?"

WHEN I sent you forth without purse and scrip . . .
lacked ye any thing? And they said, Nothing."

Every need had been supplied, every want met, because
He who sent them was with them. And so it is still, as the
experience of the China Inland Mission abundantly proves.
Facts are better than arguments. The appeal to the ledger is
conclusive. Let the records of the Mission bear their testimony in this connection, before we pass on to less material
interests.

When Mr. and Mrs. Frost left their home in Attica and
came to Toronto for the work of the Mission, what had they
to depend upon? They had plenty of needs, present and
prospective, but literally no source of supply, save the One
who had sent them and was with them. From then till now
fifty years have gone by, time enough to prove whether the
Word of God can be taken as true and reliable in our day.
For His promises were all the guarantee they had, and there
was a great work to be done.

Hundreds of missionaries sent to China and cared for through the years with their families; tens of thousands won to Christ by their labors; full equipment provided, at home and on the field, for every branch of service; and no debt incurred or overdraft at the bank—can these things be, without appeals for money, save in prayer to God alone? Let the facts speak.

On the next page appears the testimony of the ledger for the last fifty years, showing the receipts from the very beginning of the work in North America. And let it be remembered that every one of the countless gifts here represented has been voluntary, prompted by God in answer to prayer, and rewarded in blessing on the giver, according to His faithful undertaking.*

And in addition to all the donations which provide the yearly income, there have been gifts more costly still—love, friendship, fellowship in faith and prayer, comradeship in service, consecration of children, of substance other than money, of life itself—how precious it all has been!

THE TESTIMONY OF THE YEARS

". . . I will remember the years of the right hand of the most high"—Psalm 77:10.

"Many, O Lord my God, are thy wonderful works which thou hast done, and thy thoughts which are to usward: . . . if I would declare and speak of them, they are more than can be numbered"—Psalm 40:5.

---

* Each gift is acknowledged by a numbered receipt, and prayer for donors and their family and business interests is regularly and frequently offered at all the Mission centers. Every gift can be traced to the Mission exchequer, by number and amount, through the list published monthly in *China's Millions*, which also presents the annual, audited accounts. Names of donors are not published.

INCOME RECEIVED IN NORTH AMERICA

From 1888 to 1938

	Dollars
January to December 1888	3,389.55
,, ,, ,, 1889	6,841.57
,, ,, ,, 1890	16,398.72
,, ,, ,, 1891	17,014.85
,, ,, ,, 1892	21,297.78
,, ,, ,, 1893	20,823.66
,, ,, ,, 1894	27,514.25
,, ,, ,, 1895	33,320.41
,, ,, ,, 1896	31,878.33
,, ,, ,, 1897	35,912.52
,, ,, ,, 1898	35,097.45
,, ,, ,, 1899	45,814.81
,, ,, ,, 1900	40,693.70
,, ,, ,, 1901	49,798.51
,, ,, ,, 1902	61,437.14
,, ,, ,, 1903	38,699.45
,, ,, ,, 1904	46,579.02
,, ,, ,, 1905	51,786.22
,, ,, ,, 1906	65,488.19
,, ,, ,, 1907	73,451.88
,, ,, ,, 1908	50,985.00
,, ,, ,, 1909	67,508.78
,, ,, ,, 1910	62,050.51
,, ,, ,, 1911	71,448.54
,, ,, ,, 1912	73,842.52
,, ,, ,, 1913	81,619.00
,, ,, ,, 1914	73,410.78
,, ,, ,, 1915	88,170.25
,, ,, ,, 1916	146,121.66
,, ,, ,, 1917	174,793.02
,, ,, ,, 1918	151,518.41
,, ,, ,, 1919	151,878.11
,, ,, ,, 1920	173,219.59
,, ,, ,, 1921	172,059.01
,, ,, ,, 1922	163,443.83
,, ,, ,, 1923	173,734.54

				Dollars
January to December			1924	225,696.93
"	"	"	1925	227,719.32
"	"	"	1926	311,785.44
"	"	"	1927	272,695.54
"	"	"	1928	339,789.13
"	"	"	1929	502,017.90
"	"	"	1930	231,652.00
"	"	"	1931	253,682.33
"	"	"	1932	205,072.46
"	"	"	1933	169,927.29
"	"	"	1934	200,853.04
"	"	"	1935	248,155.54
"	"	"	1936	202,653.40
"	"	"	1937	227,316.24
"	"	July	1938 (through July 31)	119,973.48

Reference has already been made to the gift of a home in Norristown, the first center of the work in the United States. The generous co-operation of the giver continued and increased, though a few years later it proved desirable to move the Mission headquarters to a more central location. Those years had been rich in a new way, as regards the experience of Mr. and Mrs. Frost themselves—rich in trial, working patience and leading to fresh discoveries of the grace of God. Not that they had been without trial in the early days of the work in Canada; but this was different. It had been hard to part from the large and warm circle of the Mission which had grown up around them in Toronto. The Council there had been most reluctant to spare them for the States. It was only the conviction that the Lord was Himself leading in this direction that gave grace and courage for the separation. And then, coming to Philadelphia full of hope and expectation, it all turned out so differently! For there proved to be little interest in the Mission, beyond the immediate circle in Norristown. Daily, Mr. Frost and Miss Brayton went to the office in the city, only to meet with disappointment. Nobody seemed to know or care about the work so much on their hearts. Few letters and fewer callers or invitations to speak in meetings made the days heavy. Altogether, those first years (1901-02) would have been hard indeed to live through, but for the inner life of dependence upon God and for certain tokens of His unfailing care.

Chief among these was the increasing interest of the friend whose provision of a home had brought the Mission to the States. For that friendship was one of those God-given blessings which are for ever. A visit also from Mr. D. E. Hoste—who had succeeded Mr. Hudson Taylor as General Director of the Mission—brought strong encouragement, one of repeated visits by which he kept in touch with the work in North America. Then there was the warm co-operation of the Rev. D. M. Stearns of Germantown, a northern suburb of Philadelphia, who was at the flood-tide of his far-reaching ministry. Radiant with the love of Christ and overflowing with the precious things of His Word, Pastor Stearns had a heart big enough to take in the needs of all the world, and no small part of his sympathies went out to China and the Inland Mission. So the silent, seemingly buried years were enriched in a way which prepared for larger developments.

The Prayer Union of the Mission, started in Canada, was no little comfort to Mr. Frost at this time. Already it had over two thousand members, besides offshoots in similar Unions started by Mr. Taylor in England, Australia, and New

Zealand. More than ever, Mr. Frost was impressed with the vital connection between prayer and blessing in the work of God. *Men Who Prayed* was the title of a book he published, outcome of those silent years, followed later by his widely known and valued work, *Effective Praying.** One sign of spiritual growth for which he was most thankful was the increase in the number of prayer meetings held regularly by friends of the work, to intercede for China and the Mission. Already there were nine such gatherings in Canada and thirteen in the United States. In connection with one of these, Mr. Frost went to New York month by month, not only for the meeting at Mrs. Cortlandt de Peyster Field's, but for classes with her students at Hephzibah House on the fundamental doctrines of Scripture.

Slowly but surely the Mission was becoming known and its principles appreciated in the United States. The widespread deputation work carried on by Mrs. Grace Stott of Wenchow, and other workers on furlough, contributed largely to this result; and after his memorable visit to China in 1904, Mr. Frost had the joy of finding important openings for his ministry in the States, as previously in Canada. That his testimony to the faithfulness of God and the reliability of His Word was valued in Philadelphia is evident from the action of one of the Presbyteries of a great church in ordaining him to the ministry. Quite apart from his own seeking, he was unanimously accepted by this body, after a searching investigation as to his position in matters of faith and doctrine. The ordination took place in July, 1904, at a special

---

* These and Mr. Frost's later publications (see list at the end of this volume) may be obtained through the offices of the Mission, 237 West School Lane, Philadelphia, and 150 St. George Street, Toronto.

meeting held in the Witherspoon Building, Philadelphia. Dr. W. J. Erdman was living then in Germantown, one of whose sons was a member of the Presbytery.

All this, with the active sympathy of Pastor D. M. Stearns, was drawing Mr. Frost more and more to Germantown as the permanent headquarters of the Mission. The Church of the Atonement was attracting missionary-hearted people connected with Mr. Stearns' many Bible Classes, and Mr. Frost was a welcome speaker both there and in the adjacent home of Miss Charlesanna L. Huston. Although a comparatively new friend, Miss Huston had taken China and the Mission so much on her heart that she had rented a house near her own for Mr. Frost's young colleagues, Mr. and Mrs. George Howell, from Shanghai. Their zeal and brightness, as well as their experience in China, made them valued helpers, and soon the house was full of candidates and missionaries on furlough.

In the light of these providential indications, Mr. Frost, in consultation with Mr. H. C. Coleman, decided at length to fall in with the wishes of friends in Germantown, who urged the advantages of that suburb as a center for the Mission. In line with these suggestions, Mr. Coleman made a further generous contribution by purchasing the Norristown property from the Mission for his own residence. He was by this time Treasurer of the Council in Philadelphia, and rejoiced that the money thus donated should go direct to China. For prayer had been wonderfully answered with regard to Germantown. Within a few days of Mr. Frost's ordination, a home near Miss Huston's was purchased and given to the Mission, one of two semi-detached houses on

PRESENT HOME AND OFFICES OF THE MISSION IN PHILADELPHIA

PRESENT HOME AND OFFICES OF THE MISSION IN TORONTO

West School Lane, the second of which became a later gift. Here then Mr. and Mrs. Frost made their home early in 1905. The rented place was given up and the work consolidated.

"When I sent you forth without purse and scrip . . . lacked ye any thing?"

It was in the midst of these developments, when Mr. Frost's speaking engagements took him to Chicago, that he had the joy of making two of the most fruitful contacts of his life. How little could he have expected all that was to grow out of both the one and the other! The young Christian editor, who heard him speak at the Moody Church on *Prevailing Prayer*, was none other than Thomas E. Stevens, who received from that address impressions which led, in time, to his founding The Great Commission Prayer League, used of God in blessing to the ends of the earth. With that beloved man of God, Mr. Frost had much fellowship in later years.

And what shall be said of the contact with a recently converted society woman, also connected with the Moody Church? Through a faithful, searching address on *The Spiritual Condition of the Heathen*, Mrs. William Borden was so much impressed that she sought an introduction to the speaker. It was not of creeds or dogmas that Mr. Frost had spoken, but of the fact of universal sin and of its one and only remedy. The great "Without" written by God's own hand—"Without Christ . . . having no hope, and without God in the world"—was so brought home to the heart of this responsive hearer that she was ready to take an earnest part in the work he represented. In her beautiful home near the lake Mr. Frost became a welcome visitor, and there the friendship was begun with her younger son which proved one of the richest in all Mr. Frost's experience.

William Borden is known today as the young missionary who, dying in Cairo on his way to China, left a million dollars to the work of God, but who gave far more than this in the consecration of a life of splendid opportunity to the Master he loved and the good of those He came to save. While in his Sophomore year at Yale he founded a mission for the down-and-outs of New Haven—discharged prisoners, tramps, and hopeless drunkards for whom no man cared —which became a means of blessing to the University no less than to the hundreds redeemed for this life and the next. When asked what had impressed him most on his visit to America, a distinguished English Churchman said:

"The sight of that young millionaire on his knees, in the Yale Hope Mission, with his arm around the shoulders of a broken-down prodigal."

Three times over, Borden definitely expressed his desire to join the Mission before Mr. Frost could feel it right to regard him as a candidate for China. The first time was while he was a Sophomore at Yale.

But I felt that he was then too young to come to a positive conclusion as to the country in which he should serve, and I advised him to postpone considering the matter.

At the end of his university course he again consulted me about going to China. Once more I advised him to defer the decision and urged him to prepare himself further by taking the seminary course at Princeton.

Toward the end of his studies at Princeton, he once more offered himself for work in China. This time I was persuaded that God was indeed in the matter of his application. But to further test him, I asked whether he had considered offering himself to the

Board of his own Church rather than to us. He replied that he had; that he esteemed the Presbyterian Board, but that there were three reasons why he felt more drawn to the China Inland Mission— firstly, on account of its interdenominational character; secondly, because of its emphasis on evangelistic work; and thirdly, because it held the personal and premillennial coming of Christ. So at last we considered his application and accepted him for service in China.

Two years before this, however, Borden had been connected with the Mission as a member of its Philadelphia Council. This association had been a great joy to Mr. Frost, who valued his strong, sane point of view, freshness of thought, and enthusiasm of spirit. His hesitation about encouraging the young man's offers for China had not been on account of the sacrifice involved. How could it be a sacrifice to follow in the steps of the Lord Himself, in the full enjoyment of His companionship and love? Such a life was the highest of all privileges. This was the conviction Mr. Frost had expressed some years before, in lines written while Borden was still at Yale:

COMMISSIONED

Out from the realm of the glory-light
Into the far-away land of night;
Out of the bliss of worshipful song
Into the pain of hatred and wrong;
Out from the holy rapture above
Into the grief of rejected love;
Out from the life at the Father's side
Into the death of the crucified;
Out of high honor and into shame
The Master, willingly, gladly came:—

And now, since He may not suffer anew,
As the Father sent Him, so sendeth He you!

The early death of one so full of promise was a mystery that pressed sorely on the hearts of those who loved him.* To Mr. Frost came the sad privilege of using such funds as he had left to the Mission, specially for the care of its superannuated workers, but nothing could make up for the loss. Times of trial lay ahead, of which that great bereavement was a precursor—for the work in North America was to be tested by many changes at this period.

Only a few months after Borden's death in 1913, the Mission family in Toronto suffered a great loss. They were gathered in the dining room for a meal, and Mrs. Helmer entered as the bell rang. Returning from town just in time, she had hastened to lay off her wraps, and perhaps the stairs to her room had tried her. But she was bright and calm as usual as she took her place at the long table, bowed her head for the blessing—and in a moment was with the Lord. Anything more wonderful than the peace of that sudden passing could hardly be imagined, but the loss to her loved ones was irreparable. Mr. Helmer was so stricken that it was not long before he began to fail physically, though as helpful as ever in spirit. The Lord's providing care was very manifest as this situation developed, in the arrangements made some time previously in view of possible need. For the ideal helpers were there, at Mr. Helmer's side, to take over responsibility.

On a visit to Montreal in 1910, Mr. Frost had been entertained in the home of young married people, Mr. and Mrs. W. Y. King, who had long been interested in the Mission.

---

* For details of this event, in Cairo, see the biography, *Borden of Yale, '09,* by one of the present writers.

They had even visited China, for Miss Margaret King of Yangchow, so much used of God in work for young educated women, was their sister.* Mr. Frost, while fully alive to Mr. King's position and business prospects in Montreal, could not but feel that the work of God needed him, and that as a life-investment it offered far higher rewards. He coveted both his young hosts to strengthen the staff in Toronto, but how would they receive so unexpected and daring a suggestion?

However, Mr. Frost had seen some remarkable things that God had done in bringing about such changes, and so one evening when they were alone together he made the venture about which he had been much in prayer. He found it easier than he had expected to put the matter before them.

I saw Mr. King, as I was speaking, look meaningly at Mrs. King, and when I had finished my frank tale of profit and loss, and given my pressing invitation, was surprised to hear him say that if I had not asked them to join the work they would have asked me to allow them to do so.

So the Kings came to Toronto, gladly giving up their lovely home for just one room in the Mission House; leaving a large circle of relatives and friends, to become helpers to Mr. and Mrs. Helmer. While self-supporting and accustomed to leadership, so beautifully did they fit in, by the grace of God, that the relationship was a perfect one, and they were there three years later when Mr. Helmer's sad bereavement made their presence doubly valued.

More than this: an even greater need arose in Germantown a little later. Mr. F. H. Neale, the able and devoted

---

* For the story of her outstanding life and service, see *Margaret King's Vision*, also by one of the writers.

Secretary who relieved Mr. Frost of a world of detail in a way that made him everywhere a blessing, was stricken with serious illness. When he had to seek a more favorable climate and quieter surroundings, the Philadelphia center was so understaffed that Mr. Frost had to fall back upon Mr. and Mrs. King to take charge of both Home and offices. Set free from Toronto by the coming of Mr. and Mrs. F. F. Helmer to live with their father, this arrangement was made possible.

But the Mission was again sorely bereaved by the death of Mr. Helmer, Senior, in 1916. It had been hoped that his son might succeed him, but Mrs. F. F. Helmer's indifferent health necessitated their moving to a home of their own, while continuing to give invaluable help in other ways— Mr. Helmer as editor of *China's Millions*. The gap left in the Mission House was hard to fill, and in the end Mr. and Mrs. King had to be spared to return to Toronto, where they were already known and loved.

Meanwhile, Mr. Frost was finding in Mr. and Mrs. Roger B. Whittlesey of Cleveland, home on furlough from West China, colleagues of no little promise. All was working well, for the Whittleseys were indeed God's good gift to the Philadelphia center, when a telegram from Toronto brought tidings of the sudden death of the beloved Secretary, Mr. W. Y. King.

No words can tell the shock (wrote Mr. Frost) that his passing was to me. For years my friend had eased me of every possible burden, being the strong man physically. . . . Now he was gone and I left. How great were the mysteries of God!

But there was One who had foreseen this unexpected sorrow. Was it not His hand that had brought two young but experienced missionaries back from the Kan River, the Rev. E. A. and Mrs. Brownlee, in time to give needed help in Toronto? That was in 1917, and the long years that have passed since then have only proved how good was God's choice, both for them and the position they still so devotedly fill. Mrs. King, in her widowhood, found consolation in following the call of God to direct missionary work in China, in which she continues to be blessed and made a blessing.

In sorrow and bereavement, "lacked ye anything?" And, even through falling tears, the answer is, "Nothing, Lord."

During the years of the Great War, Mr. Frost had been absent from Germantown. Leaving the Home in charge of Mr. and Mrs. King, he had moved to the quiet town of Summit, not far from New York, partly on account of his family—seven lovely young people—and partly for greater freedom for the general oversight of the work. There he passed through most of the sorrows touched upon above, and there he had the encouragement of visits from Mr. D. E. Hoste, Mr. Walter Sloan, and other leaders in the work, with whom time was given to prayer and consideration of the Mission's great task at home and abroad. One result was the opening, in 1916, of a much-needed center in Vancouver, where the Lord had been using Mr. and Mrs. Charles Thomson—beloved workers on furlough from Chekiang— to awaken interest which was to prove singularly fruitful and lasting. There, through a remarkable series of providences, they were enabled to open the Home for outgoing and returning missionaries so much needed at the gates of the West, fulfilling in a most helpful way purposes which Mr. Frost had long cherished.

And there were other plans, much prayed over, which came to fruition at Summit—notably the revival of the greatly missed Niagara Conference of former years. No other gathering of the kind had taken its place, and Mr. Frost had long felt that the Mission had a contribution to make in this connection to the spiritual life of both Canada and the States. Experience had taught him that many, even devoted Christians, were cast down and defeated through looking within, or at circumstances, instead of to the Lord Himself.

Back in Germantown days a friend had called upon him who was utterly discouraged and depressed.

He was a noble man and doing a noble work, but was failing to receive the comfort and joy of God's salvation, and wondered if light would ever again dawn on his darkened soul. I asked him whether there was any known sin permitted in his life, and found that there was not. I inquired as to his physical health; but there was nothing along that line to account for the depression that weighed him down. I then asked what he desired and hoped for. His one longing, he told me, was for a sense of God's presence, and the joy that flows from it. But this he knew not how to obtain. He had tried everything, and everything had failed.

Happily for him and for me, I had gone through the whole sorry business and had found the way out. So I handed him my Bible, asking him to read the fifth verse of the thirty-fourth Psalm. This he did aloud, pausing over the words: "They looked unto him, and were lightened." I asked him to stop there, and then said:

"What happened?"

He answered, "They were lightened, as I long to be."

"What did they do to be lightened?"

"They looked," he said. And I remarked that there is nothing easier that God can give a man to do.

"How did they look—down or up, inside or outside, at themselves or at someone else?"

He glanced at the passage again, and replied, "They looked at God."

"Yes," he was saying to himself as he read it over and over, "they did not look at themselves, their insides or their feelings, they only looked at God."

He was not an emotional man, but his voice trembled as he questioned, "Is it possible that that is all?"

"Yes," I assured him, "that is all. And the reason is that *it is enough.*"

My friend went out into the dark that night, seeing a great light. And from that day to this he has walked with raised head and eyes uplifted—a joy to his victorious Christ, and a blessing to everyone he meets. Oh, it is a simple lesson, but its results are infinite! And it is for all who will receive it.

That a cure of souls had been entrusted to Mr. Frost was very evident from the many who came to him for just such help, and from the consequent burden on his heart about reviving the Niagara Conference. The old pavilion and conference grounds were still there, on the shores of the lake, and when he at last broached the matter to the Council and other friends, the response was more than encouraging:

All I had to do, after that, was to stand on one side and see our helpers at Germantown and Toronto put into effect the necessary arrangements. This they did with such good success that when in June, 1915, two to three hundred friends gathered for the meetings, one had the impression that not a detail had been forgotten.

It was deeply moving to some of us to be back at the Queen's Royal Hotel, in the old pavilion, under the old spreading trees, and down by the river and lake. We felt that we had returned to a spot made holy by God's presence and power, where He might once more reveal to us the divine glory. And we were not disappointed.

For six consecutive summers the Conference continued, with great and increasing blessing. Then the place with its precious associations was no longer available, and it did not seem possible to recommence elsewhere. But work had been done which was spreading out in ever-widening circles of blessing. Echoes of those days come back to us from far-away places, where lives are being lived out that were filled and transformed then, such as the recent testimony of a guided pen in that wonderful story, *Goforth of China.*

One day I went to the meeting rather reluctantly (Mrs. Goforth wrote at the time), for it was so lovely under the trees by the lake. The speaker was a stranger to me but from the first his message gripped me. Victory over sin! Why, that was what I had fought for, hungered for all my life! Was it really possible?

The day after returning home, I picked up a booklet which I had not read, entitled *The Life that Wins.* This I took to my son's bedside, telling him it was the personal testimony of the speaker (Dr. Charles G. Trumbull) whom God had used at the Conference to bring blessing into my life. I then read aloud as far as the words: *"At last I realized that Jesus Christ was actually and literally within me."* There I stopped, amazed. The sun seemed to come from under a cloud and flood my whole being.

How blind I had been! I saw, at last, the secret of victory— simply Jesus Christ Himself, His own life lived out in the believer. But the thought of victory was for the moment lost sight of, in the inexpressible joy of realizing Christ's indwelling presence. Like a tired wanderer reaching home at last, I just rested in Him, rested in His love, Himself. And oh, the peace and joy that came flooding my whole being! A restfulness and quietness of spirit, that I never had thought could be mine, took possession of me so naturally! A new life, literally, had begun for me, or rather, in me—the life that is Christ, no longer I.

The Exchanged Life, and therefore the Victorious Life— as the beloved writer was to prove! So the need was met in this and other hungry hearts through the Niagara Conferences of the Mission, and Mr. Frost's long desire turned to

OFFICERS OF THE MISSION AND MEMBERS OF THE UNITED NORTH AMERICAN COUNCIL, AT NIAGARA-ON-THE-LAKE, JUNE 1916.
Seated (left to right), H. C. Coleman, Rev. D. M. Stearns, Dr. W. J. Erdman, J. S. Helmer, Rev. H. W. Frost, D. E. Hoste, W. B. Sloan, Principal O'Meara, Principal McNicol.

Standing (left to right), J. O. Anderson, Rev. F. A. Steven, Prof. C. R. Erdman, F. F. Helmer, Rev. R. Wallace, W. Y. King, Dr. D. McTavish, J. J. Gartshore. T. Edward Ross, Rev. A Imrie.

thanksgiving, in the spirit in which he had previously
written:

PRAISING

Do you hear the angels singing
Up on high?
Do you hear their voices ringing
Through the sky?
Oh, the fulness of their song
As their praises they prolong,
Yea, the voices of that choir
Never tire!

Do you hear the saints all praising
Round the throne?
Do you hear them hymns upraising,
One by one?
Praising is their glad delight,
So they rest not day nor night,
Crying, "Holy!" o'er and o'er,
Evermore!

Do you hear the saints adoring
Here below?
Do you hear them praise outpouring
Midst earth's woe?
Hark, they sing their sweet refrain
Through their joy and through their pain,
Praising, ever, in their love,
God above!

Oh, then, add your note, rejoicing,
To the praise,
Thanks to God for all things voicing,
Through the days;
Till the earthly singing's done,
Till the heavenly is begun,
Till the anthem, round Christ's feet,
Swells complete!

CHAPTER

XXX

EVACUATION
AND ADVANCE

HOW often "man's extremity" proves to be "God's opportunity"! It was so in the experience of two much-tried members of the Mission at this time (1917) and in the decade that followed with regard to the whole work. Crises had come before in the life of A. R. Saunders, the first Canadian to join the Mission; indeed, it was the terrible summer of 1900 that had induced the eye condition which faced him now with total blindness. It did not make it easier that Mrs. Saunders, who had suffered with him through the Boxer troubles, was very hard of hearing from the same cause. Yet two more cheery, useful people it would have been hard to find. "They looked unto Him and were radiant"; so much so that their lives deeply impressed the student body in the Bible Institute of Los Angeles, numbering hundreds of young people, when they came to that city to seek professional aid.

Blind and Blessed is the title of the booklet which tells of the loss of the last hope that sight might be recovered, and of the wonderful outcome for others as well as themselves. It had been hard to leave China with the prospect of being laid aside from their life work, for they were in the midst of great opportunities. But much earnest, believing prayer was being made that God might be honored and His will done, at whatever cost, and this it was that carried them through "not somehow, but triumphantly." The whole experience was so precious, and so prophetic of what was coming on the larger scale, that we do not hesitate to recall it somewhat in detail, in Mr. Saunders' words:

On arrival in the Unites States, the advice of one of the most eminent specialists was sought, who, after five examinations declared that there was no hope of recovering my sight. During the long, lonely wait in the consulting room, my wife, far from being cast down, was wonderfully upheld by a song the Lord gave her, the words of which kept coming to her heart:

> "Rejoice, for He is with us always,
>   Lo! even to the end.
>   Look up, take courage and go forward;
>   All needed grace He'll send."

We had reached a parting of the ways. When we returned to our upper room in the Bible Institute and quietly faced the situation, three alternatives lay before us: One was to retire from active service, another to work for the Mission in North America, and the third to face seemingly insurmountable difficulties and return to China. . . . How very thankful we may be that in such crises God does not leave us to our own devices, but gives promised wisdom and the assurance that we shall hear a voice behind us saying: "This is the way, walk ye in it."

Together we knelt down as so often before, and in the simplest possible way told the Lord that once again we made absolute surrender for any service He might appoint—and when we rose from our knees, it was with the clear conviction that we were to return to China in the following October. The parting of the ways was passed. For us there was but one way, and Satan, who for a whole year had done his utmost to turn us aside, was defeated. The path before us was by no means easy, but the Lord had made the choice, so it was for Him to deal with each obstacle as we came to it. And He truly did.

The story of the months that followed reads more like romance than reality. "I thank God from my heart," wrote Dr. R. A. Torrey, "that your steps were ever directed to the Bible Institute of Los Angeles," of which he was then Dean. "Eternity alone will show what great things have been done by your presence among us."

Immediately after the fresh surrender had been made (Mr. Saunders continued), and blindness accepted as permitted by God, we began to experience in a new way the sufficiency of His never-failing grace. Doors of opportunity seemed to open to us of their own accord. Not only among the students of the Bible Institute, but in the churches of Los Angeles and the neighborhood we found abundant openings for our ministry. Wide and effectual doors constantly swung open, and seldom had we known days so full of happy service. Not with stories of missionary romance did we seek to arouse interest, but with the sterner facts of missionary suffering, blended with incidents showing the power of the Gospel and triumphs of God's grace. Such testimony was blessed in a remarkable way.

Permission was given to the students to visit us up on the tenth floor, whenever their classes would allow, and before long numbers were coming to inquire about work in China. Our room became a veritable center of the Mission. At that time we had none nearer than Philadelphia, three thousand miles away, though Dr. Torrey and Dr. F. W. Farr, who had moved to Los Angeles, were both members of the North American Council. So it was decided that all candidates for the Mission should be dealt with by us, in conjunction with these valued friends—and we were busier than ever, but supremely happy. Out of the considerable number who desired to serve the Lord in China, twelve young people were prayerfully chosen; and when our action was approved by the executive in Philadelphia, they were admitted by Dr. Frost to the fellowship of the Mission.

But it was war time.   America had joined the conflict; and even if funds had not been lacking, difficulties as to passports and transportation blocked the way, "difficulties calling for careful handling," as Mr. Saunders put it, "and unwavering faith in God."

The young people knew that we planned to leave for China in October, and if they were to sail with us three formidable obstacles must be removed. . . . But "is anything too hard for the Lord?" He who had planned their paths and ours, again proved to be El Shaddai, *The God that is Enough*—Hallelujah!

While we prayed in Los Angeles, the Lord laid it upon the heart of a lady in Philadelphia to give all the money needed for the passages of the accepted candidates.   Further, the United States Government granted passports to the young men, though the streets of every city were placarded with posters showing the familiar figure in stars and stripes pointing to the passer-by and saying, "Uncle Sam wants you!"   Accommodation on steamers seemed unobtainable, but fourteen berths were offered on one and the same boat—and early in November we all landed in Shanghai.   Truly this was the Lord's doing and marvelous in our eyes!   Why do we not trust him more?

The scene in the Mission compound on the arrival of Mr. and Mrs. Saunders, "blind and blessed," with twelve new workers was indeed memorable—the largest party from North America since Mr. Hudson Taylor had brought out the original group, thirty years previously.   At the steps of the Mission House they formed a circle with those who had come to meet them, and sang from overflowing hearts:

> "How good is the God we adore,
>   Our faithful, unchangeable Friend,
> Whose love is as great as His power,
>   And knows neither measure nor end!
> 'Tis Jesus, the first and the last,
>   Whose Spirit shall guide us safe home;
> We'll praise Him for all that is past,
>   And trust Him for all that's to come."

More than this, the best was yet to be. For in wonderful ways the Lord led each of that little band and gave to Mr. and Mrs. Saunders the most fruitful years of all their long and varied service. And the whole experience was but a foretaste of deliverances that lay ahead for the entire Mission, soon to be called upon to face the most serious emergency that had yet come upon it in China.

For that great country, brought through Revolution and many costly changes, was falling upon evil days. Disappointed and disillusioned in the Peace Conference (Versailles) at the close of the Great War, China had come to realize that little help was to be expected from most of her European Allies in resisting the steadily pressed and alarming encroachments of a neighbor near at hand. Instead of returning the Kiaochow area, taken from Germany, to its rightful owners, that important territory and harbor had been handed over to Japan, which resulted in a ferment of indignation throughout China. Russia seemed to be the only hope—the one Power in Europe that responded to her appeals for help in training a modern army. The result was that Canton was soon bristling with Russian officers, while Borodin and his associates were flooding the country with Bolshevic propaganda. And, as opposing these forces, there was but a decadent Government in Peking, and the growing power of war lords who rule for personal advantage rather than the peoples' good.

"All would confess," wrote a reliable historian, "that up to the present the Republic has been a failure, and that politically China is in a state of disintegration. At the same time, there are many movements in progress indicating that out of the old China a new one is slowly being evolved."*

---

* F. L. Hawks Pott, D.D., in *A Sketch of Chinese History*, p. 226.

The suffering from banditry was terrible. Fierce hostilities had broken out between the North and South, and the worst of it was that large bodies of unpaid soldiers, deserting from the regular forces, went off on their own account, fully armed, to harry the defenseless population! In Szechwan alone, Bishop Cassels said that there were a hundred and twenty thousand well-armed brigands, looting and pillaging at will. "Trade was ruined and agriculture neglected, the inns were destroyed, the cities sacked and roads deserted." Yet, in the midst of it all, there was a widely open door for Christian testimony.

It will be long ere I forget the whiz of those dreadful shells (came from a city in that province, bombarded for thirty-eight hours). Refugees crowded in, their faces pinched with terror; our compound was filled with women and children. Sleep seems to go at such times. But I must be brave; for yesterday, after my meeting, the women said:

"Only let us come to you, and we can bear it."

Dear trustful souls! They little know what lies, sometimes, behind a smiling face. . . . Many outsiders are now interested in the Gospel, and some have burned their idols.

But with the increase of Russian influence in China, changes came which put the missionary in a very different light. Two great Christian assemblies, held in 1922, seem to have been regarded as a challenge by Communist and antichristian forces, for they were immediately followed by one of the bitterest attacks upon Christianity that the world has ever known. "It is hardly possible to exaggerate the fury and ability with which the assault was pressed. The Boxer persecutions had been largely the work of mobs, but this campaign was the work of intelligentsia."*

---

* Mr. Marshall Broomhall, in *By Love Compelled*, p. 89.

Anti-christian literature simply poured from the press. Mass meetings and great demonstrations were organized everywhere. Behind this subtle propaganda were many able scholars. Their aim was to poison the minds of the people against Christianity. Truth was so mixed with error that even sincere believers were led astray. Christianity was confused with politics, evangelism with imperialism. The history of Spain and her alliance with the Vatican, the story of the Inquisition and the Papal Bull which gave Spain and Portugal power over the East and West, and many other historical facts were so twisted and manipulated that history was made to witness against the truth. The real message of Christ was exchanged for a fable, with a semblance of justification.

A careful analysis of ninety-seven pamphlets revealed that thirty-six were directed against Christian education, thirty-four against Christianity generally, eleven against Christians, five against the Church, five against missionaries, two against Christian literature, three against Christ Jesus Himself, and one against the Bible. Truth was so distorted, or so mixed with untruth, that to deceive the people was simple, but to enlighten them by no means easy. . . .

Meanwhile, the sufferings of the people could not be described. They were harried and harassed by extortionate soldiers and lawless brigands. Cities were sacked by the score. Thousands of Chinese were held for ransom, and the missionary body did not escape. During 1922 more than a dozen missionaries were taken captive, three were shot, and many robbed. In 1923 China was without a President for four months, and almost without a Government. Foreign ships were fired on and several were looted by pirates. . . . Pages could be filled with the lawless deeds of troops and bandits alike.*

It is a relief to turn from the dark side of the picture to some of the signs that were not lacking of the Lord's own presence and blessing. James Lawson was gone from Yüan-chow, in the Kan River district, where he had so long and faithfully labored, but a church numbering thousands re-

_____
* Ibid., pp. 90, 91.

mained to carry on the testimony.† With forty outstations amid a population of a million, Robert Porteous and his fellow-workers were overwhelmed with opportunities for making known the Gospel. To their help had come one of the preaching bands born of Dr. Frank Keller's faith and vision in the neighboring province of Hunan. Thirteen men in each band with a trained leader, giving part of the day to systematic Bible study and the rest to carefully planned evangelism, were ready to come on invitation to any given district, and remain as long as might be necessary to bring the glad tidings of salvation to every home, in every city, town, and village, through personal work. Band Number Six had been greatly used of God in the Yüanchow district, and by Dr. Keller's generous arrangement, its assistant leader, young Mr. Eo-yang, had remained as Pastor of the growing church. At the Bible Conference for men (1924) he was in his element. Two hundred and seventy delegates, many of them his own children in the faith, overflowed the Mission compound. Some had relatives in or near the city, with whom they stayed, but thirty-two tables, each accommodating eight hungry guests, taxed the commissariat department. And they were hungry for spiritual things as well—the Bible teaching and all the helpful intercourse of that full week. Truly there is nothing in the social or religious life of non-Christian lands to compare with the blessed fellowship of those who are one in Christ.

---

† This beloved pioneer died in American in January 1915. When tidings reached Yüanchow, "nothing would satisfy the Christians but that memorial services should be held for three days. On the fourth day, the whole church, in mourning, marched in procession through the city. It was touching to see old ladies of eighty following. . . . Many of the officials and gentry spoke in praise of the useful and upright life Mr. Lawson had lived among them."

How our hearts rejoiced (wrote Mr. Porteous) to hear the early bursts of praise from various companies "gathered together, praying"! This was followed by two hours of Bible study. Addresses from our local leaders and the Band workers filled the afternoon, with open-air meetings in various parts of the city. The evenings were given to lantern lectures on the life and parables of our Lord, the stories of Joseph and others.

Before the conference closed, we had the joy of baptizing seventy-two men . . . who with more than two hundred church members sat down together at the Lord's Table. . . . How I wish you could have been with us as one after another, trophies of the Band work, came forward to make public confession of Christ!

"How did you come to know about trusting the Lord Jesus for salvation?" was asked of not a few.

"*They* came to our place," was the frequent reply, indicating the Band, "and we heard them preach."

Can you imagine how our hearts overflowed with thankfulness to God for guiding Dr. Keller to this effective method of soul-winning? Would that every part of China had such Bands at work in all weathers, to seek and save the lost.

Very different, but none the less encouraging, were the labors of Dr. Edward Fish, who had joined James Adam of Kweichow in reaping the harvest among the tribespeople of southwest China. Backed by the prayers of his Canadian constituency, this young doctor faced the claims of a province with ten or more million people, among whom he was the only physician. In intervals of study—for he had at least one language to learn—he made medical journeys with his senior missionary, who rejoiced in being able to help his dearly loved Miao in any and every way possible. Happily, it did not need elaborate preparation to vaccinate babies, extract aching teeth, and care for a large part of the prevailing ailments—though even the mountain people suffer also from deeply rooted troubles, including tuberculosis and leprosy. And how grateful they were for the doctor's willing, if limited, service! Of the first of these journeys Mr. Adam wrote:

We traveled over four hundred and forty miles, visiting twelve regular outstations and many Christian villages. Our hearts were greatly encouraged in seeing the way the churches are being built up and the believers walking in the comfort of the Holy Spirit. Dr. Fish accompanied me . . . and saw over one thousand two hundred patients—all sorts and conditions, coming from near and far.

The doctor was very loving and patient with the most dirty and rude of the wild hill men. Judging from the number of oxen killed in order to treat the doctor, and the mutton, pork, chickens, eggs, honey, and oatmeal presented to him, the gratitude of those benefited was certainly remarkable.

At one place, as Dr. Fish wrote himself, he received over five hundred eggs, by actual count.

At another, visited the same week, as soon as I had made necessary preparations I began to examine the patients who were waiting our arrival. There was one continuous stream all day long. Our first mail reached us here, and I sat down on a bench to read my letters, but was soon completely surrounded by those in need of help. One man handed me a fowl, another a basket of eggs. This proved too much, and I arose and took my place where for three days I sought to minister to their needs.

On this journey Mr. Adam baptized a hundred and ninety-four believers, belonging to five different tribes, and large numbers met together for most blessed Communion Services.

It is like a bit of glory (he wrote) to hear a thousand or more saved Miao singing,

> "O joyous hour when God to me
> A vision gave of Calvary:
> My bonds were loosed, my soul unbound—
> I stand upon redemption ground."

"There is a fountain filled with blood" is also a favorite at our big meetings. The chorus, "I do believe, I will believe" goes splendidly. Think of it! These dear believers were once unrighteous, fornicators, demon-worshipers, adulterers, unclean, drunkards, and revilers. "Such were some of you: but ye are washed, but ye are sanctified, but ye are justified in the name of the Lord Jesus, and by the Spirit of our God." Oh, why do we ever limit the saving power of our God? All these Miao, saved and washed, to the glory of His great Name!

Well might his heart rejoice, for God had made him a father, spiritually, to thousands of these mountain people. Their love for him was something that never could be told—or their grief, when a year or two after Dr. Fish had joined him, this true Apostle of the Miao was taken from them in one fateful moment, by a stroke of lightning. But the movement he had inaugurated, which had already spread to the adjacent province of Yunnan, went right on—Dr. Fish, Mr. and Mrs. Isaac Page, and a group of devoted German sisters from Friedenshort taking up the work that had fallen from his hands, and many others carrying it farther and farther afield, even to the far frontiers of Burma and Tibet.

But to return to the troubled conditions that prevailed in most parts of China. Great was the opportunity, in spite of Communist propaganda, that came to doctors and nurses in mission hospitals, as they ministered to the suffering, whether wounded soldiers, civilians, or bandits. But it was overwhelming too, as Dr. Jessie McDonald could tell. Just returned from furlough, she found the staff at Kaifeng, capital of Honan, unavoidably depleted. Dr. D. M. Gibson was taking needed furlough, Dr. Whitfield Guinness had been called to meet an urgent need elsewhere, and their young colleague, Dr. R. N. Walker, was engrossed in language study.   How thankful the young Canadian must have been for the prayer group behind her in Toronto, when she had to take the lead in caring for a sudden influx of two hundred wounded soldiers!   Happily Dr. Jessie was a surgeon of unusual ability and courage, for the sufferers were all serious cases, passed on by overcrowded military hospitals.

On Wednesday night they began to pour in (she wrote in May, 1922).   Forty-five arrived, in almost half an hour.   Imagine the bustle!   They came on beds, stretchers, barrows, and on foot. . . . Several of our old students came in to help, but Dr. Walker and I were the only doctors, and I saw the men as if they had been women. There was nothing else to be done.   We got them classified, dressed, and put to bed, then operated till late in the night, removing bullets and setting fractures.   And we have been at it ever since.   They streamed in until we had nearly two hundred.   The chapel floor was crowded.

Now we are left with over a hundred on hand, all more or less serious cases.   Several have died and more are dying—awful conditions, as you may imagine!   Some of the faces haunt one.   Their only hope is in us.   There is so little time to tell them of Him in whom to put their trust.   But as I write the Gospel service is going on, and they are singing: "I do believe, I will believe, that Jesus died for me."*

This is May 17.   The work continues; operations every day.   How we do praise God for your help by prayer!

But while missionaries were availing themselves of the unusual opportunities of this period, the tide of antiforeign feeling fostered by Russian propaganda was reaching the danger point.

Early in the summer of 1925 serious riots broke out in Shanghai. The students sought to rush the police station and capture the arms stored there.   In their extremity, the police fired on the students,

---

* In the wards of that hospital, in one season (1918) a hundred and sixty men recorded their names as new believers.

killing twenty-one of them and wounding sixty-five others. This was like a match to gunpowder. The whole country blazed with indignation and rioting spread to other centers.*

Communist influences did not fail to make the most of the situation, and other deplorable incidents followed, making the position of missionaries throughout the interior perilous in the extreme. Then came the time when the modern-equipped army with its Russian instructors was ready to advance from Canton against the Northern war-lords, many of whom were playing into the hands of Japan. Nothing seriously impeded their progress until Nanking was reached. But there Chiang Kai-shek found himself unable to restrain the Communistic elements the southerners themselves had invoked. Terrible tragedy followed, as his army looted and massacred throughout the city, and but for the intervention of foreign gunboats the whole European community in Nanking would have perished. Their eyes opened to the real nature and objectives of Communism, Chiang Kai-shek and his party lost no time in sending their Russian advisers, including Borodin and his staff, back to their own country, and ridding themselves as far as possible of Chinese Communists also. But the dread influences that remained were not so easily dealt with, and the concern of foreign powers was serious in consequence.

For this was the situation that called forth the order for evacuation that came like a thunderbolt upon missionaries throughout the interior. British and American authorities required the withdrawal of their nationals to the coast, as war with China seemed an imminent possibility. This may

---

* Broomhall, *Love Compelled*, p. 94.

have been the only course open to them, but the difficulty and danger involved were incalculable.

Thus we come to the ever-memorable year, 1927, when six hundred and fifty members of the China Inland Mission had to leave their inland stations and travel to the coast. Many had children with them, too young to be at the Chefoo schools, and the country was seething with unrest, civil war, and banditry. At such a time, the wonder was not that some precious lives were sacrificed, but that the large majority were brought through in safety.

From Mr. Adam's station of Anshun, three American workers with two children set out for the railway, in the neighboring province of Yunnan. Crossing the mountainous borderland between, they were attacked by a band of armed robbers who soon overpowered their escort. Terrible were the experiences that followed. One of the bandits fired at Mrs. Morris Slichter, who was holding little Ruth in her arms. The bullet wounded both mother and child. At the same time, another attacked Mr. Slichter from behind, the dagger piercing his heart. He fell without a word, and little Ruth died a few minutes later. The anguish of bereavement under such circumstances was terrible enough, but there was also the agonizing suspense that followed. For it was not until three weeks later that Mrs. Slichter, Miss Mary Craig, and little John obtained their freedom.

No less serious was the loss the Mission sustained in the death of Dr. George King, on the way down from the far northwest. Physician in charge of the Borden Memorial Hospital and the only medical man in the whole province of Kansu, a thousand miles across, Dr. King was most reluctant to leave for the coast. But a party of thirty-seven missionaries and twelve children had to travel by raft down the Yellow River, including his own family. Young and strong, a good swimmer, and proficient in Chinese, Dr. King's help was invaluable, especially when the rafts were stranded on sand banks, after an exciting escape from bandits. Twelve hours in the water, doing heroic work, told upon his strength, and when all but one of the rafts had been floated, he was caught in a treacherous current with many eddies.

"Can you make it?" called an anxious watcher.

"I don't know," came the answer, before the brave swimmer disappeared, not to be seen again.

Just as heartbreaking was the loss of the beloved chief of the Kaifeng hospital, Dr. Whitfield Guinness, who was desperately ill with typhus fever when it became necessary to evacuate for Peking. The only accommodation on the last train available was a box car shared with twelve other foreigners. It was no small comfort that Dr. Jessie McDonald as well as Dr. Gibson and more than one trained nurse were among the number. But the noise and jolting of the crowded car, endured for two days and nights did not help matters, and all that love could do was unavailing.*

Such friends of China are hard indeed to replace.

> "We can but wait;
> Life's mystery deepens with the rolling years,
> Life's history, hardly read through blinding tears,
>   Seems dark and vain;
> But a kind Father's hand controls our way,
> And when that hand has wiped the tears away,
>   All shall be plain."

---

* For the full story of this beautiful life, see *Guinness of Honan*, by his sister, Mrs. Howard Taylor.

Many were the parties, harassed and weary, traveling thus to the coast. Some of the refugees were sick in body, some newly bereaved, and all were homeless—wondering where they were to find shelter. And was the Father's heart unmindful of His suffering children? Had He, who alone could foresee the emergency, failed to provide? If ever there was a time, we say it reverently, when the faithfulness of God was put to the test, it was surely in those days in Shanghai.

And what was the actual outcome? Not once did a party arrive before there was a roof to cover them and a welcome waiting. Not one account for expenses was presented that could not immediately be settled. Many thousand of dollars were needed to cover the unavoidable outlay of those months —the rent of fourteen emergency homes, and all the losses that had to be made good. But every need was met, without delay and without incurring debt. Yes, our God is a real Father. He cannot fail; He cannot forget His trusting children.

As to the financial side, long before the emergency arose, the Lord had made provision. A generous donor in America had some time previously placed a considerable sum at the disposal of the Mission for certain, specified buildings. When the trouble came, this friend cabled to say that the money was to be used for any urgent need. A little later, a legacy became available from another friend in the States, which was no little help. And, strangely enough, the exchange turned markedly in the Mission's favor. Silver became cheap when the need was greatest! "It is no vain thing to trust in God," wrote Mr. W. H. Warren, of the Executive in Shanghai, "and it seems to those of us who have been behind the scenes during the whole period that no body of missionaries in China has been more adequately provided for."

And there was more, much more than this. He who cared for the needs of the body, did not fail to minister to tried and suffering spirits. So many refugees together, away from their accustomed work with all its claims, might have reacted unhelpfully on one another. But quite the reverse was the case. For, as they gave themselves to prayer, much prayer for the Christians left behind, for the whole great country in its need, and for light upon the situation that faced the Mission, new faith and love filled many hearts and new confidence was awakened in the overruling wisdom and power of God.

In a word, Satan overreached himself. True, "ye meant evil against me; but God meant it for good . . . as it is this day, to save much people." Instead of retreat and dismay before so terrible an onslaught of the enemy, the ranks of the Mission were steadied at home and in China, by the grace of God, and before long His hand led to a glorious advance.

CHAPTER

XXXI

THE TWO HUNDRED

NO FEWER than five thousand missionaries, representing many societies, left China in that fateful year, 1927. Some were taking furlough to relieve congestion at the ports, but about two thousand of the number were never to return. It was a devastating crisis, and apart from faith the outlook was gloomy indeed. Surely the best that could be hoped for was that the evacuated workers who remained might be able, gradually, to get back to their inland stations. How could any Mission be thinking of *advance*?

This was the view generally taken, it would seem, not only by outsiders who openly declared that missionary work in China was at an end, but by responsible leaders at home, to whom consolidation of the little that remained seemed the best hope. Talk of retrenchment was heard of on all hands, for a period of financial depression soon set in which was to be long continued.

But quiet waiting upon God has a wonderful power to change the aspect of things. "I am the resurrection and the life" is the word that still breathes through our most hope-less hours. Jesus was just as truly there, among His stricken and perplexed servants, as He was at the grave of one He loved, long ago. And the result was the same—resurrection! overcoming life, to the glory of God.

That was what lay behind the new movement that began to be felt throughout the fellowship of the Mission. It was recognized at home as well as on the field that, "once again God had called us to take up the challenge thrown down by the adversary in China, and in His conquering Name to resume the offensive, giving ourselves as never before to the unfinished task committed to us as a Mission."

And that task was seen in a new light as spiritual vision cleared through the very troubles. The objective of the Mission from the beginning had been to establish self-governing, self-supporting churches, and in some districts this goal had been notably attained, but in others the missionary was still too much the leader and authority. This meant that he was taken up with the detailed care of churches which should have been on their own feet as regards support and spiritual ministry. Chinese leadership had not yet come to its own, nor had Christian giving taken its rightful place. But with their missionary friends suddenly snatched away, the local Christians had to carry on alone, and in many cases they did so with marked devotion and ability. It takes the tempests of winter to root great trees deeply, and the Chinese Church was being "stablished, strengthened, settled" by the very storms that threatened to uproot it.

Those were days of heart-searching and humbling before God for the evacuated people at the coast, as they waited upon Him about the situation. Why had He permitted this tremendous upheaval, and what was to be the outcome? For surely it meant blessing and the advancement of His purposes.

"We reëxamined ourselves and our methods," said one of the workers from Szechwan in a recent conversation, and the words meant much. "Realizing that we had had a mistaken attitude," in this matter of missionary control, "we tried faithfully to make needed adjustments. The advance of the Chinese Church, since then, has been phenomenal."

Another outcome of those days of waiting upon God was the new sense of urgency which invested the great task about which the workers at the coast were praying. Amid the strenuous labors of inland stations, the tendency had been to center on the near and immediately pressing. Now it was seen that, with church affairs in the hands of Chinese leaders, the missionary might concentrate upon forward evangelism—including village work around existing centers, planning for and helping in tent missions, training the Christians as personal workers, developing special efforts among children, and preparing attractive literature and posters for visual evangelism. It was seen also that large reinforcements would be needed to cover effectually the great field left by general consent to the China Inland Mission—the vast, inland districts in which no others were working. The burden of the unreached multitudes for whom we were in this way responsible pressed heavily upon men and women who knew from close contact the sorrows and darkness of heathenism. "Unable to go to the people with the Gospel, we went to God for them with strong crying and tears."

And so it was that the appeal took shape which, before long, was to startle the home churches with its faith and vision. But it was no arbitrary setting of a goal—when the whole Mission joined in prayer for two hundred new workers. A well-qualified group had been appointed at the request of the evacuated missionaries to go over the whole field, noting just where reinforcements were needed, and how many. Gradually the estimated number rose until, to the surprise of all concerned, it reached a hundred and ninety-nine. These findings were then prayerfully considered by Mr. D. E. Hoste and the China Council, and not until it was clear that every one of the number was really needed was the appeal sent home to be approved by the Councils in England, North America, and Australasia.

But, even so, it was something of a shock to the home constituencies to see the statement made public in 1929, that the Mission was praying for and expecting *two hundred new workers within the next two years.*

"What could the China Inland Mission be thinking of," was the reaction of even some of its best friends, "to come out with such an appeal at such a time?"

What indeed—if not the Master's clear and unrevoked Commission; the need of perishing millions for whose souls no man cared; and the Eternal Faithfulness which makes of every divine command, a promise? Go! carry the Glad Tidings to every creature . . . "Lo, I am with you alway." Was not that enough?

There are some advances that can only be made on our knees (wrote Rev. W. H. Aldis, Home Director of the Mission in England). This call comes to us as the result of continued prayer over many months, of a careful survey of the field and its needs, and of mature consideration on the part of Mr. Hoste and the China Council. It comes also as a confirmation of an ever-deepening conviction, shared by many, that the recent time of testing and tribulation is to be the prelude to some great new thing in connection with the Lord's work in China.

"Some great new thing"—and so it proved, as we rejoice to record. For the two hundred asked for in faith in 1929 were all given before the close of 1931; and within five years from the time the appeal went out, more than five hundred young men and women were added to the ranks of the Mission. *Two hundred asked for and five hundred given*—at a time of unusual depression at home as well as difficulty and danger in China—what a testimony it was and is to the faithfulness of God! "Is there anything too hard for the Lord?"

> "Where reason fails, with all her powers,
> There faith prevails and love adores."

Not a few of the Two Hundred, and those who followed them, came from North America, where Dr. Frost entered heartily into the new advance.* The difficulties of a situation never hindered his prayers. Long years had passed since his first quest of faith in connection with the Mission had seemed to fail, only to bring larger blessing than any he had asked or thought. Trials had never been lacking, but as Dr. Frost wrote after the sailing of the Saunders' party:

Nothing was plainer than this, that God had faithfully kept every promise He had made to us, and from first to last had been to us the God of grace and glory. What more could we desire than this? For we knew that what He had been, He would be. One gracious act was the promise of another, and a thousand gracious acts the

---

* In recognition of his contribution to Christian life and literature, the degree of Doctor of Divinity had been conferred on Mr. Frost by Westminster College, representing the United Presbyterian denomination.

promise of a thousand more. So then we knew that the God of grace and glory would go before us and lead us from grace to grace and from glory to glory. I confess that this is boasting. But why should we not boast, when it concerns such an One as our God?"

But now a new experience had to be faced in his own life —that of advancing age and declining strength. This too the Lord had anticipated, as Dr. and Mrs. Frost were to find, just thirty years after they had left their home in Attica. It had seemed only another trouble when the owner of the house they were renting in Summit had an opportunity to sell, and so wind up the estate to which it belonged. It meant another move, and they had had so many! Princeton was the only place they would have cared to go to, for it was near Philadelphia and associated with the happiest years of Dr. Frost's early life. But houses for rent in that university center were few and far between. After a discouraging search, Dr. Frost was about giving it up when he had occasion to call on Miss Huston at Germantown, and she surprised him by inquiring into the matter. It was no use trying to evade her kindly interest, and before long it was explained.

"I am glad that you will need to buy a house in Princeton," she said quietly, "for I have set aside money for that purpose. I do not want Mrs. Frost ever to have to move again."

"An hundredfold now in this time."* Truly, it is wonderful to deal with God!

Among the first visitors Dr. and Mrs. Frost had the pleasure of receiving in their own home at Princeton was Dr. Robert Hall Glover, whom they had long known as a pioneer and leader in missionary work. Dr. Glover's practical experience in China and other fields fitted him for the under-

---

* Mark 10:29, 30.

taking about which he wished to consult Dr. Frost; for he
was considering an invitation from Dr. James M. Gray of
Chicago to direct and enlarge the Missionary Department
of the Moody Bible Institute. Dr. Frost warmly encouraged
the proposal, though even then he was feeling how desirable
it would be to have this very friend as his colleague. But the
time had not come for any such development, and it was
not until some years later, after a ministry of teaching and
personal counsel among a great body of students, over two
hundred of whom actually entered foreign missionary service,
that Dr. Glover, with an enlarged and enriched experience,
was brought by the Lord Himself into the fellowship of the
Mission.

Those years, 1921 to 1927, had brought sorrow and
changes through repeated bereavements. Two valued Secre-
taries of the Mission in North America had been taken—
Mr. F. H. Neale from Ventnor and Mr. R. B. Whittlesey
from Germantown. Dr. W. J. Erdman, friend of a lifetime,
was gone from the Council, and the large place filled by the
beloved Miss Charlesanna Huston was sadly empty. But for
the brave spirit of Mrs. Frost and the ability and devotion
of Miss Mary Brayton, the Germantown work and Dr. Frost
himself could hardly have come through those days of strain
and sorrow. But succor was being sent from China, and six
months after Mr. Whittlesey's lamented death Mr. H. E. V.
Andrews and Mr. W. A. Schlichter arrived, with their families, to fill the posts of Secretary and Treasurer respectively.

By this time the difficulties growing out of the evacuation
period were having to be faced, and it was whole-heartedly
that Dr. Frost responded to Mr. Hoste's proposal that Dr.

Glover, newly appointed as Assistant Home Director, should visit China, to become better acquainted with the personnel of the Mission and to share the counsels of its leaders with regard to its problems and interests. Mrs. Glover accompanied him on this journey, taking their son of fifteen with them, while the daughters remained at college. It was no time, then, to think of age-limits, rest, or retiring, so— although he had passed his seventieth year—Dr. Frost held on in his responsible position, finding daily renewal in the long-tried way of fellowship with God.

It is anticipated events (he wrote in this connection) which make us fear. The realized ones, when we walk with God, make us satisfied and brave. For God is ever the revealer of goodness, and His ways encourage us to hasten onward to wider and richer experiences of grace. In spite of declining years, therefore, I found myself full of hope and courage.

CHAPTER

XXXII

"A NEW THING"

THE new things that God was doing in China became evident as the workers returned to their stations after the evacuation of 1927. It was not all encouraging, by any means, for the independent church movement had begun, which took on an antiforeign expression in not a few places. There was need for humility and patience in mutual adjustment, but the joy with which the missionaries, generally speaking, were welcomed back was very cheering.

"Have you been away only two years," said the Tonghsu women, crowding around Miss Maybeth Standen, "it seems more like ten or twenty! You will never go away again, will you? We need you here so much!"*

Among the crowds of women that first Sunday (wrote their beloved missionary), how glad I was to have my faithful Mrs. Suen! She has been a real help and support to the other women during these testing years. I wish you could have seen that Sunday congre-

---

* Tonghsu, and other outstations of Kaifeng, Honan, had been Miss Standen's special care since she had been obliged to move from the Kwangsin River to a more bracing climate.

gation, gathered in the school courtyard for the service, our old chapel not being large enough to hold them. There must have been at least three hundred—and it was a hot day, too! Then followed our monthly Communion Service, when eighty to ninety of us met to remember the Lord's death. . . . What a bond the love of Christ is, and how it holds us together!

It was good to find, as did so many others, that the work had been extending during the foreigners' absence, in spite of the cruel depredations of soldiers and bandits. In a village a mile or two from Tonghsu, where there had been eight baptized Christians, they now had a congregation of some fifty people on Sundays, meeting in their own chapel.

It was only a small, whitewashed building (Miss Standen continued, the joy-bells ringing in her heart), but they had made a little platform, on which was placed a table and chair for the speaker, and there were backless benches for the congregation, and bright Gospel texts on the walls. It could not have been plainer, but the beauty of it was that it had all been done by themselves, without help from the missionary, and one thanked God and took courage.

That the spirit of God was working in many places was manifest. A converted stonecutter in northern Anhwei was winning many to Christ in a gracious revival movement near Fowyang; and farther north, in Pastor Hsi's old district, rivers of living water were flowing, as Miss Römke wrote from Chaocheng. This was the center in which Mrs. Hsi had spent the long years of her widowhood and from which she passed to be with the Lord in the fall of 1929. Her life of love and prayer had been a blessing to the whole church, and her Home-going was followed by times of wonderful revival. Miss Christensen was conducting missions in many places, and of Chaocheng itself Miss Römke wrote:

At the request of one of the Elders, who was hungry to see souls saved, two weeks of special meetings were held, when many came in from the villages. Never shall I forget the stillness of those gatherings, and how the people were drinking in the Word of Life! On the third day we could see how the Holy Spirit was using the Word. Men and women were burdened with their heavy load of sin. The next day, the first was gloriously set free, and has since been a living witness in his own and the neighboring villages. A demon-possessed woman was delivered and got right with God, rejoicing in her freedom. . . . For eight days, after that, we were dealing with seekers from morning till night, between the meetings. What a privilege it was to see our Chinese brothers and sisters helping their own people, and to share their joy as these converts, one after another, cast their burden at the foot of the Cross!

I could not but regret being the only foreigner there with them, so was glad when Mr. H. M. Griffin came down from Pingyao to share the blessing with us. Those were days never to be forgotten, when the sound of prayer and praise went up from almost every room in this courtyard.

"We have open heaven, open hearts, and open doors," wrote Mr. Griffin of that visit. And it was so elsewhere, not in Shansi only. A remarkable movement was taking place at the same time, quite apart from missionary activities.

The action of the Government in destroying idols in many of the temples (wrote Mr. C. H. S. Green from Hopeh) is having the effect, very markedly, of arousing an interest in the Gospel, and both we and our Chinese fellow-workers are seeking to enter this widely open door. It seems that the floodtide of opportunity is upon us, and our earnest hope is that a great ingathering of believers may result.

And on the last day of the year (1928) Mr. Macpherson, now of the Executive in Shanghai, wrote from Chekiang:

The idols in ten of the temples of our city and suburbs were destroyed by members of the local Nationalist Bureau, acting under instructions from the Central Bureau at Nanking. Next day we presented to every shop in the city a booklet setting forth the Lord Jesus Christ as the supreme need of the Chinese people, both nationally and individually.

Another striking way in which God was overruling this crisis for blessing was the development of a wholly new series of attractive, colored posters of large size, for visual evangelism. Among the hundreds of missionaries driven to Shanghai in 1927, was one little woman from far-off Kansu whose presence carried inspiration. Quiet and unassuming as she was, Miss S. J. Garland, by her clear thinking, breadth of outlook, and intensity of zeal and devotion, "was always in the very front rank of advance."* Taking advantage of the prayer-power concentrated in Shanghai and of the experiences of evacuated fellow-workers, Miss Garland led the way in designing the posters and accompanying publications, of which a representative of The Religious Tract Society wrote:

The Visual Evangelism material of all kinds has met with such a wonderful reception that we have been working overtime at the depot and press, and can scarcely keep pace with the orders. Eight hundred and forty thousand *Week of Evangelism* tracts have almost all gone out. Cannot get another print done in time. Five thousand *sets* of accompanying posters have also been sold. And all this demand, please remember, is *before* the forward movement of any Mission has been launched. What will it be when these movements are in full swing?

A remarkable answer to prayer, too little known, is connected with one series of posters produced about this time— those which combined Arabic with Chinese, for use among the millions of Moslems scattered throughout the country.

* The Rev. Frank Houghton (now Bishop in West China) in *The Two Hundred*, p. 15.

Mohammedans, the world over, set much store by the beauty of their written character, and the style developed in Persia is reckoned the most perfect of all the Arabic scripts. Chinese Moslems read the Persian script more easily than any other, as Persian influence is strong in the Mohammedanism of China. They cherish unbounded admiration for its strong, flowing curves and artistically grouped dots and circles, to reproduce which requires years of training, for the art is regulated by the most exacting requirements.

This was the despair of George Harris, the young American artist upon whom had fallen, in large measure, the mantle of William Borden. Borden had consecrated his life to the evangelization of Chinese Moslems, and had died in Egypt while studying Arabic with a view to this great task. Harris was then a student in the Art Institute in Chicago, little dreaming that his talent and training were to be used to the same high ends. He knew nothing of Borden at that time, but received his definite call to Moslem work on the third anniversary of Borden's death, when (as he discovered later) Mrs. Borden and a few friends were met for prayer in her New York home that someone might be raised up to carry on her son's missionary work. During his course at the Moody Bible Institute, young Harris learned of the China Inland Mission from Mr. F. A. Steven, and of the opportunity it offered for reaching Chinese Moslems. And now with his young wife, Mr. Steven's daughter, he was facing the actual problem in Kansu—the province to which Borden had been dedicated—of how to bring home to Moslems hearts the precious and all-important truths of the Gospel.

In the city of Sining and later in Hochow, the Mecca of China, he had friends among all classes of the large Mohammedan population. He had learned Arabic as well as Chinese and found ready acceptance for Christian literature in mosque and school, as on the crowded streets. His picture scrolls, painted by hand, always gathered an audience for the message, but he longed to make more use of the beautiful written language, with its peculiar appeal to readers of Arabic. Subtle and delicate as it was, he knew that he could reproduce that writing, if only he had knowledge of the rules that controlled it with absolute precision. But just there he was checkmated. No Mohammedan teacher or friend could be persuaded to divulge those secret rules to an outsider. They had themselves spent years in learning them—twelve years to become a proficient writer—and even then, few could achieve the large bold strokes and spacing needed for the posters Harris longed to produce. He had to go home on his first furlough defeated, so far as that was concerned.

But the Lord had not prepared His instrument and given the vision in vain. In New York City, Harris was passing a second-hand bookstore one day, little thinking that, not in China, but among those piled shelves and tables his prayers were to be answered. His love of books impelled him to step in and, finding that he was acquainted with strange languages, the owner of the store brought forth a thin volume he had little chance of selling.

"You might be interested in this," he said, handing it unsuspectingly to the one man in that great city who could most appreciate its value.

For to his amazement, Mr. Harris found upon looking into it that it was not only a book on Arabic writing, but actually *a key to the Persian script!* There it lay open before him— exact instructions as to joining any combination of letters in a proper way, so as to be accurate and beautiful. Fifty years before, an English diplomat had obtained the information in Persia; the book had found its way to an obscure corner of New York; and a baffled missionary from Northwest China thanked God as he turned its pages and saw the divine purpose in his life more clearly than ever before.

For, with that treasure, purchased for a dollar, the artist in Harris was able to reproduce that Persian script so perfectly that the Kansu Moslems, astonished at those beautiful Gospel posters, could not and would not believe that a missionary, a foreigner, had written them. They could find no fault with the artistry, and great was the appeal of the Scripture truths and passages thus presented. For the posters carry their message widely. Prized for their beauty, they find their way into mosques and homes that no preacher could enter, and attract crowds on street and market—even *ahongs* (Moslem priests) being found to listen, furtively, to the explanations given in Chinese and Arabic. Should not this seed-sowing be watered by our prayers?*

Another development rich in spiritual results belongs to this period of new beginnings. Many years previously, Mr.

---

* Even yet, Chinese Moslems reject the thought that an outsider can produce their cultured and artistic script—"the tongue of the angels and the language of heaven." "Up in our district," Mr. Harris said recently, "they do not believe that I do the writing myself. They say I secretly bribe some *ahong* to do it for me. A paper in Peking, a Moslem monthly, had a full-page representation of our posters and tracts, requesting fellow-Moslems to discover and inform them as to who was selling their religion to the Christians. That was about 1933.

and Mrs. F. C. H. Dreyer had been led to open the first Bible Institute in North China, sacrificing for this purpose their much-loved evangelistic and station work. Students had flocked to them at Hungtung in increasing numbers, and the course of study had grown with the graduates, who returned to strengthen the churches in Shansi and neighboring provinces. As he taught his classes, Mr. Dreyer, quite unconsciously to himself, was doing a double work which was to bear fruit in all parts of China. For he soon found that it was not possible for his students to grasp the lessons given and at the same time take adequate notes in the cumbersome Chinese characters. So, to help them, he made it a habit to dictate his own full outlines after every lesson to a quick writer who put them on the blackboard for the students to copy at leisure. Mr. Dreyer had no thought at that time of the invaluable *Mandarin Bible Commentary* in forty volumes that was to grow out of this small beginning. He only knew that the notes were needed and valued, as they began to find their way into Christian magazines, and he received requests from editors in various parts of the country for fuller articles.

At the same time, a new version of the Bible in the everyday language of the large majority of the people was brought to completion, and a nation-wide movement was set on foot by the Government to popularize the use of this Mandarin colloquial instead of the classical and little-understood Wenli. The hour was ripe for the appearance of a Commentary which would fit the new Bible text, and Mr. Dreyer was approached by The Religious Tract Society with a view to publishing his notes in this form. Several volumes both on the Old and New Testament had appeared before the Evacua-

tion, when Mr. and Mrs. Dreyer went home on furlough.
Seriously impaired health made it impracticable for him to
return to Shansi. Able and devoted successors had taken
over the Bible Institute, in the persons of Mr. and Mrs.
Graham Anderson. The Religious Tract Society was urging
that Mr. Dreyer's whole time should be given to the Commentary, which was meeting a widely felt need—and "assuredly gathering" that the Lord was shutting one door to
open another, Mr. and Mrs. Dreyer went to Chefoo to continue the great task.

And now, as the closing volumes of this *Mandarin Bible
Commentary* are eagerly looked for, Mrs. Dreyer's words
come to us as an urgent call to prayer:

> This Commentary is not a translation of any one Western book,
> but is an entirely new and independent study and exposition of the
> Word of God adapted to Chinese modes of thought and expression,
> though helpful material has been drawn from all available sources.
> Practical applications, homiletical hints, Bible reading and sermon
> outlines, useful illustrations, general summaries, together with dis-
> cussion of exegetical problems, Biblical difficulties, and apparent
> discrepancies, are introduced in addition to the introductions and
> expositions.
> All is written from the standpoint of faith in the inspired Word
> of God. In these days when destructive criticism is coming into
> the Church of China like a flood, we are glad to be privileged to
> help to establish the faith of the Christians. . . . We would earn-
> estly ask prayer that the Lord may give all needed strength and wis-
> dom, that these expositions may be in line with His will and be
> made spiritually helpful to many throughout this land.

It is a far cry from the China of a Commentary in forty
volumes to the China of the mountain-tribes, whose languages were not even reduced to writing. But a wonderful
work of God was spreading in those regions of the far west,

in which North American members of the Mission were privileged to have no small part. Starting like a prairie fire in Kweichow, as we have seen, it had kindled faith and love in thousands of hearts, and was being carried by the tribes-people themselves into regions hitherto untouched by the Gospel.

At the time when Shanghai was filled with evacuated missionaries, a few who had been enabled to stay at their stations two thousand miles away, near the borders of Burma and Tibet, were encouraged by a new development which was to bear rich fruit. Mr. J. O. Fraser, used of God through years of prayer and loving, patient labor, to win hundreds of Lisu from their demon-worship and degradation to Christ, was not there at the time, and his place had been taken by Carl G. Gowman of Ontario, whose experience in work among tribes-people had been long and varied. He already spoke four tribal languages, and was a great strength to Mr. and Mrs. Allyn Cooke and other young workers whom he had joined in the Muchengpo district. The Lisu church was by that time sending out its own volunteer missionaries who, without purse or scrip, like the early disciples, went far afield seeking the unevangelized of their own tribe especially.

No one unfamiliar with such regions can ever know what those devoted pioneers had to face of loneliness, suffering, and danger, as they traveled on foot, for weeks and months together, over mighty mountain ranges and through deep ravines and fever-stricken valleys. Often their hearts went back with longing to the homes so far away, and to the loved ones whom some of them were never to see again. But the joy of finding precious jewels for the Lord Jesus, in many a busy market and village clinging to the mountainside, richly rewarded all the toil and sacrifice. And what true Apostles to their own people many of these simple Lisu preachers became!

I pray constantly in the Name of the Saviour for the believers (wrote one of them), and am also laboring in prayer for the heathen. And in answer, God has given many believers in many villages; and I praise the Lord Jesus because none has backslidden. The believers hold regular midweek and Sunday services in our fourteen meeting-houses. . . .

And now, through the grace of God, I have put in three years' time away from home as a preacher. I feel I should return to my family after Christmas. But if God wants me to stay on here, I shall be pleased to do so. . . . Pray that I may be fitted to do God's work and may be enabled to endure through the help of the Holy Spirit, and that I may always be holy and clean. I too am praying for these things.

The writer is Job, the slave of the Lord.

This man was one of four unpaid evangelists who, encouraged by Mr. Gowman, had set out from the mother-station, in 1928, to seek the Lisu of the Mekong Valley. Five days they traveled northward to the city of Yungchang, where they surprised the young missionaries one morning (Mr. and Mrs. De Witt Payne) at breakfast on the porch of their little home.

Three weeks later (wrote Mr. Payne) they were back with a sad tale. The Lisu in the Mekong Valley had refused to believe that they were preachers of good news. Taking them for robbers, they had treated them roughly, and four discouraged men were ready to return to their farms. But I took them aside, and talked with them about Acts 18:9,10, "Be not afraid, but speak, and hold not thy peace . . . for I have much people in this city."

Then we prayed, and the Lord led us to go to the Salween River. For seven long days we pushed our way westward, travelling through mountain jungles, and coming at last to the edge of the Lisu country. There my Lisu companions said:

"These people have never seen a white man. You stay outside the villages, while we go and get in touch with the folk." . . .

One whole day I spent in prayer, down on the sandy bank of the river, almost under the shadow of the mighty mountains of Tibet, pleading with God both to fulfill His promises and to gladden our hearts by doing a saving work in that region. I then decided to retire into the background, returning home by a different route.

Some weeks later I revisited the Salween. Praise the Saviour! Twenty to thirty families (about a hundred people) had made a clean-cut turn to the Lord, throwing out all objects of idolatry. Many had purchased Lisu books and were learning to read, while some could sing a few hymns. The four preachers had scattered to different villages and were hard at work teaching. After the day's labor in the fields, crowds would gather in the little homes, and by the light of pine splinters study far into the night. . . .

We praise our heavenly Father for each and every one of them. And we are looking upward for yet greater things—for did not the Lord Jesus promise *"rivers* of living water"?

Such was the beginning of the great and blessed movement by which the Church of Christ was established on the Upper Salween—where Mr. and Mrs. Allyn Cooke, Mr. and Mrs. John Kuhn, and others have since devotedly labored, translating the entire New Testament into the Lisu language, to the joy of thousands of believers.

CHAPTER

XXXIII

UNCHANGING

FAITHFULNESS

BUT these developments were only part of the Forward Movement which was well under way in several provinces, even before the last of the Two Hundred could reach China, and this in spite of the most adverse conditions. For Communism, banditry, and civil war were on the increase, causing untold suffering and peril. Of 1930, one worker wrote, "No words can describe the awful conditions that have existed here throughout the year"; while from another came, "We have never known such a period of testing."

In Kiangsi, thirty-seven out of eighty-one counties were under the control of the Reds, while thirty-eight others were infested with brigands. Twenty out of the thirty-eight stations in this province were looted. And so the record of sorrows could go on, but this will suffice. It seems almost a miracle that the missionaries could hold on, still more so that they should plan advance.*

---

* *By Love Compelled,* p. 111. Mr. Broomhall also quotes from another province (p. 115), "It is impossible to estimate the number of people ruthlessly killed during the Red occupation. In a mulberry grove, adjoining the Mission compound, were found thirty-six pits into which hundreds of dead bodies have been thrown. We were horrified to see a similar pit in our back garden."

Famine and flood added to the national distress and took heavy toll of the ranks of the Mission. Up in Kansu, where a fierce Mohammedan rebellion was raging, five valued workers were carried off by typhus fever, including Miss Susie Garland, who was caring for over two thousand starving people at Hweihsien. Three of the five were from North America—Dr. Leighton P. Rand of Cornell University and the Borden Memorial Hospital, Miss Dorothy Bidlake of Seattle, a specially promising young missionary, and Mr. Lloyd R. Rist of Toronto, who had already given eighteen years to the work in China. Keen for advance, he and Mrs. Rist had returned to the interior even before the call went out for a Forward Movement. In the unopened city of Chungwei, far up the Yellow River (Kansu), they had the joy of seeing the first converts won to Christ. For five strenuous but rewarding months they so prayed and labored that over two hundred men gave in their names as believers, and the self-propagating church was founded which is witnessing brightly today in that long-neglected region. "And so passed to his reward a brave, earnest soldier of Christ—a man of God, beloved by all who knew him."

Very many were the Chinese Christians who laid down their lives at this time for Christ's sake. It was the churches of Kiangsi that suffered most, for there and in the neighboring province of Hunan the Communists had their chief successes. Five separate Red armies, under independent generals, established a reign of terror in as many districts which they held as "kingdoms," making those rich and populous provinces run with blood. Without going into detail, we have it on reliable authority that millions of lives were sacrificed and millions more made homeless under that awful regime. For it was years after the break with the Soviet party (1927) before the National forces under Chiang Kai-shek could dislodge these strongly entrenched Red armies —and then it was only to spread the terror in neighboring provinces and even to the tribal regions of the West. John and Betty Stam, beloved young American workers, suffered death at the hands of one group that escaped into Anhwei, while another captured and held the much-prayed-for members of the Mission, Hayman and Bosshardt, for more than a year and for eighteen months, respectively.*

In Kiangsi itself, three associate workers of the Mission were martyred near Kian, and many stations had to be vacated. A tide of blessing had been flowing through the Yüanchow district, where Dr. Keller's Band Number Nine was being much used of God. Seven of these young evangelists were captured by the Communist General, Peng Teh-hwai. Two were ultimately liberated, but five sealed their testimony with their blood.

"It is not that we are afraid to die," said a faithful Kiangsi Christian, speaking for many others, "it is the slow and awful tortures beforehand."

And to the missionaries who loved them, this was the worst of their sufferings, when they too were at the mercy of Communist captors. For Mr. and Mrs. R. W. Porteous, of Yüanchow, were themselves taken by Peng Teh-hwai when he looted the city. For a hundred days, hurried hither and thither to strongholds in the mountains, they had to witness

---

* See *The Triumph of John and Betty Stam;* also, *The Restraining Hand,* by R. A. Bosshardt. To be ordered from the Mission, 150 St. George Street, Toronto, or 237 School Lane, Philadelphia.

the suffering of their fellow-prisoners, not knowing when it might be their turn to die. Indeed, they faced death many times, proving the protection and sustaining grace of God in such wonderful ways that their enemies marveled, and it seemed as if they could not kill them.* The whole heart-moving story is told in the pages of the booklet worth its weight in gold, *Is Thy God Able?*, with the eventual deliverance brought about, humanly speaking, by the devotion of Pastor Eo-yang and others who risked their lives repeatedly to save their beloved missionaries.

Yet from this baptism of fire, the Christians of Kiangsi emerged, as Mr. William Taylor wrote on his return to the province, "more mature, steadier, sturdier, wiser, less dependent on foreigners, with more initiative, yet manifesting full love for their missionary friends."

But valued leaders were missing, alas! in many places. Seized by the Communists at Iyang, as Miss Rebe Mackenzie afterwards learned, Pastor Yen had been required to hand over the church roll, with the names of all members under his care. Bound and imprisoned, he was left to await their return at night, which meant death unless he complied with their demands.

"Father," called his young daughter, held in captivity in the room above, "Father, tell them, or they will torture and kill you."

---

* The hand of God was no less seen in the liberation of Miss Nina E. Gemmell of Bellingham, Washington, who for eleven days was held with Mr. and Mrs. Porteous, and in the narrow escape of their American colleagues, Mr. and Mrs. Russell H. Glazier and Miss Gertrude Rugg. Very noteworthy has been the blessing of God upon the labors of these beloved workers, in Kiangsi and elsewhere, since that distressful time. "We went through fire and through water: but thou broughtest us out into a wealthy place."

The pleading voice went to Pastor Yen's heart, but the reply was unwavering:

"Never, never can I betray my brethren."

Through the boards of the rough floor between them, the girl heard his brave testimony that evening—silenced by a cruel death. "Notwithstanding, the Lord stood with me and strengthened me."

"Shall Suffering and Danger Halt our Missionary Work?"

To ask the question is to answer it, as Dr. Glover did in his convincing article under that title. After a year in China (1928) he had returned to take over the responsibilities of Home Director in North America, just as the appeal went out for two hundred new workers.

Conditions in China for the present grow no better (he wrote). Lawlessness abounds, and bandit hordes continue their daring and atrocious deeds. . . . Within the last three years, four missionaries and a score or more of our Chinese workers have been cruelly done to death. The Communist menace has grown steadily more serious . . . the efforts of Government troops to dislodge the Red forces having been ineffective. . . . All this is sad and serious beyond words. It not unnaturally raises the question in some minds as to whether missionary work should continue under such conditions, and particularly as to whether the Mission is justified in undertaking a forward movement at such a time as this.

Searchingly the whole situation was brought under review, in the light of the example and teachings of Christ and His Apostles.

In the inspired account of the missionary work of the first generation of the Church, we find opposition, persecution, hardship, suffering, violence, imprisonment, and martyrdom running through the entire record. One can scarcely open the book of Acts anywhere without seeing some such feature upon the page. Five distinct gen-

eral persecutions are cited up to the twelfth chapter, and then immediately follow the foreign missionary campaigns of Paul and his
companions, attended as they were with constant experiences of in-
sult, peril, bodily attack, and suffering of every kind. Who can
read thoughtfully those categories of the great Apostle's afflictions
for Christ as given in 2 Corinthians, chapters four and eleven, and
not be profoundly stirred.

Two things particularly impress us with regard to missionary experience in The Acts. The first of them is the clearly apparent fact
that suffering is no mere accident or incident in missionary work,
but a very part of the missionary program, indeed a most prominent
and fruitful part. At the very outset, Stephen was stoned to death.
What a blow of Satan, aimed at crushing the movement at its start!
But Satan miscalculated, for instead of extinguishing the Gospel
fire he only succeeded in spreading the embers on every hand, so
that we read: "They that were scattered abroad went everywhere,
preaching the Word." As a result, a multitude in Jerusalem believed,
and the work extended far afield. . . .

And this is but one of the many instances throughout the book
of the same result of suffering, for a careful reading will reveal that
every recorded persecution imparted fresh impulse to the Christian
movement, and was followed by a large ingathering of souls.

The other impressive thing we observe in Acts is that the Apostles
and early Church, far from being dismayed by suffering, regarded it
as something to be expected and rejoice in. It never once seemed
to occur to them that persecution, distress, or even the martyrdom of
one of their number should prompt them to suspend operations or
diminish their efforts. They went steadily on in spite of everything
that happened. After having been beaten by the Council and dismissed with a serious warning not to preach again, "they departed
. . . rejoicing that they were counted worthy to suffer shame for his
name. And daily in the temple, and in every house, they ceased
not to teach and preach Jesus as the Christ." When Peter and John
were similarly released after an effort to intimidate them, they joined
their company and a prayer meeting was held. Observe how the
united petition ran: "And now, Lord, behold their threatenings,
and . . ." And *what?* How should we be disposed to finish that
prayer in like circumstances? By praying for condign punishment
upon our persecutors? By pleading for exemption from further

ROBERT HALL GLOVER
Home Director in North America from 1930

trial and suffering? The early Church did not pray thus. Listen to their words, "And now, Lord, behold their threatenings: and grant unto Thy servants that with all boldness they may speak Thy word . . . " They prayed to be made good soldiers, to be kept courageous and faithful to their trust, ready to endure all that might come to them. And God abundantly answered their prayers, for "they spake the word of God with boldness," great power and grace were upon them all, and as a result a multitude believed and were added to them. . . .

That every reasonable safeguard and precaution for the safety and welfare of our missionaries should be taken, and that anything savoring of foolhardiness or recklessness should be avoided, we shall all agree. But in the face of our Lord's unrevoked commission to carry the Gospel to every creature, and of the fact that multiplied millions in China have never yet heard that Gospel, must we not conclude that, so long as the door of opportunity is open, we are justified, nay more, we are obligated, at any cost, to continue our missionary effort?

The practical answer of the Mission to all such questions was the steady sailing of party after party of the Two Hundred. America supplied almost half the entire number. After Dr. Glover's return from China, he was so much occupied with meetings in many parts of the country that Dr. Frost consented to continue his leadership of the work for another year. Dr. Glover's official appointment to sole responsibility, in January 1930, left the beloved Director Emeritus more free for spiritual service in correspondence, interviews, and the publication of book after book on fundamental truth.* No one valued more than Dr. Frost himself the provision thus made for strong, experienced leadership in carrying forward the great advance to which the Lord was leading. For not only were five hundred new members and

---

* The list of Dr. Frost's works given at the close of this volume will be of value to Bible students.

associates added to the Mission in the decade that followed 1927; more than a hundred new central stations were opened in long neglected places, and no fewer than sixty-five thousand new converts—men, women, and young people won to Christ—were added by baptism to the churches of the Mission.

Who could have foreseen and provided for such developments ten years ago, save the unfailing Leader who, in giving His Great Commission, met every possible need arising from it by saying, "Lo, I am with you alway, even unto the end of the world"? To give one illustration, only, of His faithfulness at that time.

The Mission premises in Shanghai, originally the gift of Mr. Orr-Ewing, had not grown with the growing work. Indeed, there was no room for growth, for a downtown district had sprung up around the green and quiet compound, with its precious associations of forty years. The buildings were quite inadequate for the influx of new workers and the increase of all manner of service. But how to improve the situation, without debt or mortgage, was the question? Clearly a move was desirable to some part of the Settlement where larger premises could be erected; but, without funds to draw upon, how could such a move be made?

Years of prayer, it need hardly be said, lay behind the unexpected developments that took place just in time to meet both the seen and unseen emergency of 1931. A cash-down offer was made by a Chinese syndicate for the purchase of the old property, of no less than sixty-five times its original price, enough to put up all the premises needed, without cost to the Mission. And even before this, a legacy from the

United States had made it possible to secure the site which had been selected as desirable for the new headquarters.

"And now, Lord, what wait I for? My hope is in thee."

Wonderful it was to have abundant room and comfort for party after party pouring in from the home lands, and still more wonderful to see in it all the unfailing faithfulness of God. For trouble that had long been brewing came suddenly to a head at the close of 1931, and the premises vacated only a few months previously were in the vortex of the attack when the last party of the Two Hundred arrived to find that section of the city in flames. The Japanese were for the first time bombarding Shanghai. But the Home of the Mission to which the young men were taken was in comparative safety, three miles away.

Yes, and unworthy as we are, our hearts still say, "This God is our God for ever and ever: he will be our guide even unto death."

CHAPTER

XXXIV

GOD'S VOICE FROM CHINA

DO we hear it speaking above the babel of confused, heart-rending cries from that great land today? Only six years have passed since the first invasion of Shanghai by Japanese forces, but they have stabbed China wide-awake and have welded it in one as never before in the furnace of suffering. And has this no meaning for us? Have we no part in the destiny of a nation that comprises one-fourth of all the people in our troubled world?

Destruction in China has been awful (writes a missionary from Kiukiang). Homes and hearts have been broken. People are sad and lonely. There is sickness, suffering, sorrow, and heartache—yet a real hope in the hearts of the people and a unity we have not seen before. As Madame Chiang Kai-shek said: "China is fighting for her very life, but is unafraid. China has found her soul and will defend her people and her rights. She knows only too well the sorrow, the suffering, and the horrors that confront her—but China is unafraid."

Pray that peace may soon come to this land. Her people need your interest and your prayers more than ever before. They call you their friends, and they need you in this awful struggle.

Have we access to a throne of grace, through the precious blood of Jesus? Are we using it as we ought "to *obtain* mercy and to *find* grace to help" our fellow-believers, and the multitudes who, in this extremity, are feeling their way to the Saviour of whom they so late have heard? Surely the leader of one of our Associate Missions voices all our hearts when he says:

If we have ever felt responsible for the spiritual welfare of this nation, we do so in the present time and with greater faith than ever, for *China is groping for the Eternal.* In a radio message spoken by a Chinese in Hankow, people were exhorted that they should give up, as far as possible, the festivities of the present Chinese New Year, and face rather the present most pressing need of the nation, and that they should go and—Pray!

A nation trying to pray—*to whom?* Oh, that they might feel after and find Him who has created and redeemed them! And here lies our responsibility, our opportunity—and *yours too.*

Opportunity is written large over the missionary outlook in China today. Not only is the work unhindered in many provinces, but even where the horrors of war are at their worst, wonderful access is being given to the hearts of sufferers. For all are suffering—soldiers and civilians alike. In Shanghai alone, more than eighty thousand non-combatants are crowded in Refugee Camps. An April letter says:

It had been hoped that after the winter conditions would be such as to make it possible to restart them in life. But now there seems no prospect whatever of this. Funds are getting used up; and what is to happen to these thousands of absolutely homeless, destitute people of all ages, with no place to go to or means of support?

God is working in many hearts. We have heard such interesting stories of one and another. On Sunday, the speaker at a service we attended told of an incident that will ever live in his heart. They were leaving their station at Kiangyin—shells screaming overhead and bombs falling within two hundred yards of the house—when a bright young officer (Chinese) came, asking for baptism. He had a premonition that he would soon be killed, and wanted to avow his faith in Christ. In the study, he wrote out such a clear statement of his belief that Mr. Allison baptized him, in the midst of all the uproar. He has heard nothing further of the young man and feels sure that he is no longer living.

Some who have escaped almost unbelievable cruelties and dangers are now preparing for the service of the Lord they love. Bible schools are carrying on, amid flaming destruction through bombing raids, as Mr. Robert Porteous writes recently from Nanchang:

Although we had frequently to vacate the classroom and find a place of safety, the forenoon classes were usually through before the warning signal sounded. . . . Altogether we have had seventeen actual raids. How we praise our heavenly Father for His constant watchful care and protecting power around us. Praise His Name! We do realize how much the earnest prayers of you, His dear servants, have prevailed on our behalf, for which we are deeply grateful!

There has been no let-up in the work. The Central Gospel Hall is still in full swing. I think it would be quite safe to say that in the daily Gospel meetings held there, hundreds have been brought to a definite decision for Christ within the last few months, the larger proportion being wounded soldiers. The work in the military hospitals has also kept us busy. Only the day before yesterday Mr. Wang and I had the joy of baptising seven of these men. They were leaving shortly to rejoin their divisions. One of them remarked,

"I have lots of pocket-money now that I have given up gambling. If I am spared to return I will surely come to visit you; if not, we shall meet in heaven!"

These are only a small fraction of the many thus won to a knowledge of the Lord Jesus as their own personal Saviour.

We are working now in five military hospitals which we visit regularly each week. . . . On our first visit to one of the largest of these, we were shown by the officer-in-charge into an open courtyard.

One of the orderlies ran for seats for Mrs. Porteous and Mrs. Mc-Culloch; Mr. Wang and I hung up our hymn sheets on the parallel bars, and soon the strains of my English concertina and the singing of the choruses brought a huge crowd of soldiers round us. Wang and I then rang out the Message of the Cross, with suitable illustrations from camp life. Quite a few score of hands were raised in response to the closing challenge to accept Christ. Amongst them I noticed a handless stump. I gave the poor fellow a special smile of recognition, to which he immediately responded. Then I looked upwards, thinking of our heavenly Father's smile resting upon him. After the appeal, those who had raised their hands were asked to follow us in a short closing prayer, which they repeated sentence by sentence, asking for cleansing and forgiveness in the precious blood of Christ.

"I know a fount where sins are washed away;
I know a place where night is turned to day;
Burdens are lifted, blind eyes made to see;
There is wonder-working power in the Blood of Calvary!"

What a lovable people our dear Chinese are! Our hearts go out to them as we pass through the busy streets—all the more so in these days of suffering and deep distress. Our Central Hall and the new Bible School building (Coleman Memorial) are housing seventy of our Father's suffering saints, driven from their homes in Anhwei and Chekiang. What a joy it is to shelter these and show them any little kindness for His Name's sake!

That this is a day of opportunity for Christian witness could not be more manifest. From all over the country, letters come telling the same story:

We rejoice that we are able to carry on with our work in the hospital (writes a lady doctor in Shansi). People are eager to hear the Gospel. It seems as though the very difficulties and distresses through which they are passing were softening many hearts and making people more willing to listen.

There has been a remarkable response among the wounded (comes from our Kaifeng hospital). Services are conducted each day, and personal work is going on continually. The men are keen, for the most part, to read the Word of God and to listen. We are thankful to the Lord for bringing to us really prepared hearts—for which we had been definitely asking.

At least a hundred and twenty bombs were dropped on our city (this is from Wuhu on the Yangtze). When there was a respite, we seized the opportunity to distribute tracts on the streets. Never have I seen people so eager to receive them—to grasp anything that might give a ray of hope, like a drowning man catches at a straw.

Tracts are gladly received and hearts are open for conversation on spiritual things. (This from behind the Japanese lines in Hopeh.) God is preparing many for a deep work of the Spirit. Christians have been drawn nearer to the Lord . . . and the Church is being cleansed through these troubles.

God is indeed answering prayer (writes a member of our China Council, from Hankow). It is an undoubted fact that there were never before such opportunities for preaching the Gospel as we have now, and that never have people listened with such eagerness. This applies to all classes. I believe that during the last six months (since the invasion by Japan began) more people have been brought to Christ in China than in any previous six months of her history. Thus God is bringing good out of evil.

Sorrow everywhere (writes a young American worker from Honan). China is like a broken-hearted child—and now is the time for the Church to advance. We are so glad we are here and in the midst of all this trouble. To be able to stand by these people is a privilege. It may be dangerous, but while in the place of the Lord's will we are safe and happy. . . .

Psalm 57:7—If our hearts are fixed in Him, we cannot help but rejoice, even if it should mean death.

How are we sustaining and sheltering these precious workers by our prayers? Prayer is the controlling element in this whole situation—prayer in the Spirit, according to the will of God. How are we using this great opportunity for turning

dark, bewildered, perishing souls to Christ?   Listen to the
cry of a burdened heart, burdened for "the hundreds and
thousands of villages in Honan."

My time is practically all spent in country work, up against the
fact that in most of these villages the people have had *no* opportunity of hearing the Gospel, especially the women and girls.   There
never was such a wide-open door—the people eager to hear, asking
intelligent questions, and coming around hungry for that which will
satisfy the heart.   Doubtless the war conditions have opened the
eyes of many to the futility of the things of the world, and produced a preparedness of heart not seen before.   We are not touching the fringe of the opportunity.

. . . . . .

"If Thee we never sought, we seek Thee now;
    Thine eyes burn through the dark, our only stars;
We must have sight of thorn-pricks on Thy brow,
    We must have Thee, O Jesus of the Scars.

The other gods were strong, but Thou wast weak;
    They rode, but Thou dids't stumble to a throne;
But to our wounds, God's wounds alone can speak,
    And not a god has wounds but Thou alone."

"Wounded for our transgressions . . . bruised for our
iniquities."   And He is trusting us to make the Message
known.

A word as to the future:—What is to be the outcome of
all that is taking place in China?   Politically we may not
know, but in far more important and enduring ways we need
be in no doubt.   An experienced member of the Mission,
returning recently to China, said some things on this subject
well worth bearing in mind.   Appealing to facts, he re-

minded us that this is not the first crisis in China that has
threatened the very existence of the Mission. Have there
not been at least three great emergencies in which it looked
as though the work had received an irreparable blow: the
Boxer Troubles of 1900; the Revolution Period of 1911, followed by the European War; and the Evacuation Crisis of
1927? And yet, each period was followed by wonderful
advance, as we have seen. The reason is an open secret.
Prayer, much prayer, world-wide prayer was called forth by
these emergencies. This is the vital fact. In other words,
God was able to work as never before, in answer to the
volume of prayer that was going up to Him for China.

Is it not also true that the present unparalleled crisis is
calling forth more prayer than all the former crises put together? All round the world and from countless hearts in
China, prayer is going up day and night, for deliverance and
blessing. And it is more *united* prayer than in any previous
time of need, dividing lines being lost sight of in the overwhelming disaster and distress. It is prayer also in which
China herself, through her leaders, is taking a new part—
China, awakening to the knowledge that there is only one
Name "under heaven given among men, whereby we must
be saved."

We may be sure of the outcome. "Call unto me, and I will
answer thee, and will shew thee great things, and difficult,
which thou knowest not." Are we ready to reap the harvest,
a spiritual ingathering such as we have never known?

Already we are rejoicing in developments that mark advance of a new, important kind. In her recent notable address to a company of missionaries in Hankow (April 6),

Madame Chiang made the announcement that the law had
been rescinded which forbade religious teaching in registered schools. Bible study can thus be brought into the
curriculum of practically all institutions of learning; and
what this means to the *ninety-nine million* young people of
school-age in China, who can tell? Madame Chiang went on
to speak of the influences that had brought about this change.
After expressing deep appreciation of the prayers of Christians at this time, and enumerating many ways in which missionary work had brought temporal as well as spiritual
blessing to China, this gracious lady continued:

> The Generalissimo and I feel that no words we can speak could
> sufficiently express our debt of gratitude to the missionary body all
> over China, who have been a help to the distressed and the best of
> friends to the hundreds of thousands of refugees. . . .
> But noteworthy as your work has been (in relief measures of all
> sorts) I want to add one thing. The most effective and worthwhile
> contribution you have made to the good of my country is not so much
> the work itself, as the spirit in which you are working. Why do
> I say this? A few years ago, our people were very much against
> Christianity, and the Government promulgated a law whereby re-
> ligion was forbidden to be made a required study in any school.
> . . . I am very glad to tell you, now, that those who criticized
> Christianity in years past are the very ones who are—what shall I
> say—vociferous?—articulate in their praise of Christianity today.
> You have won these men over by the work you have done and the
> spirit in which you have done it. You have all had a leading part
> in making this change in the law possible, because you have shown
> what true, practical Christianity means in its widest sense.

Deeper still was the note struck by the same speaker on
another occasion when she said: "At the heart of our faith
are hardship, endurance, suffering, a Cross. Without these,

there cannot be any Christian faith." It is this spirit which is telling in China in these momentous days.

"Are you a Christian?" was asked of a Cabinet Minister.

"No," was his reply, "but I can see that the most self-sacrificing people in our country are Christians, so there must be something in Christianity."

Even a Communist leader is reported to have said in a recent speech: "I have studied Marx and Lenin, but now I know that only the spirit of Christ can help us to bring world-peace and teach us the way of life through sacrifice."

Truly, "I, if I be lifted up, will draw all men unto me."

When the Generalissimo first threw open military hospitals to the visits of missionaries, he sent a memorable message to the group in Nanchang which was undertaking the work. "He asks you to remember," said Madame Chiang, "that these men are suffering, many of them dying, and that what they need to hear about is the suffering, dying Saviour."

Wonderful has been the ingathering from among the wounded since then, and it still goes on. For the door is open wide, it cannot be too much impressed, for faithful, loving witness to Christ, in this suffering land, today.*

---

* Since the above was written, letters have poured in from many parts of China telling the same story. Dr. Jessie McDonald, who with Miss M. Soltau returned in April (1938) from furlough, writes from the Kaifeng hospital:

"I am sure the Lord brought us here at the right time. The staff does look tired. The wounded soldiers do appreciate all that is done for them: it is really a Christian task and privilege. The Gospel is received eagerly and tracts and books are begged for. God is working out His purposes of blessing for this land, and people are ready to listen and eager for teaching. Multitudes are being reached who, otherwise, would never have heard the Gospel. Pray for the wounded; pray for the staff in this strenuous service during the great heat. Pray for the leaders and people of China and Japan. Pray for the open door to be opened even wider. Pray that this terrible war may soon come to an end; and pray for all who are now hearing the Gospel."

"Forty new workers," reads the recent cable from Shanghai that rejoices our hearts—"forty new workers" may be sent forward this fall! And they are ready. For many months a number of accepted candidates have been waiting, and it is a joy to celebrate our Jubilee in North America by sending out *in faith* a contingent of eighteen. For faith was never more needed than in this hour.

Fifty years have passed since our beloved Director Emeritus and Mrs. Frost took those first steps of faith which led to the developments we have traced. Rich has been the fruitage of those years; and as we go forward, now, it is with unchanged faith in the unchanged Word of God. We are no stronger, no richer, no more adequate in ourselves than at the beginning. God is still our only trust; and we have no resources, either temporal or spiritual, but in Him. Our task is no easier than in early days. It has always been impossible —save to faith. But "Christ has never relinquished," as Dr. Glover reminds us, "either the force of His Great Commission or His power to guard those who undertake to fulfil it."

As to present conditions in China and whatever may grow out of them, our confidence is that recently expressed by Dr. Frost, backed by the unchanged calm and steadfastness of his life:

Mr. Hudson Taylor used to be fond of quoting the lines:

"God nothing does nor suffers to be done
But thou would'st do the same, could'st thou but see
Through all the event of things as well as He."

Yes, that is it. There is One over all, "blessed forever." His will is infinitely good, and even His permissive will is perfect. We need then to surrender and trust, putting all things into the hands of our heavenly Father, to order as pleases Him, whatever it may mean to us. Then shall we follow on to know the Lord, and then shall we find that He understands how to lead the blind by a way that they know not.

If we trust without limit in the Infinite One, we shall find that He will do infinite things for us. So to Him, in all that He is, does, and permits, let us say a glad and confident, Amen!

Facing our situation as it is, but also facing God's promise to the Redeemer of the World (Psalm 2:8) and all His glorious purposes yet to be fulfilled, the worship, love, and longing of our hearts pass beyond words. "He shall see of the travail of His soul, and be satisfied."

Lord, here am I. Use me, in prayer, in gift, in service, just as Thou wilt and on to the very end.

PAMPHLETS AND BOOKS
by Henry W. Frost, D.D.

•

Poetical

Heart Songs   Songs of Life

Devotional

Intercession
Little Sermons from the Pentateuch
Men Who Prayed
Effective Praying

Doctrinal

Faith's Final Authority   Miraculous Healing
The Gift of Tongues   About the Old Faith
Outline Bible Studies   Who Is the Holy Spirit?

Prophetical

The Seven Dispensations
Matthew Twenty-Four and the Revelation
The Second Coming of Christ

Missionary

Do You Know?
The Kinsmen Who Never Heard
Missionary Motives
The Spiritual Condition of the Heathen
The Great Commission
The Heathen

The above publications may be ordered from the offices
of the China Inland Mission, at 237 West School Lane,
Philadelphia, Pennsylvania, or at 150 St. George Street,
Toronto 5, Ontario, Canada.

Date Due